STRAT INVESTMENT TIMING

HOW TO **PINPOINT** AND **PROFIT** FROM SHORT- AND LONG-TERM CHANGES IN THE ECONOMY

REVISED EDITION

DICK STOKEN

PROBUS PUBLISHING COMPANY
Chicago, Illinois
Cambridge, England

ISBN 1-55738-491-6

Printed in the United States of America

1 2 3 4 5 6 7 8 9 0

ONCE AGAIN:

To Antigone, Andre, Kingsley
and "the little one,"
Deidre.

With Love

Acknowledgments

I would like to thank all those who have helped in the writing of this book. I express my gratitude to:

Haskel Benishay and Joel Weisman for reading parts of the manuscript and offering many valuable suggestions.

Sue Kurman for patiently editing and typing the manuscript.

Shaila Zeilman who performed the painstaking task of typing the tables.

Isaak Grazutis for the chart graphics.

Dominick Abel, my agent, for his faith in the project.

Kingsley Stoken for doing the much needed stock market research.

Antigone Stoken for checking over my figures.

Thaila Poulos and Jean Emling for their help in getting the updated copy of *Strategic Investment Timing* out.

Andre and Deidre Stoken for their encouragement.

And to Sandre Loebe, friend and soul mate, thanks for your helpful suggestions and support.

Contents

Chapter 1

Introduction

Investment success depends upon three important factors . . . timing . . . timing . . . and timing.

Generally speaking, most people act as if they haven't heard of the financial law of gravity: that which goes up, comes down! Whether we are talking about stocks, real estate, or gold, it is not until the rise in price is far along that most people—even sophisticated investors—become interested. Year after year of relentless climb convinces investors, along with nearly everyone else, that prices can only go up. But they are dead wrong!

In the late 1920's, a raging speculative fever unlike anything experienced before or since gripped this nation. Years of "Coolidge prosperity" had whetted the public appetite to own stocks. Stories of fortunes made overnight were on everybody's lips. Brokerage houses from New York to Oregon were jammed with crowds of men and women, ranging from corporate executives to chauffeurs, seamstresses, and bootblacks, all willing to pay outlandish prices just to participate in this great new game. The stock market was going to make them rich—or so they were all convinced. But in October 1929, hard reality intervened. In a handful of days, the bubble burst and sobered investors realized they had squandered their life's savings.

The story of the stock market crash of 1929 has become a legend, told in chilling tones to each new generation of Americans. The clear lesson of that financial disaster—there is a time to buy and a time to sell.

By the 1930's, Americans in droves had deserted the stock market, and for many years, the traffic on Wall Street was subdued. But following World War II, prosperity reappeared. By the mid-1960's, literally millions were lured into the stock market in search of what appeared to be easy profits. Clearly forgetful of the lesson their parents had learned so painfully in the 1930's, they thought they had found the easy road to riches. They became swept up in a mounting enthusiasm and bid up the price of so-called glamour stocks to ridiculous heights, far beyond anyone's wildest expectations.

In that supercharged atmosphere of the late 1960's, the stock market went into another tailspin. In successive waves of selling that continued into the early 1970's, many former wide-eyed stock market enthusiasts were nearly wiped out. Never before, not even in 1929, had so many Americans bet on a brighter future and lost. Surely, now people would learn that what goes up, comes down.

But no! The red ink had barely dried on the ledgers of the nation's stockbrokers before millions of Americans discovered a new boom in gold, real estate, diamonds, and collectibles of nearly every sort. Their rationale: inflation was here to stay, setting off an unquenchable thirst for real assets. But those who did not get out in 1980 were taken to the woodshed to learn the lesson once again—that there is a time to buy and a time to sell.

Most people, it seems, have read a very short history book—at least when dealing with investments. Time and time again, they become caught up in the latest fad, the latest shortcut to riches, and when reality intrudes, as it always does, they find their dreams shattered and their pocketbooks emptied. It never dawned on them that there is a time to buy and a time to sell.

Of course, we all want to buy just before a market is poised to take off, and unload near the top. But can it be done? Can ordinary investors spot the elusive turning points in investment markets? Can they recognize when to buy stocks and sell real estate, when to move in or out of gold, or when to sell everything and go into cash?

Investment timing is not a random factor. The simple truth is that markets, like most other things, operate in accordance with certain laws. In this book, we will show you four fundamental indicators that measure the key forces at work in the economy. Unlike the so-called technical indicators that most methods of market timing are based upon, these fundamental tools are easy to understand. But most importantly, they can be combined into a model that has pinpointed all the important turns in investment markets. Consider this: when the Dow finally cracked the 1000 barrier in November 1972, the investment community was bubbling with enthusiasm. According to the sages of Wall Street, the sky was now the limit. Yet just one month later, in mid-December, with the Dow at 1027, these four tools flashed a sign to sell stocks and buy gold, silver, real estate, commodities, antiques, stamps, and even vintage wines, as inflation was about to take off. Barely three weeks later the Dow reached a peak of 1051, which was to stand for nine years. Then a lengthy retreat began, smashing the hopes and dreams of millions of investors. During the following year and a half, stock market investors saw the value of their stocks plummet by a numbing 45 percent, but prices of real assets were marching to the tune of an inflationary spiral. Gold, which sold for $63 an ounce in London at the time inflation broke out, reached $179 an ounce. An investor following the model and participating in this inflationary boom would have gotten a signal to sell in early August 1974, at $156 an ounce, just before the inflationary bubble crested.

In early October 1974, when the Dow was at 604, just 5 percent above what was to be the low, these indicators spoke again. The signal to buy stocks was flashed. During the following two years, inflation moderated and most inflation hedges plunged; gold fell more than 45 percent from its high and there was an across-the-board decline in the value of tangible assets. But the stock market roared back, and by the time the next sell signal was given in March 1977, the Dow stood at 965, and our investor was ahead by about 60 percent.

According to the model, this was the time to make the switch from stocks to gold (then selling at $146 an ounce) and other real assets, as inflation was on the runway, ready for another major takeoff. During the following three years, as inflation kept gaining momentum, gold soared to an incredible price of $850 an once, and most tangibles rose to dizzying heights. But on Wall Street there was nothing to cheer about. All that time, the stock market meandered in the wilderness below 900.

On January 22, 1980—just one day after the top in gold—the indicators flashed red. Investors would have gotten $737 an ounce for their gold, or about 405 percent more than what they paid for it before withdrawing to the sidelines.

Another signal to buy stocks flashed in early May of the same year. The Dow stood at 816. Had our investors ventured out and bought stocks, they would have caught nearly all of the following advance, selling out in mid-April 1981 at 1015, just one week before the top, for an eleven-month profit of 24 percent. During the following sixteen months, as nearly all investment markets went into a deadly free fall, they would have been on the sidelines, snugly and securely, collecting 14 percent to 16 percent in money market funds.

Once again, in August 1982, when the economy was flat on its back, the stock market blasted off on record-shattering volume. Within a matter of weeks, the Dow was back into a new all-time high. When did we get a buy signal? Try August 3, 1982, when the Dow stood at 816—just 5 percent and seven days before the low (see Chart 1). The Dow then made a gargantuan move, nearly straight up until September of 1987 (see Chart 1a). When did the sell signal appear? It

Chart 1   Stock Market and Gold   1971-1983

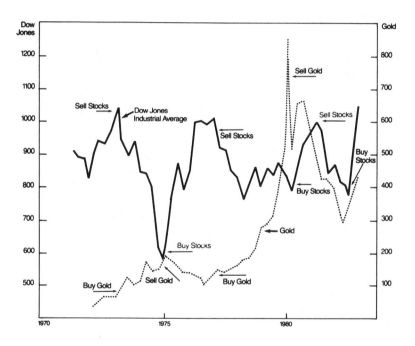

Chart 1a   Stock Market and Gold 1984-1989

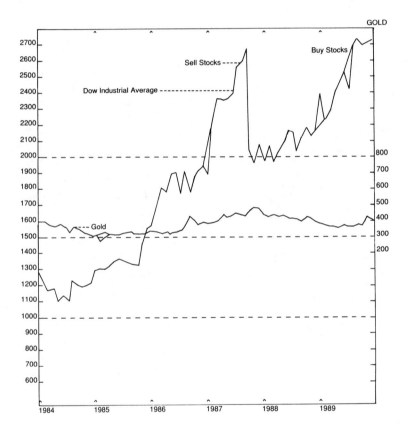

appeared September 9, 1987, within 6 percent of the high. The investor who followed this signal and sold had a Dow based profit at 212 percent.

Sound incredible? A once-in-a-lifetime favorable circumstance of history? If you have been around the investment scene for a while, you will be skeptical. No doubt you have noticed that most investment advice floating around is based on something that has worked for a relatively short period of time but does not stand up to the test of history. Is this just another piece of advice based on a slice of history?

Well, we have put these indicators to the test: sixty-three years of history! And the astonishing result is that these tools have worked with almost pinpoint accuracy. They flashed a signal at the beginning of each bull and bear market—without exception—within an average of 6 percent of the exact high or low. In this book, you will see how the model has proved itself. If this is not enough, you will also learn how to pick stocks that normally outperform the Dow by a wide margin.

But this is not just a stock market book. You will also learn to recognize when inflation, that nemesis of our time, begins to heat up and when it is likely to cool; when interest rates are primed to move either up or down; and how to predict the winner of a presidential election. Also Chapter 13, which deals with the effect of disinflation was written for this new edition

But above all, by the time you finish this book, you will be able to identify the important turning points in stocks, bonds, gold, and other investment markets before they become obvious to most others. This can open the door to the kind of success most investors only dream of. Let us begin.

Chapter 2

The Investment Climate

The most significant fundamental factor affecting the economy, the stock market, and other financial markets is the investment climate. Shifts in this climate foreshadow, early and clearly, the major turning points in the business cycle. When this climate turns favorable, investors can feel confident that there is a powerful economic force operating to drive the stock market higher. Most stocks, even those with the shabbiest fundamentals, will do well. On the other hand, when this climate turns hostile, investors can be pretty sure that the current bull market is nearly over and that stock prices, even those of the best companies, are about to suffer a nasty plunge.

The key to the investment climate is the rate of interest. There are basically two types of interest rates: short-term and long-term. The most sensitive measure of short-term rates is probably the rate on 90-Day Treasury Bills (T-Bills) at the weekly Monday auction. The best guideline to long-term rates is the weekly average of Prime AAA (the highest quality rating) Corporate Bonds.

A fall in the 90-Day T-Bill rate to its lowest level in fifteen months—that is, lower than all of the preceding sixty-five weekly auction prices—is an indication that a turn in the economy and stock market is at hand. There is also another sign. This occurs when AAA Corporate rates fall into a fifteen-month low. If one or the other occurs, if either short- or long-term interest rates fall to their lowest level in fifteen months, it means that a powerful expansionary force has been unleashed, a force that will propel the economy and the stock market much higher.

In order for the investment climate to turn hostile, both the 90-Day T-Bill rate and the AAA Corporate rate must reach a seven-year high. It takes more to fuel a hostile investment climate because there is a bias in our economy that favors growth. When both short- and long-term rates have recorded a seven-year high, it is a surefire sign that the economy is becoming fragile and that a nasty stock market plunge is imminent.

All the fifteen-month lows and seven-year highs in 90-Day T-Bill and AAA Corporate Bond rates since 1946 are listed in Tables 1 and 2. A complete record of these rates on a weekly basis is provided in Appendixes B and D.

Table 1   Interest Rates Fall into a 15-Month Low

90-Day T-Bills	*AAA Corporate Bonds* [a]
July 11, 1949	January 28, 1949
September 21, 1953	February 19, 1954
December 30, 1957	January 31, 1958
June 6, 1960	August 19, 1960
March 13, 1967	[b]
September 21, 1970	February 5, 1971
September 30, 1974	February 13, 1976
May 12, 1980	[b]
August 2, 1982	August 27, 1982
December 10, 1984	January 31, 1985
[b]	June 9, 1989

Note: See Appendix D.

[a] Date report was released, which was six days after AAA Corporate Bonds reached a fifteen-month low.

[b] Failed to make a fifteen-month low.

Table 2   Interest Rates Reach a 7-Year High

90-Day T-Bills	AAA Corporate Bonds [a]
[b]	January 9, 1948
April 24, 1950	June 22, 1951
November 21, 1955	August 31, 1956
August 24, 1959	February 6, 1959
January 17, 1966	December 17, 1965
May 20, 1968	July 7, 1967
July 23, 1973	July 12, 1974
September 10, 1979	April 27, 1979
December 15, 1980	December 5, 1980

Note: See Appendix D.

[a] Date report was released, which is six days after AAA Corporate Bonds reached a seven-year high.

[b] Short-term rates had reached a seven-year high prior to 1946.

Where do you get the information to keep tabs on interest rates? The rate for 90-Day T-Bills at the weekly Monday auction is reported in *The Wall Street Journal* and in most major newspapers the following day. The St. Louis Federal Reserve Bank reports the weekly average rates on AAA Corporate Bonds in the *U.S. Financial Data* bulletin,[1] which is released every Friday afternoon. This report contains both a preliminary figure, based on the first three days for the current week, and the corrected figure for the prior week. As the preliminary figure is subject to revision, it should be disregarded. The figure to focus on is the one for the previous week. For instance, the corrected figure for the week ending Saturday, March 20 would be available to us in the bulletin released on March 26. This, of course, means that there will be a six-day delay before we can be sure the rate for a particular week indicates a turn in the investment climate.

[1] The St. Louis Fed will put those who are interested on the mailing list for their weekly *U.S. Financial Data* bulletin without charge.

Both short- and long-term interest rates are also reported in the *Federal Reserve Bulletin*, published monthly by the Federal Reserve Bureau, and the *Survey of Current Business Conditions*, put out monthly by the Government Statistical Office. However, as these publications are released late, the information will be dated by the time it reaches the investor. The chief value of these publications is in the background information they carry.

Clearly, interest rates are the single most important factor affecting the climate for investments. But there is another consideration. That is politics, which also plays an important role, especially during periods preceding presidential elections. Many stock market commentators have pointed out that there is a four-year cycle operating in the economy and the stock market, wherein periods preceding a presidential election have generally been characterized by a prosperous economy and a booming stock market, while those periods immediately following the election have usually been a time of sagging business and falling stock prices.

This election cycle is not a mystery, nor is it an accident. It is deeply rooted in politics. Ever since the incumbent president was defeated in 1932 because of a depressed economy, politicians have attempted to dress up the economy before an election. They see to it that a great deal of fiscal and monetary stimulus has been applied so that when voters go to the polls on election day, they will be impressed by a booming economy. (It is not necessary that the incumbent be eligible to run for another term. The engineering job can be conducted just as well by the heir apparent, who will have attained a great deal of influence.) Soon after the election, the new administration slams on the brakes to compensate for the earlier excesses, derailing the economy.

The really juicy part of the election cycle is the fifteen-month period beginning in early October, two years before the presidential election, and lasting until early January of the election year (say from October 1,

Table 3 Political Cycles: 15-Month Favorable Phase

October 1	Dow	January 2	Dow	Gain (%)	Gain/Loss During Remaining 33 Months
1934	90	1936	144	60	(1)
1938	143	1940	151	6	(28)
1942	109	1944	131	24	30
1946	171	1948	181	6	26
1950	228	1952	269	18	33
1954	359	1956	485	35	9
1958	530	1960	679	28	(16)
1962	571	1964	766	34	(1)
1966	757	1968	906	20	(16)
1970	760	1972	889	18	(32)
1974	604	1976	858	42	(2)
1978	871	1980	824	(5)	10
1982	907	1984	1252	38	8
1986*					
		Average Gain		25%	2%

Note: Negative numbers are indicated by parentheses.
* No favorable phase because it did not have a prior slump.

1974, until January 1, 1976). It is during this period that politicians have the easiest time of it.[2] As you would expect, it has been a very favorable period for investments. Since 1932, the average gain on the Dow during this favorable phase of the political cycle has been 25 percent (see Table 3). Interestingly, *no* reces-

[2] Politicians are not always successful in producing a booming economy at election time. Sometimes the economy heats up too soon, and the administration, facing an economy threatening to boil over, cannot stay the course. The stimulus must be withdrawn before the election, as we saw happen in 1980. But, and this is the important part, the reigning party has never had trouble igniting the fire. The first fifteen months of their engineering effort have always been successful.

sion has begun during this favorable period. In fact, in 1967, the one time when we appeared headed in that direction, a one-quarter slowdown in GNP was stopped dead in its tracks before it became a bona fide recession. On the other hand, the average gain on the Dow during the remaining thirty-three months of the political cycle was a puny 1 percent. A note of caution: without a stock market slump early in a new administration's reign to cool things off, it is questionable whether they will be able to provide the stimulus necessary to keep the stock market and the economy on an upward course prior to the next election (see Chapter 13).

The level of interest rates can be disregarded during the fifteen-month favorable phase of the political cycle. The climate turns favorable on the first day of October two years before an election, no matter what the level of interest rates. The climate remains friendly until January 1 of the election year.

Normally, a favorable investment climate begins when either short- or long-term interest rates have fallen to a fifteen-month low. This climate will not turn hostile until both rates have reached their highest level in seven years. For instance, 90-Day T-Bills made a fifteen-month low on June 6, 1960, (see Tables 4a and 4b). This was the sign that the stage was set for a recovery in both the economy and the stock market. The climate was to remain friendly to investors for more than five years. The first hint of trouble on the interest rate front came when long-term rates made a seven-year high in December 1965. But this was not enough to derail the favorable investment climate: short-term rates had to reach a seven-year high as well. When they did on January 17, 1966, it meant the economy and the stock market were in for a period of stormy weather.

A friendly investment climate will also be triggered when the favorable phase of the political cycle begins, even if neither short- nor long-term rates have fallen into a fifteen-month low. This occurred on October 1, 1966, and the climate was to remain friendly to investors until short-term rates make a new seven-year high on May 20, 1968. The reason this favorable investment climate lasted beyond January 1, 1968, was because 90-Day T-Bills fell to their lowest level in fifteen months in March 1967. This, of course, meant that both short- and long-term rates would have to reach a seven-year high before another period of stormy weather was signaled.

Even if both short- and long-term rates make a seven-year high during the favorable phase of the election cycle, the onset of a hostile investment climate will be delayed until January 1 of the following election year. This happened in 1979. AAA Corporate Bonds made a seven-year high during April of that year, and their counterpart, short-term rates, followed suit in September. But these highs rates of interest could be disregarded until January 1, 1980. It was at that time the investment climate turned sour.

All in all, there have been nine favorable investment climates since World War II (see Table 5). The average length of these friendly climates was forty months. All began during a time of business contraction and provided the clue that the forces of recovery were being set in motion. Anywhere from two to nine months later, the gears of business and industry were churning again. In fact, no recovery was able to get under way until the investment climate turned favorable. Clearly, a friendly investment climate is a prerequisite to a period of vigorous economic growth.

The onset of a hostile investment climate sounds the alarm that the gears of business are about to grind

Table 4a 90-Day T-Bills at Weekly Auction

1959		1960		1961		1962		1963		1964		1965		1966	
Jan 05	2.678%	Jan 04	4.602%	Jan 03	2.234%	Jan 02	2.703%	Jan 07	2.920%	Jan 06	3.534%	Jan 04	3.829%	Jan 03	4.532%
12	2.808	11	4.590	09	2.385	08	2.823	14	2.884	13	3.549	11	3.814	10	4.585
19	3.035	18	4.436	16	2.358	15	2.770	21	2.923	20	3.538	18	3.821	17	4.673 7-year high
26	2.975	25	4.116	23	2.230	22	2.688	28	2.917	27	3.501	25	3.848	24	4.596
				30	2.299	29	2.705							31	4.638
Feb 02	2.721	Feb 01	4.039	Feb 06	2.374	Feb 05	2.695	Feb 04	2.946	Feb 03	3.505	Feb 01	3.888	Feb 07	4.650
09	2.810	08	3.563	13	2.462	12	2.759	11	2.944	10	3.540	08	3.903	14	4.695
16	2.726	15	4.045	20	2.496	19	2.849	18	2.905	17	3.534	15	3.936	21	4.696
24	2.589	23	4.168	27	2.594	26	2.664	25	2.870	24	3.547	23	3.989	28	4.661
		29	4.278												
Mar 02	2.816	Mar 07	3.641	Mar 06	2.485	Mar 05	2.721	Mar 04	2.897	Mar 02	3.589	Mar 01	3.982	Mar 07	4.620
09	3.062	14	3.451	13	2.352	12	2.804	11	2.870	09	3.534	08	3.948	14	4.718
16	2.763	21	3.033	20	2.278	19	2.689	18	2.902	16	3.538	15	3.917	21	4.576
23	2.766	28	2.792	27	2.392	26	2.719	25	2.919	23	3.550	22	3.922	28	4.555
30	2.841									30	3.525	29	3.921		
Apr 06	2.948	Apr 04	2.731	Apr 03	2.470	Apr 02	2.757	Apr 01	2.922	Apr 06	3.503	Apr 05	3.942	Apr 04	4.531
13	3.075	11	3.622	10	2.360	09	2.720	08	2.913	13	3.484	12	3.937	11	4.618
20	3.105	17	3.306	17	2.292	16	2.723	15	2.917	20	3.463	19	3.946	18	4.664
27	2.831	25	3.317	24	2.186	23	2.740	22	2.884	27	3.446	26	3.916	25	4.630
						30	2.748	29	2.898						
May 04	2.935	May 02	3.003	May 01	2.300	May 07	2.720	May 06	2.905	May 04	3.482	May 03	3.901	May 02	4.674
11	2.722	09	3.274	08	2.232	14	2.646	13	2.903	11	3.491	10	3.893	09	4.630
18	2.869	16	3.793	15	2.264	21	2.700	20	2.922	18	3.482	17	3.897	16	4.626
25	2.878	23	3.497	22	2.354	28	2.656	27	2.974	25	3.475	24	3.889	23	4.638
		31	3.184	31	2.438									31	4.641
Jun 01	3.149	Jun 06	2.776 15-month low	Jun 05	2.516	Jun 04	2.691	Jun 03	3.028	Jun 01	3.478	Jun 01	3.870	Jun 06	4.573
08	3.283	13	2.292	12	2.295	11	2.671	10	2.975	08	3.462	07	3.781	13	4.575
15	3.276	20	2.613	19	2.325	18	2.721	17	2.997	15	3.496	14	3.799	20	4.470
22	3.281	27	2.399	26	2.219	25	2.792	24	2.979	22	3.478	21	3.789	27	4.435
29	3.164									29	3.479	28	3.784		

1959		1960		1961		1962		1963		1964		1965		1966	
Jul 06	3.266	Jul 05	2.307	Jul 03	2.305	Jul 02	2.930	Jul 01	3.011	Jul 06	3.492	Jul 06	3.853	Jul 05	4.731
13	3.401	11	2.567	10	2.322	09	2.974	08	3.164	13	3.448	12	3.883	11	4.876
20	3.337	18	2.307	17	2.200	16	2.983	15	3.192	20	3.503	19	3.833	18	4.996
27	3.047	25	2.404	24	2.244	23	2.892	22	3.206	27	3.475	26	3.803	25	4.818
				31	2.300	30	2.874	29	3.263						
Aug 03	3.043	Aug 01	2.131	Aug 07	2.366	Aug 06	2.802	Aug 05	3.253	Aug 03	3.488	Aug 02	3.832	Aug 01	4.834
10	3.150	08	2.215	14	2.519	13	2.867	12	3.335	10	3.510	09	3.846	08	4.826
17	3.417	15	2.278	21	2.503	20	2.837	19	3.355	17	3.511	16	3.813	15	5.048
24	3.824	22	2.518	28	2.321	27	2.806	26	3.396	24	3.513	23	3.855	22	5.020
31	3.889	29	2.550							31	3.512	30	3.886	29	5.087
Sep 08	3.979	Sep 06	2.520	Sep 05	2.392	Sep 04	2.834	Sep 03	3.384	Sep 08	3.514	Sep 07	3.898	Sep 06	5.155
14	4.166	12	2.654	11	2.328	10	2.789	09	3.343	14	3.541	13	3.887	12	5.447
21	3.958	19	2.434	18	2.262	17	2.796	16	3.409	21	3.542	20	3.905	19	5.586
28	4.194	26	2.286	25	2.233	24	2.749	23	3.379	28	3.555	27	3.983	26	5.503
								30	3.408						
Oct 05	4.007	Oct 03	2.473	Oct 02	2.302	Oct 01	2.752	Oct 07	3.459	Oct 05	3.582	Oct 04	4.050	Oct 03	5.408
12	4.262	10	2.698	09	2.389	08	2.760	14	3.458	12	3.580	11	4.006	10	5.471
19	4.099	17	2.406	16	2.382	15	2.749	21	3.488	19	3.592	18	4.034	17	5.424
26	4.022	24	2.129	23	2.325	22	2.742	28	3.452	26	3.567	25	4.040	24	5.246
		31	2.127	30	2.280	29	2.686							31	5.234
Nov 02	4.137	Nov 07	2.390	Nov 06	2.349	Nov 05	2.841	Nov 04	3.517	Nov 02	3.562	Nov 01	4.082	Nov 07	5.432
09	4.089	14	2.624	13	2.516	12	2.801	11	3.565	09	3.574	08	4.045	14	5.459
16	4.332	21	2.396	20	2.537	19	2.833	18	3.524	16	3.600	15	4.097	21	5.252
23	4.279	28	2.326	27	2.606	26	2.853	26	3.480	23	3.758	22	4.104	28	5.202
30	4.501									30	3.868	29	4.115		
Dec 07	4.638	Dec 05	2.328	Dec 04	2.625	Dec 03	2.861	Dec 02	3.531	Dec 07	3.815	Dec 06	4.344	Dec 05	5.198
14	4.535	12	2.334	11	2.579	10	2.807	09	3.500	14	3.864	13	4.391	12	5.048
21	4.670	19	2.222	18	2.670	17	2.861	16	3.538	21	3.868	20	4.505	19	4.842
28	4.516	27	2.148	26	2.594	24	2.894	23	3.522	28	3.867	27	4.457	27	4.747
						31	2.926	30	3.524						

Table 4b   AAA Corporate Bond Rates

1959 Week Ended		1960 Week Ended		1961 Week Ended		1962 Week Ended		1963 Week Ended		1964 Week Ended		1965 Week Ended		1966 Week Ended	
Jan 03	4.10%	Jan 02	4.61%	Jan 07	4.34%	Jan 06	4.43%	Jan 05	4.22%	Jan 04	4.37%	Jan 02	4.43%	Jan 01	4.73%
10	4.09	09	4.61	14	4.33	13	4.42	12	4.21	11	4.37	09	4.44	08	4.73
17	4.11	16	4.61	21	4.32	20	4.42	19	4.20	18	4.38	16	4.43	15	4.74
24	4.12	23	4.61	28	4.31	27	4.41	26	4.21	25	4.38	23	4.43	22	4.74
31	4.16	30	4.61									30	4.42	29	4.74
Feb 07	4.15	Feb 06	4.60	Feb 04	4.30	Feb 03	4.42	Feb 02	4.21	Feb 01	4.37	Feb 06	4.41	Feb 05	4.75
14	4.14	13	4.57	11	4.28	10	4.42	09	4.19	08	4.36	13	4.41	12	4.76
21	4.14	20	4.54	18	4.27	17	4.43	16	4.19	15	4.36	20	4.41	19	4.79
28	4.13	27	4.54	25	4.25	24	4.42	23	4.19	22	4.36	27	4.41	26	4.82
										29	4.35				
Mar 07	4.11	Mar 05	4.54	Mar 04	4.23	Mar 03	4.42	Mar 02	4.19	Mar 07	4.36	Mar 06	4.41	Mar 05	4.85
14	4.13	12	4.51	11	4.22	10	4.40	09	4.19	14	4.37	13	4.41	12	4.88
21	4.13	19	4.48	18	4.21	17	4.39	16	4.19	21	4.38	20	4.42	19	4.93
28	4.14	26	4.46	25	4.22	24	4.39	23	4.19	28	4.39	27	4.43	26	4.97
						31	4.38	30	4.19						
Apr 04	4.17	Apr 02	4.45	Apr 01	4.22	Apr 07	4.37	Apr 06	4.20	Apr 04	4.40	Apr 03	4.42	Apr 02	4.99
11	4.20	09	4.44	08	4.23	14	4.34	13	4.20	11	4.40	10	4.42	09	4.98
18	4.22	16	4.45	15	4.24	21	4.33	20	4.21	18	4.40	17	4.43	16	4.95
25	4.26	23	4.45	22	4.26	28	4.31	27	4.22	25	4.41	24	4.43	23	4.95
		30	4.46	29	4.28									30	4.95
May 02	4.30	May 07	4.46	May 06	4.29	May 05	4.30	May 04	4.22	May 02	4.41	May 01	4.43	May 07	4.94
09	4.33	14	4.45	13	4.27	12	4.29	11	4.22	09	4.41	08	4.43	14	4.95
16	4.36	21	4.46	20	4.25	19	4.28	18	4.21	16	4.41	15	4.45	21	5.01
23	4.39	28	4.47	27	4.27	26	4.27	25	4.22	23	4.41	22	4.43	28	5.02
30	4.42									30	4.41	29	4.44		
Jun 06	4.44	Jun 04	4.48	Jun 03	4.29	Jun 02	4.28	Jun 01	4.23	Jun 06	4.41	Jun 05	4.45	Jun 04	5.04
13	4.47	11	4.44	10	4.31	09	4.28	08	4.23	13	4.41	12	4.46	11	5.06
20	4.46	18	4.45	17	4.33	16	4.28	15	4.23	20	4.41	19	4.47	18	5.06
27	4.47	25	4.45	24	4.34	23	4.29	22	4.22	27	4.41	26	4.47	25	5.07
						30	4.29	29	4.22						

	1959	1960	1961	1962	1963	1964	1965	1966
	Jul 04 4.48	Jul 02 4.44	Jul 01 4.36	Jul 07 4.32	Jul 06 4.23	Jul 04 4.40	Jul 03 4.46	Jul 02 5.10
	11 4.48	09 4.44	08 4.39	14 4.34	13 4.24	11 4.40	10 4.47	09 5.12
	18 4.47	16 4.43	15 4.41	21 4.33	20 4.27	18 4.41	17 4.48	16 5.14
	25 4.46	23 4.40	22 4.41	28 4.35	27 4.29	25 4.40	24 4.48	23 5.17
		30 4.38	29 4.42				31 4.48	30 5.22
	Aug 01 4.45	Aug 06 4.34	Aug 05 4.45	Aug 04 4.37	Aug 03 4.29	Aug 01 4.40	Aug 07 4.47	Aug 06 5.24
	08 4.43	13 4.30 (15-month low)	12 4.45	11 4.36	10 4.29	08 4.41	14 4.48	13 5.25
	15 4.42	20 4.26	19 4.45	18 4.36	17 4.29	15 4.42	21 4.50	20 5.31
	22 4.42	27 4.23	26 4.44	25 4.34	24 4.29	22 4.41	28 4.51	27 5.37
	29 4.44				31 4.29	29 4.41		
	Sep 05 4.47	Sep 03 4.23	Sep 02 4.44	Sep 01 4.33	Sep 07 4.30	Sep 05 4.42	Sep 04 4.51	Sep 03 5.44
	12 4.49	10 4.23	09 4.46	08 4.33	14 4.31	12 4.42	11 4.52	10 5.52
	19 4.52	17 4.26	16 4.46	15 4.32	21 4.32	19 4.42	18 4.52	17 5.51
	26 4.54	24 4.26	23 4.45	22 4.31	28 4.32	26 4.42	25 4.52	24 5.49
			30 4.45	29 4.31				
	Oct 03 4.57	Oct 01 4.27	Oct 07 4.43	Oct 06 4.29	Oct 05 4.32	Oct 03 4.42	Oct 02 4.53	Oct 01 5.47
	10 4.57	08 4.28	14 4.42	13 4.28	12 4.31	10 4.42	09 4.57	08 5.44
	17 4.56	15 4.29	21 4.42	20 4.27	19 4.31	17 4.42	16 4.57	15 5.43
	24 4.56	22 4.31	28 4.42	27 4.27	26 4.32	24 4.43	23 4.57	22 5.41
	31 4.56	29 4.30				31 4.43	30 4.57	29 5.37
	Nov 07 4.57	Nov 05 4.30	Nov 04 4.40	Nov 03 4.26	Nov 02 4.32	Nov 07 4.43	Nov 06 4.58	Nov 05 5.35
	14 4.57	12 4.29	11 4.39	10 4.25	09 4.33	14 4.43	13 4.60	12 5.35
	21 4.57	19 4.30	18 4.39	17 4.25	16 4.33	21 4.42	20 4.61	19 5.36
	28 4.55	26 4.32	25 4.39	24 4.24	23 4.33	28 4.44	27 4.61	26 5.36
					30 4.33			
	Dec 05 4.55	Dec 03 4.33	Dec 02 4.38	Dec 01 4.25	Dec 07 4.33	Dec 05 4.45	Dec 04 4.60 (7-year high)	Dec 03 5.37
	12 4.56	10 4.35	09 4.39	08 4.26	14 4.34	12 4.45	11 4.64	10 5.38
	19 4.59	17 4.34	16 4.42	15 4.25	21 4.36	19 4.43	18 4.69	17 5.38
	26 4.59	24 4.34	23 4.44	22 4.24	28 4.37	26 4.43	25 4.71	24 5.39
		31 4.35	30 4.44	29 4.23				31 5.40

Table 5

Favorable	Unfavorable	Favorable Climate (Length in Months)	Economic Recovery Begins	Months after Climate Turns Favorable	Recession Begins	Months after Climate Turns Unfavorable
	January 9, 1948				November 1948	10
January 28, 1949		36	October 1949	9		
	January 1, 1952[b]				July 1953	18
September 21, 1953		35	May 1954	8		
	August 31, 1956				August 1957	10
December 30, 1957		25	April 1958	4		
	January 1, 1960[b]				April 1960	3
June 6, 1960		67	February 1961	8		
	January 17, 1966				December 1966[c]	11
October 1, 1966[a]		19	April 1967[d]	6		
	May 20, 1968				December 1969	19
September 21, 1970		46	November 1970	2		
	July 12, 1974				November 1973	[d]
September 30, 1974		64	March 1975	6		
	January 1, 1980[b]				January 1980	0
May 12, 1980		7	July 1980	2		
	December 15, 1980				July 1981	7
August 2, 1982		61	November 1982	3		
	September 9, 1987[e]				[f]	
June 9, 1989						
	Average	40		5		8

[a] The favorable phase of the election cycle began.
[b] Extended until the favorable phase of the political cycle ended.
[c] Same month.
[d] Minirecession estimated.
[e] Eight months before climate turned unfavorable.
[f] No recession.

to a halt. Eight of the nine business contractions since 1946[3] began after the investment climate turned hostile.[4]

What happens is that a business contraction reduces the demand for funds, and as a consequence, interest rates tumble. However, the lower cost of borrowing soon encourages a wave of consumer spending along with a resurgence of business investment, and this lifts the economy out of recession and launches it on an upward course.

A booming economy, on the other hand, produces hefty increases in the demand for funds, and this sends both short- and long-term interest rates soaring. Rates reach painfully high levels, and this, of course, discourages spending by businesses and consumers. The economy will soon come to a screeching halt and the earnings of the nation's business firms will hit the skids.

The most striking relationship is that between the investment climate and the stock market. An investor who bought stocks on the day after the climate turned favorable and sold on the day after the climate turned hostile would have bought very close to a major bottom and sold near a bull market high (see Table 6 and Chart 2). Such an investor would have bought on June 7, 1960, when the Dow Jones Industrial Average, the most widely followed stock market index, was at 645. This investor would have sold on January 18, 1966, when the Dow was at 994, less than one Dow point from what was to be the actual top, pocketing profits of 45 percent. All purchases made at the beginning of

---

[3] Although the slowdown in GNP during the January to March quarter of 1967 was not officially designated a recession by the National Bureau of Economic Research, which serves as the arbiter of when a recession begins and ends, corporate earnings did decline for three consecutive quarters, and many economists and financial observers persist in calling it a "minirecession." It is shaded in along with other recessions on their charts and graphs.

[4] The record shows a recession began in November 1973, eight months before the investment climate turned unfavorable. But during that span, the slump was unusually mild. For instance, the index of industrial production, a fairly reliable indicator of the nation's output of goods, continued to post gains up until July 1974, the same month that the warning bell sounded.

Table 6   Major Stock Market Signals

Buy	Dow	Sell	Dow	Gain (%)
1. January 29, 1949	179	January 2, 1952	269	50
2. September 22, 1953	261	September 4, 1956	507	94
3. December 31, 1957	435	January 4, 1960	679	56
4. June 7, 1960	645	January 18, 1966	994	54
5. October 3, 1966	757	May 21, 1968	896	18
6. September 22, 1970	747	July 15, 1974	786	5
7. October 1, 1974	604	January 2, 1980	824	36
8. May 13, 1980	816	December 31, 1981	918	13
9. August 3, 1982	816	September 9, 1987	2549	212
10. June 19, 1989	2479			
			Average	59%

the nine favorable investment climates were very profitable, the average gain being 59 percent (not including dividends). On the other hand, the Dow experienced an average loss of 11 percent during the eight hostile climates. On October 19, 1987, the Dow lost 22.6 percent in a single day. This represented more than a half trillion dollars in lost values. Though comparatively short-lived, this hostile phase was worth avoiding. The effects of interest rates can be important.

However, an investor must be careful if long-term rates do not make a fifteen-month low. If only short-term rates fall to a fifteen-month low, the friendly investment climate will not be lengthy. This is because there will not be enough of a window to allow business firms to convert short-term borrowing into long-term debt. Balance sheets will remain tattered, and as a result, the business community will not be in a position to finance a major expansion.

This happened in the climates that began in 1966 and 1980, and in both cases, the economic recovery soon fizzled out and the advance in the stock market proved modest. These two short friendly climates lasted an average of thirteen months, as opposed to an average of forty-seven months for those climates wherein

Chart 2   The Investment Climate[*]
Dow Jones Industrial Average   1945-1984

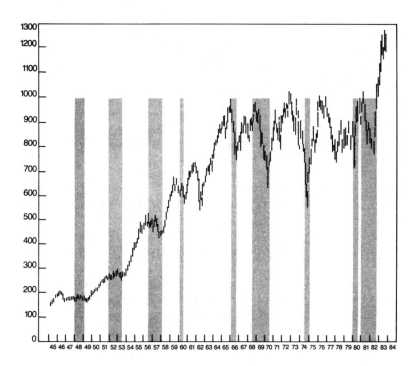

[*] Unfavorable periods are shaded.

long-term rates registered a fifteen-month low. In order for the recovery to broaden into a full-fledged expansion and the bull market in stocks to have staying power, long-term rates must touch a fifteen-month low.

The message to investors is clear. Keep your eyes on the investment climate. When this climate turns favorable, investors are given the green light to strike out and seek their fortunes. This is the time to put one's money at risk—the secret being that in reality there is very little risk at the time. On the other hand, the onset of a hostile investment climate is a red light, indicating trouble looming on the horizon. It is a time for investors to pull in their horns and become defensive. Those who ignore the warning will in all likelihood end up with at least one black eye.

The investment climate is the most important factor affecting the economy and the stock market, but it is not the whole story. Sell signals in 1974 and 1980 came well after the Dow had topped out, and investors who relied solely on the investment climate would have been short-changed. Such investors would have emerged from the 1970-73 bull market, when the Dow appreciated by 67 percent, with a meager 5 percent return.

Luckily, there are two other factors, which, when considered along with the investment climate, will allow investors to spot turning points with almost pinpoint accuracy. The first of these factors is inflation, which will be taken up in the following chapter.

Chapter 3
Inflationary Spirals

In the previous chapter, we saw how the stock market usually benefits from a friendly investment climate. However, there are times during a favorable investment climate when the stock market proves disappointing, and the dominant force in investments becomes an unquenchable thirst for real assets such as gold, commodities, real estate, art, antiques—any asset considered scarce and thought to be of lasting value. This occurs during an inflationary spiral. A period of galloping prices has an important and still not completely understood effect on investment markets.

The best way to keep tabs on inflation is to watch the Producers Price Index, formerly the Wholesale Price Index[1] (see Table 7). Its movements tend to precede changes at the consumer level by several months. Early each month, the Bureau of Labor Statistics reports the Producers Price Index for the previous month. It is picked up and reported in most major newspapers.[2]

To measure inflation, it is necessary to look at the year-to-year change in this index. That is, how does

[1] In 1978, the Bureau of Labor Statistics substituted the Producers Price Index for the Wholesale Price Index as the primary indicator of prices at an early stage of the production process. When dealing with the pre-1978 period, we will refer to the Wholesale Price Index.

[2] It also reported in the *Federal Reserve Bulletin* and the *Survey of Current Business Conditions,* but by the time these publications are released, the figures will be several months old.

Table 7   Wholesale Price Index 1944-1978 (1967 = 100)

Year	Ann. Avg.	Jan.	Feb.	Mar.	Apr.	May	June	July	Aug.	Sept.	Oct.	Nov.	Dec.
1944	53.6	53.3	53.4	53.5	53.5	53.6	53.8	53.7	53.5	53.6	53.7	53.8	54.0
1945	54.6	54.1	54.2	54.3	54.5	54.7	54.8	54.7	54.5	54.3	54.6	55.0	55.2
1946	62.3	55.2	55.5	56.2	56.8	57.2	58.2	64.4	66.5	64.0	69.2	72.1	72.7
1947	76.5	73.2	73.9	75.7	75.2	74.8	74.8	75.6	76.6	78.1	79.1	79.9	81.4
1948	82.8	82.9	81.3	81.3	82.0	82.4	83.0	83.7	84.3	84.2	83.3	83.1	82.6
1949	78.7	81.6	80.3	80.1	79.3	78.6	77.9	77.8	77.9	78.0	77.7	77.7	77.6
1950	81.8	77.6	78.0	78.1	78.1	79.1	79.5	81.7	83.5	85.0	85.5	86.7	89.0
1951	91.1	91.2	92.5	92.5	92.3	92.0	91.3	90.7	90.2	90.0	90.2	90.2	90.1
1952	88.6	89.7	89.3	89.2	88.7	88.6	88.2	88.7	89.1	88.7	88.2	87.8	87.0
1953	87.4	87.2	87.0	87.3	86.8	87.2	86.9	88.0	87.7	88.1	87.5	87.2	87.4
1954	87.6	88.0	87.7	87.7	88.1	88.0	87.3	87.7	87.7	87.3	87.1	87.3	86.9
1955	87.8	87.4	87.7	87.3	87.7	87.2	87.6	87.7	88.0	88.7	88.6	88.2	88.3
1956	90.7	88.8	89.2	89.5	90.2	90.8	90.7	90.5	91.0	91.7	91.7	92.0	92.3
1957	93.3	92.7	92.8	92.7	93.0	92.9	93.2	93.8	94.0	93.7	93.5	93.7	94.1
1958	94.6	94.3	94.4	95.0	94.7	94.8	94.6	94.6	94.5	94.5	94.4	94.6	94.6
1959	94.8	94.8	94.8	94.9	95.2	95.2	95.0	94.8	94.5	95.0	94.5	94.3	94.3
1960	94.9	94.7	94.7	95.2	95.2	95.0	94.8	95.0	94.6	94.6	94.9	94.9	94.8
1961	94.5	95.2	95.2	95.2	94.7	94.3	93.8	94.2	94.3	94.3	94.3	94.3	94.6
1962	94.8	95.0	94.9	94.9	94.6	94.4	94.3	94.6	94.7	95.4	94.8	94.9	94.6
1963	94.5	94.7	94.4	94.2	94.0	94.3	94.5	94.8	94.6	94.5	94.7	94.9	94.5
1964	94.7	95.2	94.7	94.6	94.5	94.3	94.3	94.6	94.5	94.9	95.0	94.9	94.9
1965	96.6	95.2	95.4	95.5	95.9	96.2	96.9	97.0	97.0	97.1	97.2	97.5	98.1
1966	99.8	98.6	99.3	99.3	99.4	99.5	99.6	100.3	100.7	100.1	100.1	99.8	99.8
1967	100.0	100.1	99.9	99.6	99.2	99.7	100.2	100.3	100.0	100.1	100.1	100.1	100.8
1968	102.5	101.1	101.9	102.1	102.1	102.4	102.5	102.8	102.5	102.9	102.9	103.3	103.6
1969	106.5	104.3	104.8	105.4	105.5	106.3	106.8	107.0	106.9	107.1	107.4	108.1	108.6

Year	Jan.	Feb.	Mar.	Apr.	May	Jun.	Jul.	Aug.	Sep.	Oct.	Nov.	Dec.
1969	3.2	2.8	3.2	3.3	3.8	4.2	4.1	4.3	4.1	4.4	4.6	4.8
1970	4.8	4.7	4.3	4.3	3.5	3.4	3.6	3.3	3.6	3.3	2.6	2.2
1971	2.3	2.8	2.9	3.1	3.5	3.5	3.4	4.3	3.2	3.2	3.3	4.1
1972	4.0	4.0	3.8	3.6	3.8	3.9	4.3	4.2	4.9	4.8	5.3	6.3
1973	7.1	8.2	10.6	11.1	12.7	14.5	12.2	18.6	16.2	15.6	15.3	15.4
1974	17.8	17.8	16.6	17.0	16.4	14.5	20.4	17.8	19.7	22.7	23.5	20.9
1975	17.2	14.6	12.5	12.7	11.7	11.6	8.7	5.6	6.3	5.1	3.8	4.2
1976	4.4	4.7	5.5	5.3	4.7	5.5	5.0	4.0	4.0	3.6	4.2	4.7
1977	4.8	6.0	6.8	7.2	7.3	6.2	5.6	5.9	5.7	5.9	6.2	5.9
1978	6.4	6.3	6.1	6.3	6.6	7.8	8.2	8.2	8.8	9.5	9.4	9.7
1979[a]	9.9	10.3	10.7	10.4	10.3	9.9	10.1	11.1	11.9	12.4	13.0	12.8
1980	13.3	13.6	13.9	13.7	13.6	13.8	14.6	14.8	13.1	13.1	12.4	11.8
1981	11.3	10.8	10.8	10.9	10.8	10.5	9.0	8.2	8.2	7.6	7.4	7.3
1982	6.5	5.5	4.2	3.3	3.0	3.5	3.6	4.0	3.6	3.6	3.7	3.7
1983	2.2	2.2	2.2	2.1	2.3	1.8	1.4	1.3	1.4	1.3	0.7	0.6
1984	2.0	2.3	2.8	2.9	2.4	2.1	2.3	1.8	1.5	1.4	1.9	1.7
1985	1.0	0.7	0.2	0.7	1.0	1.1	0.9	0.8	0.2	1.1	1.4	1.8
1986	1.3	-0.2	-1.4	-2.0	-1.8	-1.6	-2.4	-1.8	-0.9	-1.4	-1.9	-2.3
1987	1.4	0.1	1.6	2.7	2.4	2.4	3.4	3.2	3.3	2.6	2.6	2.2
1988*	2.2	1.9	1.9	1.8	2.0	2.1	2.5	2.6	2.7	3.0	3.3	4.0
1989	4.5	5.3	5.5	5.6	6.2	5.9	5.0	4.2	4.5	4.9	4.6	4.8
1990	5.8	5.1	4.4									

[a] Producers' Price Index substituted.
* Based on a new series beginning on January 1, 1988.

one month's figure compare to the same month one year earlier—say, November 1981 as compared to November 1980? In November 1981, the Producers Price Index stood at 7.2 percent above its year-earlier reading, and this is the rate of inflation. Throughout the remainder of this book, the inflation rate will be expressed as the year-to-year change in the Producers Price Index. These rates, for the period beginning in 1945, are shown in Table 8.

An inflationary spiral begins when the rate of price increase reaches 5 percent or more and is at its highest reading in a year. But there is a catch. This rapid burst of prices will not become an inflationary spiral unless people become convinced that this escalation in the price level is likely to continue. The first indication that inflation is lurching out of control comes when the rate of price increase quickens to 5 percent or more. Though people may moan and groan about increases of a lesser magnitude, it seems that a rate of 5 percent is necessary to alter the mechanisms of the marketplace. But a 5 percent rate of inflation does not by itself indicate that an inflationary spiral is brewing. Inflation must also be gathering momentum. No matter how high the rate of inflation, an inflationary spiral will not begin unless inflation is gaining momentum.

To spot when the rate of inflation is picking up or losing momentum, we can compare the current month-to-month price increases to those during the past year. If you look at Table 8, you will see that we get a new reading on the rate of inflation each month. When the rate of price increases is the highest in twelve months, inflation is gathering momentum. Conversely, when the rate of inflation registers the lowest reading in a year, inflation is losing momentum. This indicates inflation is cooling.

A sign that inflation was gaining momentum was given in August 1971—the 4.3 percent rate of increase registered that month was the highest reading of the past year. However, as the rate was still below the 5 percent threshold, we could conclude that inflation

Table 8   Rates of Inflation

Year	Jan.	Feb.	Mar.	Apr.	May	Jun.	Jul.	Aug.	Sep.	Oct.	Nov.	Dec.
1945	1.5	1.5	2.2	1.9	1.9	1.9	1.9	1.9	1.3	1.7	2.2	2.2
1946	2.0	2.4	2.7	4.2	4.6	6.2	17.6	22.0	17.9	26.7	31.1	31.7
1947	32.6	33.2	34.7	32.4	30.8	28.5	17.4	15.2	22.0	14.3	10.8	12.0
1948	13.3	10.0	7.4	9.0	10.2	11.0	10.7	10.1	7.8	5.3	4.0	1.5
1949	(1.6)	(1.2)	(1.5)	(3.3)	(4.6)	(6.1)	(7.0)	(7.6)	(7.4)	(6.7)	(6.5)	(6.1)
1950	(4.9)	(2.9)	(2.5)	(1.5)	+0.6	2.1	5.0	7.2	9.0	10.0	11.6	14.7
1951	17.5	18.6	18.4	18.2	16.3	14.8	11.0	8.0	5.9	5.5	4.0	1.2
1952	(1.6)	(3.5)	(3.6)	(3.9)	(3.7)	(3.4)	(2.2)	(1.2)	(1.4)	(2.2)	(2.7)	(3.4)
1953	(2.8)	(2.6)	(2.1)	(2.1)	(1.6)	(1.5)	(0.8)	(1.6)	(0.7)	(0.8)	(0.7)	+0.5
1954	0.9	0.8	0.5	1.5	0.9	0.5	(0.3)	0.0	(0.9)	(0.5)	+0.1	(0.6)
1955	(0.7)	0.0	(0.5)	(0.5)	(0.9)	+0.3	0.0	0.3	1.6	1.7	1.0	1.6
1956	1.6	1.7	2.5	2.9	4.1	3.5	3.2	3.4	3.4	3.5	4.3	4.5
1957	4.4	3.8	3.6	3.1	2.3	2.8	3.6	3.3	2.2	2.0	1.8	2.0
1958	1.7	1.7	1.4	1.8	2.0	1.5	0.9	0.5	0.9	1.0	1.0	0.5
1959	0.5	0.4	(0.1)	0.5	0.4	0.4	0.2	0.0	0.5	0.1	(0.3)	(0.3)
1960	(0.1)	(0.1)	+0.3	0.0	(0.2)	0.2	2.0	0.1	(0.4)	0.4	0.6	0.5
1961	0.5	0.5	0.0	(0.5)	(0.7)	(1.1)	(0.8)	(0.3)	(0.3)	(0.6)	(0.6)	(0.2)
1962	(0.2)	(0.3)	(0.3)	(0.1)	+0.1	0.5	0.4	0.4	1.0	0.5	0.6	0.0
1963	(0.5)	(0.5)	(0.7)	(0.6)	(0.1)	+0.2	(0.2)	(0.1)	(0.9)	(0.1)	0.0	(0.1)
1964	0.5	0.3	0.4	0.5	0.0	(0.2)	(0.2)	(0.1)	+0.4	0.3	0.0	0.4
1965	0.0	0.7	1.0	1.5	2.0	2.8	2.5	2.6	2.3	2.3	2.7	3.4
1966	3.6	4.1	4.0	3.6	3.4	2.8	3.4	3.8	3.7	3.0	2.4	1.7
1967	1.5	0.6	0.5	(0.2)	+0.2	0.6	0.0	(0.7)	(0.6)	0.0	0.3	1.0
1968	1.0	2.0	2.5	2.9	2.7	2.3	2.5	2.5	2.8	2.8	3.2	2.8

(Table continues)

Year	Ann. Avg.	Jan.	Feb.	Mar.	Apr.	May	June	July	Aug.	Sept.	Oct.	Nov.	Dec.
1970	110.4	109.3	109.7	109.9	110.0	110.0	110.4	110.9	110.4	111.0	110.9	110.9	111.0
1971	114.0	111.8	112.8	113.1	113.4	113.9	114.4	114.7	115.1	114.6	114.5	114.6	115.6
1972	119.1	116.3	117.3	117.4	117.5	118.2	118.8	119.7	119.9	120.2	120.0	120.7	122.9
1973	134.7	124.5	126.9	129.8	130.5	133.2	136.0	134.3	142.1	139.7	138.7	139.2	141.8
1974	160.1	146.6	149.5	151.4	152.7	155.0	155.7	161.7	167.4	167.2	170.2	171.9	171.5
1975	174.9	171.8	171.3	170.4	172.1	173.2	173.7	175.7	176.7	177.7	178.9	178.2	178.7
1976	183.0	179.4	179.4	179.7	181.3	181.9	183.2	184.4	183.8	184.8	185.3	185.6	187.1
1977	194.2	188.1	190.2	192.0	194.3	195.2	194.5	194.8	194.6	195.3	196.3	197.1	198.2
1978	209.3	200.1	202.1	202.1	206.5	208.0	209.6	210.7	210.6	212.4	214.9	215.7	217.5

Producers Price Index 1978–1989

Year	Ann. Avg.	Jan.	Feb.	Mar.	Apr.	May	June	July	Aug.	Sept.	Oct.	Nov.	Dec.
1978	195.9	188.2	189.7	190.3	192.8	194.4	195.9	197.6	197.0	198.5	201.0	201.7	203.9
1979	217.7	206.9	209.3	210.7	212.9	214.4	215.2	217.6	218.9	222.2	225.9	228.0	230.0
1980	247.0	234.4	237.7	240.0	242.1	243.4	244.9	249.3	251.4	251.4	255.4	256.2	257.2
1981	269.8	260.9	263.3	266.0	268.5	269.6	270.5	271.8	271.5	271.5	274.3	274.7	275.4
1982	280.7	277.9	277.9	277.3	277.3	277.8	279.9	281.7	282.3	281.2	284.1	284.9	285.5
1983		283.9	284.1	283.4	283.1	284.2	285.0	285.7	286.1	285.1	287.9	286.8	287.1
1984		289.5	290.6	291.4	291.2	291.1	290.9	292.3	291.3	289.5	291.5	292.3	292.0
1985		292.3	292.6	292.1	293.1	294.1	294.0	294.8	293.5	290.5	294.7	296.4	297.2
1986		296.0	291.9	288.0	287.2	288.9	289.3	287.6	288.1	287.3	290.7	290.7	290.4
1987		291.8	292.3	292.6	294.9	295.8	296.2	297.4	297.3	296.7	298.2	298.2	296.8
1988*		106.3	106.1	106.3	107.0	107.5	170.7	108.6	108.7	108.6	109.4	109.8	110.0
1989		111.1	111.7	112.1	113.0	114.2	114.1	114.0	113.3	113.5	114.8	114.8	115.3
1990		117.5	117.4	117.0									

* Based on a new series beginning on January 1, 1988.

was still tolerable. The indication that prices had finally begun to gallop was given when the rate reached 5.3 percent in November 1972. On the other hand, it did not become apparent that the torrid inflation of 1972-74 had lost momentum until the rate fell to 12.5 percent, which was the lowest reading in a year, in March 1975.

While a 5 percent rate of inflation that is gaining momentum indicates an overheating economy, it does not always foretell an inflationary spiral. To do so, the acceleration in price level must take on a self-feeding character. That is, people must change their spending and investment habits. And they only do this when they have adopted expectations that the rapid price increases are likely to continue. Actually, it's rather easy to detect when people are likely to adopt inflationary expectations. They will become believers only after memories of the last deflation have faded. Up until now, we have focused on the rate of inflation. But to spot a deflation, we will look at the Producers Price Index itself—the actual number (Table 7). A one-year low—that is, an index number lower than any number in the past year—is a sign of an actual deflation. For instance, in February 1949 the index number fell to 80.3, and as this was a one-year low, it indicated a deflation had begun.

Since 1946 there have been four deflations, and each time inflationary expectations were killed. People thought we had entered a period of falling or stable prices, and as a result, they were slow to respond to a subsequent upturn in the rate of inflation. In general, it takes two years since the last deflation has ended before an acceleration in the price level will kindle inflationary expectations. Until that time, any quickening in the price level will be deceptive. It will be perceived as a temporary aberration or a return to normal, and people will not think inflation has become entrenched in the economy (see Table 9).

For example, in July 1950 the rate of inflation jumped to 5 percent. At first glance, this might appear to have been the beginning of an inflationary spiral.

Table 9   1946–1984

Deflationary Trend		Not Susceptible to
Begins *(1-Year-Low)*	*Ends*	*Inflationary Expectations*
February 1949	December 1949	February 1949–December 1951
January 1952	April 1953	January 1952–April 1955
November 1959	April 1963[a]	November 1959–April 1965
April 1967	April 1967	April 1967–April 1969
March 1986	April 1988	March 1986–April 1988

Note: The period began in 1946, more than six years after the last deflationary trend ended in August 1939.

[a] The deflationary trend actually ended in June 1961. However, before two years were up, the Wholesale Price Index made another yearly low and that deflationary trend lasted until April 1963.

But this flare-up in prices was not a genuine inflationary spiral because it was following too closely on the heels of a deflation. A deflation had begun in February 1949, when the Wholesale Price Index hit 80.3, and continued until December 1949. There would be a two-year grace period, or until December 1951, before inflationary expectations could be rekindled. Until that time, people would not be alarmed about the shrinking value of the dollar. But by the time December 1951 rolled around, inflation was clearly losing momentum. The rate of increase had fallen to a twelve-month low in September 1951, and when we looked in December, the rate at the last reading (the November figure) had slipped to 4 percent.

In general, we will not be susceptible to an inflationary spiral until two years after a deflationary trend has ended. On the other hand, if a subsiding rate of inflation does not turn into an actual deflation—that is, the index does not register a yearly low—it is not necessary to wait two years. This is because inflationary expectations will not have been snuffed out. They will lie dormant and can be quickly revived once the economy recovers. For instance, an inflationary spiral began in February 1977, just four months after the low point in a moderating trend.

In February 1989, the increase of the Producers Price Index hit the 5 plus mark and even went above 6 percent in May, but then appeared to settle back down. However, this appears to be more of a disinflationary period rather than deflationary (see Chapter 13 for further details on the effects of disinflation).

An inflationary spiral is signaled when the rate heats up to 5 percent and is gaining momentum—but only if two years have passed since the last deflation has ended.

When this occurs, it means that inflation has taken on a self-feeding character and is ready to roll. Demand mushrooms as people adopt a "buy now and beat the price increase" psychology. The shrinking purchasing power of the dollar also frightens people. They will shun stocks and bonds and turn to gold and other tangibles such as real estate, diamonds, art, and stamps as a means of defense. This robs the economy of the investment needed to expand business facilities, modernize plants and equipment, and increase productivity. The nation becomes unable to expand its output so as to accommodate the ballooning demand, and this fans the fires of inflation even more. The rate reaches still higher levels, further undermining confidence in the purchasing power of money, and on and on.

Each signal of an inflationary spiral is indicated in Table 10. The investment climate is altered in the middle of the following month, say, the fifteenth. This delay is because the Producers Price Index for a particular month is actually released at the beginning of the next month.

The outbreak of an inflationary spiral is bad news for stock market investors but good news for owners of real estate, "gold bugs," commodity traders, and collectors. This is because the stock market will be stopped dead in its tracks while gold and other tangibles will spring to life. The strategy for investors is obvious: sell stocks and buy real assets.

Once an inflationary spiral gets rolling, the only thing able to stop the bull market in real assets is the

Table 10 Inflationary Spirals

	Inflationary Spiral Begins	Sell Inflation Hedges	Gains/Loss	Loss of Purchasing Power
	I. July 15, 1946	January 30, 1948		
Rate of Inflation at Last Reading	6.2	12.0	29%–annualized 19%	22%
Wholesale Price Index	64.4	82.9	50%	
Cash Wheat	1.87[a]	2.81	78%	
Cash Soybeans	1.87[a]	4.11	46%	
Dow Jones Commodity Futures Index	111	162	(13%)	
Dow Jones Industrial Average	200	174		
	II. December 15, 1972	August 2, 1974		
Rate of Inflation at Last Reading	5.3	14.5	29%–annualized 19%	28%
Wholesale Price Index	122.9	167.4	145%	
Gold	$63	$156	84%	
Dow Jones Commodity Futures Index	184	338	(27%)	
Dow Jones Industrial Average	1027	752		
	III. March 15, 1977	January 22, 1980		
Rate of Inflation at Last Reading	6.0	12.9	31%–annualized 11%	24%
Producers' Price Index	178.6	234.4	405%	
Gold	$146	$737	74%	
Dow Jones Commodity Futures Index	137	239		
Homes (average price, existing single-family)	$41,000	$68,200	66%	
Dow Jones Industrial Average	965	866	(10%)	
		Average loss of purchasing power		25%

[a] Average monthly prices received by farmers.

onset of an unfavorable investment climate. Even if inflation has lost momentum, people will not be convinced the moderating price trend is for real as long as the investment climate remains friendly. The past period of runaway prices will have left a vivid impression on investors, and they will be on the lookout for a resurgence of rapid price increases. As a result, inflation hedges will continue to make headway. To turn the tide in gold and tangibles it takes the bitter medicine of high interest rates.

When the investment climate turns hostile, it is the sign that inflation is running out of gas, and the party in inflation hedges is about over. The rate of price increase will usually register its lowest reading in twelve months soon after. This loss of momentum confirms the fact that inflation has been brought to heel.[3]

The time to unload inflation hedges is shortly after the investment climate turns unfavorable. As there is likely to be a breath of life left in real assets, we can wait three weeks after the climate has turned sour before selling. For instance, although the investment climate turned hostile on January 1, 1980, indicating that inflation was running out of steam, the time to sell hard assets was three weeks later, January 22.

There have been three inflationary spirals following World War II. The first was signaled in mid-July 1946. Early in that month the Wholesale Price Index for June was released, and it showed inflation running at an annual rate of 6 percent, which was the highest reading in a year. At that time, the Dow Jones Average stood at 200, just 6 percent below its bull market high, which had been made six weeks earlier.

Although word came that inflation was losing momentum in mid-August 1947, fears about inflation remained, and this would be enough to drive real assets higher, until the climate turned sour in January 1948. During that eighteen-month span, the Wholesale Price

---

[3] Actually, it could take as long as eighteen months before we receive confirmation that inflation has moderated.

Index increased by over 29 percent. How did inflation hedges fare in that period? Let's look at cash wheat. Its price was $1.87 when this inflationary period began, and in January 1948 it stood at $2.81—a gain of 50 percent. The rise in cash soybeans was even better. From $2.31[4] in July 1946, the price rose to $4.11 during January 1948, a gain of 78 percent. An index of commodity futures put out by the Dow Jones Company increased by almost 50 percent. The price of homes leaped upward as the building boom following World War II got under way. In fact, nearly every tangible that was freely traded (gold at this time was fixed at $35 an ounce) experienced very respectable price advances. The one investment market that did not fare well was the stock market. On January 30, 1948, three weeks after we discovered that the investment climate had turned sour, the Dow stood at just 174, down 13 percent from its mid-July 1946 level (see Table 10).

Twenty-five years were to pass before inflation moved into high gear again. The signal that inflation was reaching a feverish pitch came in mid-December 1972, shortly after the release of the November Wholesale Price Index. The Dow at the time was 1027, about 2 percent below what was to be its peak. The sign that this inflationary spiral was losing its zing was given on July 12, 1974, and three weeks later, it was time to sell inflation hedges. During that twenty-month period, the Wholesale Price Index had increased 36 percent and in its wake made fools of those who saved. The Dow Jones Commodity Futures Index soared from 184 to 338—a rise of 84 percent. The gain in most tangibles, however, was even more spectacular. Gold, which was trading in London at $63 an ounce when the period of inflation began, rose to $179 an ounce—a gain of 185 percent.[5] For the first time since the early 1950's, homeowners were getting a taste of the lush increases in the values of their homes and finding they liked it. People were not long in realizing that the pur-

---

[4] Average monthly prices received by farmers.
[5] Gold had slipped to $156 an ounce by August 2, 1974.

chase of a home was perhaps the best investment they could make. Again, inflation hedges did very well indeed. The story for the stock market, however, was quite different. By early August 1974, the Dow was trading at just 752—off 27 percent from where it had stood when the period of runaway prices began.

The rate of inflation actually reached its peak level of 23.5 percent in November 1974, three months after the signal to sell real assets was flashed. And in mid-April 1975, the rate of inflation showed its lowest reading in twelve months, indicating that a moderating trend had set in. The next two years were to be a time of relative price stability.

The third period of galloping inflation was signaled in mid-March 1977 following the release of the February Wholesale Price Index number. The Dow at this time was 965, just 5 percent below its high-water mark. It would not be until January 22, 1980, which was three weeks after the investment climate turned unfavorable, that there was a sign to dump inflation hedges. During that thirty-four-month period, the Wholesale Price Index jumped 31 percent. But the quantum leap in the prices of most tangibles was simply mind-boggling. Gold, which began the period at $146 an ounce, was going for $737 when the period ended. Actually, gold reached its peak at $850 an ounce the day earlier. The Dow Jones Commodity Futures Index soared 74 percent. During this period, the average price of existing family homes zoomed from $41,000 to $68,000[6]—a breathtaking rise of 66 percent. And in some areas, the gain was even more spectacular. The western states, for instance, showed an increase of 93 percent. As real estate is a highly leveraged investment, returns were simply enormous. On a down payment of 20 percent, real estate investors in the western states reaped a gain of 465 percent, and if they had put down 10 percent, why, their gain was 930 percent. The increase in other tangibles was no less spectacular. Art, antiques, stamps, wines, and yes, even Mickey Mouse

[6] According to the National Association of Realtors.

Chart 3   Rates of Inflation* and Inflation Hedges
1945-1984

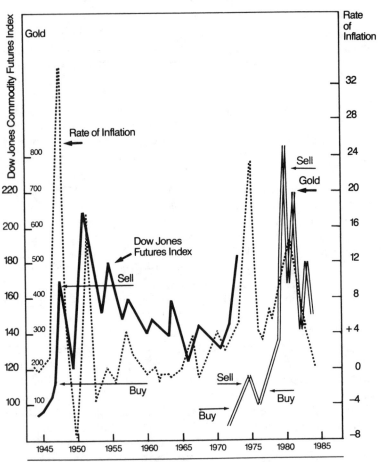

*   Wholesale price index 1944-1978
    Producer price index 1979-1984

watches, were increasing by leaps and bounds (Chart 3). Yet once again, practically the only conspicuous investment not to participate was stocks. When the sign to unload inflation hedges flashed in late January 1980, the Dow stood at 866—10 percent below its mid-March 1977 level.

The indication to sell inflation hedges came seven months before the rate of inflation reached its high-water mark of 14.8 percent in August 1980. In mid-December of that year, we got word that the rate had registered it lowest reading in twelve months, and this confirmed that inflation had lost its steam.

This was to be the longest period of rapidly accelerating inflation, and no doubt played a role in the hatching of a new economic theory, supply-side economics, designed to make the American economy more productive and therefore less prone to continued price increases. Ronald Reagan, a politician from the right wing of the Republican party incorporated this new theory into his campaign and rode it to victory in November 1980.

We can see that the outbreak of a spiraling inflation changes the complexion of investment markets. It explains why the stock market topped out in 1973 and again in 1976, well before the investment climate turned unfriendly.[7] Had investors sold their stock holdings when an inflationary spiral was signaled, they would have sold very close to the top of the 1970-73 and 1974-76 bull markets. For example, they would have gotten a sell signal on December 15, 1972, when the Dow was at 1027, about 2 percent from the peak (Table 10). This would have enabled them to pocket a respectable 38 percent on buys made in September 1970, instead of a skimpy 5 percent had they waited for the investment climate to turn hostile. Another sell signal was flashed on March 15, 1977, when the Dow stood at 96, just 5 percent from the top, and investors

---

[7] The stock market also topped out well before the investment climate turned unfriendly in January of 1948. The culprit: once again, an inflationary spiral. The outbreak of inflation was signaled on July 15, 1946, and investors who sold stocks on that date would have gotten 200 on the Dow, which was only 6 percent below the peak of 212 made six weeks earlier.

would have enriched themselves by 60 percent during that bull market.

As long as the investment climate is favorable and inflation is in check, the stock market is the best place to be. There will be a growing appetite to own stocks, and this will keep driving share prices higher. However, if the economy becomes trapped in an inflationary spiral, the stock market will become a dead issue while gold and real assets put on a glittering performance. They will continue to shine until about three weeks after the investment climate turns sour.

It should be clear by now that a new, friendly investment climate provides a period of investment opportunity. The economy recovers, the stock market booms, and sometimes there is a rapid appreciation in the price of real assets. This period of opportunity can be called an investment cycle. The stock market will be the first to respond. It marches to the tune of the economic recovery that follows on the heels of the friendly investment climate. The advance in stock prices will continue until either the investment climate turns hostile or an inflationary spiral begins. If a hostile investment climate sinks the stock market, the cycle ends with only one stage.

However, if the stock market is shot down by an inflationary spiral, a new opportunity surfaces. During this second stage of investment cycle, the stock market becomes a dead issue, while gold, silver, commodities, and real estate march to the tune of an escalating price level. As long as the fires of inflation are burning brightly, stocks will not become a buy—even if the Dow slips into a two-year low. But once the investment climate turns hostile, it indicates that inflation is running out of gas, and the cycle is about over.

When another favorable investment climate surfaces, a new investment cycle begins and stocks can be bought with confidence, even if inflation has not yet lost momentum. This is because there is often a fairly long delay—up to eighteen months—between the time we get a sign that inflation is about to lose steam and the rate of price increase actually falls to the lowest point in a year. For example, a signal that inflation was running out of gas was given in January 1980, and this, of course, spelled curtains for real assets. However, when the investment climate turned friendly four months later, there was still no visible sign that inflation had moderated. Yet it was safe to buy stocks. We could expect it to become apparent very soon that the punishingly high interest rates in effect a few months earlier had in fact punctured the balloon of inflation.[8]

An inflationary spiral is the second factor investors should consider. Since World War II, there have been three periods of runaway inflation, and each time the value of the dollar plummeted. Those who didn't protect their wealth suffered huge losses on the spending power of their savings. The average loss of purchasing power during these three periods was 25 percent. This means about $133 was needed in January 1980 to purchase what $100 would have bought in March 1977.

The indicators revealed in this chapter would have enabled investors to more than beat inflation. They could have profited handsomely instead. For instance, an investment in gold during the 1972-74 inflationary spiral would have returned investors 145 percent, which more than offset the 28 percent fall in purchasing power the dollar suffered during that time. And the 405 percent return to gold buyers during the 1977-80 inflationary spiral dwarfed the 24 percent loss of purchasing power during that period.

To beat inflation, you do not have to pack your investment portfolio with gold and other hard assets and sit on them through thick and thin, as many hard money advocates suggest. If investors take account of the investment climate and inflationary spirals, they can adopt a flexible investment strategy. They would have participated and profited in each period of galloping inflation. In addition, they could have been fully invested during the bulk of the eight post-World War

---

[8] If inflation has not lost momentum by the time a favorable investment climate surfaces, investors should not be concerned. It often takes a while before inflation visibly cools.

II bull markets in stocks, pocketing an average profit of 48 percent. And there never was a loss—NEVER!

Still, stock market timing can be improved. There are times to wait before buying stocks during a favorable investment climate. In the next chapter, we will consider the third and last factor in the model— whether the stock market is in a buy zone or a caution zone.

Chapter 4
Buying Zones

The stock market is related to the investment climate, as we have seen, but it also displays a nature of its own. That is, prices swing from cheap to dear and back to cheap again. These rhythmic swings in the stock market reflect the psychology of investors—that is, pessimism or optimism. When the investing public is pessimistic, stocks will be cheap and there is not much risk in owning securities. We can consider the stock market to be in a buying zone at this time. On the other hand, when investors are optimistic and see only a rose-colored future, most stocks will be sporting princely price-earnings ratios. As surely as night follows day, stock prices will soon suffer a nasty plunge.

Major bull markets are built on a foundation of investor pessimism. When economic prospects turn grim, there will be an exodus of investors from Wall Street. This shrinking universe of investors ensures that stock prices are driven down to levels which are considered undervalued.

But there is a cruel hoax operating in the financial world. The public will have become underinvested in equities just before the economy shows a startling improvement. The reason: when the atmosphere on Wall Street is one of doom and gloom, the mood in the business community, which is plugged into the same broad economic and political scenario, will also be downcast. Companies large and small will slash costs, pare inventories, fire workers, and most importantly, curtail borrowing. The reduced demand for funds ensures a steep tumble in interest rates, and this in turn breathes new life into the economy. Because of the dramatic cost-cutting campaign that business has just conducted, the resulting economic recovery generates breathtaking increases in business earnings.

The fuel to launch a bull market is provided when a public undercommitted to equities is caught off guard by a business recovery. In order to replenish shrunken portfolios, investors will be bidding for stocks on any market weakness, thus counteracting further decline. This underlying source of buying power provides the underpinnings to keep the stock market on an upward course that continues until it becomes apparent that making money in the stock market is easy. Once this occurs, the mood turns optimistic, and hordes of new investors flock to Wall Street. These investors, who had shied away from owning stocks when they were cheap, are now willing to pay almost any price to "join in." The prices of most stocks are bid up to levels far beyond what had been considered reasonable standards of value.

But we now encounter the other side of the hoax. That is, soon after the public has become overcommitted to equities, there will be a nasty surprise on the business front—because members of the business community are also affected by this optimism. They will have put on rose-colored glasses and thrown caution to the winds, accumulating inventories that are far too large, adding new and often inexperienced workers, and expanding into new areas, many of which are not economically viable. But most worrisome will be the enormous amount of new borrowing undertaken. The mushrooming demand for credit drives interest rates through the roof, and this in turn will put a nooselike grip on the economy. Because business firms have allowed their expenses to become bloated, a spate of dismal corporate earnings reports will surely follow.

Bear markets occur when the public, overcommitted to stocks, is caught off-balance by a slump in the economy. The overextended public then attempts to retreat before things get much worse. And this provides a great deal of overhanging selling pressure, which dampens rallies and keeps that stock market on a downward course that lasts until many investors have become disenchanted with owning common stocks once again.

The shifts from pessimism to optimism and back again are the driving force behind what Wall Street calls bull and bear markets. Bull markets rise from the ashes of investor pessimism and climb a proverbial "Wall of Worry." This prolonged period of rising stock prices is generated by a public that has become underinvested just before the economy turns up. Bear markets result when the public is caught with too much high-priced stock in the face of a flagging economy.

But how can we tell when the public has become pessimistic or optimistic? The most accurate sign that the investing public has become pessimistic occurs when the Dow closes into a two-year low. Since World War II, no sustained bull market has been able to get underway until the Dow has fallen into a two-year low. Any upswing that begins before that level is reached is likely to burn itself out rather quickly. For instance, the Dow was sinking throughout 1960, and in October of that year reached 566, which was a twenty-two-month low. However, the election of John Kennedy, who promised to get the economy moving again, buoyed the market before a two-year low was reached. A brisk advance began, which continued throughout most of 1961. But the firm foundation of pessimism was missing, and very quickly investors became giddy and lost sight of the fundamentals. Prices were bid up to levels beyond people's wildest expectations, new issues were snapped up at any price, growth stocks were sporting princely price-earnings ratios, and low-priced stocks whose prospects were iffy at best reached ridiculous heights. Investors had left themselves no leeway for surprise. So it was no wonder that the stock market collapsed when President Kennedy had a confrontation with the steel industry in early 1962 (see Chart 4). In a period of a few months, profits made in 1961 were given back, and many investors went from riches to rags.

In general, the best time to buy is one week after the Dow has closed into a two-year low. At that time we can conclude that the distressed selling is subsiding and stock prices have reached a point that is very attractive. In fact, many stocks will have been hammered down to levels that are absolutely mouth-watering. This marks the beginning of a buy zone, which will last until the mood of investors has turned optimistic once again.

The most reliable indication of investor optimism comes when the Dow closes into a two-year high. At that time it becomes apparent that investors who bought during the previous two years had made out like bandits, and speculative juices begin to flow. An army of new investors descends on Wall Street and becomes swept up in a tide of mounting speculative enthusiasm. In general, we can depend upon this buying pressure to last about nine months. After that time, the stock market can be considered to be in an area of vulnerability, *a caution zone*, and a major price break will soon follow.

A buying zone begins one week after the Dow has made a two-year low and lasts until shortly after the public's appetite to own stocks has been whetted. We can conclude that this has occurred when nine months have passed since the Dow made a two-year high. This means the stock market is in a caution zone, which will last until the Dow is again battered down to a two-year low. As far back as we care to look, we can see that the stock market has swung like a pendulum from a two-year low to a two-year high and back again to a two-year low (see Chart 4).

On June 6, 1949, the Dow closed at a two-year low for the first time since World War II. One week later, when the Dow was at 161, the stock market entered a buy zone. Although most investors were unaware of it at the time, this was to be the absolute low. On the

Chart 4   Buy Zones
Dow Jones Industrial Average 1945-1984

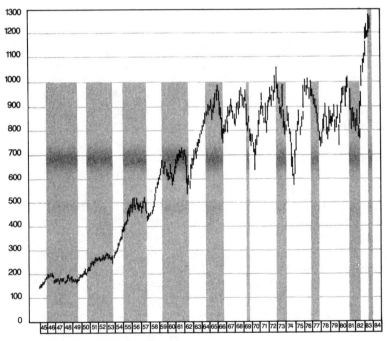

Buy Zone: White   Caution Zone: Shaded

very next day, prices began to climb, and by mid-November 1949, the Dow had made a two-year high. Nine months later, on August 18, 1950, the stock market entered a caution zone. The Dow at that time stood at 219, and those who had bought when the buying zone began had fattened their pocket books by 36 percent.

There have been nine other buy zones since 1946, and five began quite close to a major low in the stock market (Table 11). Each time, the Dow was considerably higher at the end of the buy zone than at the beginning. The purchases made when a buy zone was first indicated and sold nine months after the Dow made a two-year high would have produced an average profit of more than 34 percent. Not surprisingly, when the market was in a caution zone, it was not a particularly good time to be in stocks. With the notable exception of the recent extended Bull market, the Dow actually lost an average of 5 percent from the time a caution zone was first indicated until a new buy zone began.

Investors who confined their purchases to the time stocks were in a buy zone would have avoided buying too early. If the investment climate turns favorable before the stock market reaches a buy zone, investors should wait until one week after the Dow has made a two-year low before buying. For example, although the investment climate turned favorable on January 28, 1949, the stock market had not yet fallen into a two-year low. In that case, the time to buy was when the stock market entered a buy zone on June 13 at 161 on the Dow. According to all the vital statistics—industrial production, business orders, and unemployment—the economy was quite sick. In fact, most of the business and financial community thought that the widely heralded "depression" which, according to expert opinion, was supposed to follow World War II, had finally arrived. Needless to say, the mood of the nation was very grim, and most market watchers expected the stock market to fall into an abyss. But they were dead wrong. An investor who bought according

Table 11 Buying/Caution Zones

	Buying Zone Begins			Caution Zone Begins				
2-Year Low	Dow 1 Week Later	% from Actual Low	2-Year High	Dow 9 Months Later	Gain %	Length of Buy Zone in months	% Gains/(Loss) from Beginning of Caution Zone to Following Buy Zone
June 6, 1949	161	—	November 18, 1949	219	36	14	18
September 14, 1953	258	1	February 4, 1954	366	42	14	19
October 17, 1957	436	4	September 15, 1958	624	43	20	(12)
June 14, 1962	550	3	September 5, 1963	806	47	24	(2)
August 16, 1966	790	6	October 3, 1968	886	12	35	(7)
July 25, 1969	826	31	April 5, 1972	1047	27	41	(23)
November 27, 1973	803	39	January 7, 1976	965	20	34	(16)
October 13, 1977	814	10	July 17, 1980	1015[a]	25	42	(20)
June 17, 1982	810	4	October 20, 1982	1227	51	13	46
October 19, 1987	1794[b]	3	August 24, 1989			31	
			Average		34%	27	

[a] On April 29, 1981; the NYSE was closed on April 17, 18, and 19.
[b] Actually only a year and a half low, but down 36 percent from high. See Chapter 13 on disinflationary environment.

to our method would have gotten in at the exact low just as a major bull market was beginning.

Our investors would also have held off buying when the investment climate turned friendly in June 1960. It was not until June 21, 1962, that the stock market entered a buy zone. And investors would have paid 550 on the Dow, which was just 3 percent above the low that was to come three days later. As we can see, the ideal time to buy is when the investment climate has become friendly and the stock market has also reached a buy zone.

Investors might also have avoided selling too early by waiting for the stock market to reach a caution zone. For instance, the stock market was still in a buy zone when the investment climate turned hostile on December 15, 1980. Time would not run out on this bull market until it reached an area of vulnerability on April 20, 1981.[1] Investors who sold on that later date would have received 1015 on the Dow, just 1 percent below the peak that was to come one week later.

However, investors should not ignore a hostile climate indefinitely. After seven months of a perilous investment climate, recessionary clouds will be gathering over the economy, and the stage will be set for a chilling decline in stock prices. Investors should not delay selling any longer, even if the stock market has not yet reached a caution zone. For example, the stock market was in a buy zone when the investment climate turned sour on May 20, 1968, and seven months later, on December 20, 1968, market watchers could conclude that prices would soon fall victim to the brutally high interest rates. It was time to sell even though the stock market had not yet reached a caution zone. Investors would have gotten 966 on the Dow, just 2 percent less than the peak that was reached ten trading days earlier.

Market watchers should be aware of one more thing. There is a time when investors can jump the gun and buy before the investment climate turns friendly. It occurs just after the level of investor pessi-

[1] There was no ruling on April 17, 18, or 19.

mism reaches an extreme level. If that should happen, it will discourage borrowing, and we can expect a fall in interest rates to be imminent.

The sign that pessimism has reached excessive levels occurs when the Dow closes into a five-year low. Breaks of that magnitude mean that people throughout the economy have become so thoroughly demoralized that it is safe to bet that the steep drop in the demand for credit has already begun. Once five months pass since the Dow reaches this extreme level, it is not necessary to wait any longer, even if the climate has not yet turned friendly. We can buy stocks immediately, anticipating that interest rates will soon tumble. This happened only twice in the past thirty-eight-year period, but both times provided investors with a rare opportunity to purchase stocks at prices that would soon seem dirt cheap (see Table 12 and Chart 4).[2]

Investors in the know would have bought on June 30, 1970, when the Dow stood at 683. This would have enabled them to get in on the ground floor of a major bull market just five weeks after the bottom instead of having to wait until September 27, 1970, when the Dow was at 747.

Although the stock market also sank to a five-year low in September 1974, the investment climate turned favorable before five months had passed. As a result, the buy on October 1 of that year was not altered. But no doubt this five-year low provided further confirmation that stocks had reached bargain-basement levels and an explosive rally was imminent.

Investor pessimism and optimism are the two masters that govern in Wall Street. They are not merely the technical indicators that most of Wall Street likes

---

[2] The stock market registered a level of extreme pessimism five other times during this century. Four times a bottom was made within five months and was followed by explosive rallies. Investors who bought at that time would have made an average profit of 46 percent (including dividends) during the following year. The only time in this century that prices continued to slide for more than five months after reaching a level of excessive pessimism was in 1931, during the Great Depression. But even then it was not too long before prices rebounded back to levels well above those in effect when extreme pessimism was first indicated.

Table 12   5-Year Lows

5-Year Low (Extreme Pessimism)	Dow (5 Months Later)	Caution Zone	Dow	Gain	Months Later
January 30, 1970	683	January 5, 1973	1047	54%	32
September 13, 1974	726	October 7, 1976	1976	33%	20
		Average		44%	26

to think them. They are important, perhaps the most important, fundamental factors. This is because there is a paradox operating in our economic and financial world. When most people agree that the future is bleak, they create the conditions for a startling improvement in the economy. A psychology of pessimism ensures that the public will become underinvested and securities undervalued. Yet it will also set off a fall in interest rates, which in turn provides the thrust to launch a broad business recovery.

On the flip side of the coin, when there is widespread agreement that the future is risk-free, you can be pretty sure that stormy weather is on the way. This is because investor optimism leads to an overinvested public and overvalued stock prices. But this optimism will also promote sky-high interest rates, which will choke off economic growth.

To sum up, an attractive opportunity to buy stocks emerges when most people see the future as bleak. We can tell this has occurred when stocks have had a significant break, *to at least a two-year low on the Dow.* If the break has been unusually steep, to a five-year low, it means investor pessimism is rampant, and nothing else is needed. Stocks become a buy within five months. On the other hand, if the break has not been to a five-year low, investors should wait for the investment climate to turn favorable. This is the time to jump in with both feet. Investors can be pretty sure that a major bull market is on the launching pad and ready to take off. And there will be no need to worry until either the investment climate sours or an inflationary spiral begins.

Chapter 5

The Investment Cycle:
Putting It All Together

An investment cycle begins about the time either long- or short-term interest rates have fallen into a fifteen-month low and lasts until the onset of a hostile investment climate points to stormy weather ahead. During this time there will be a prolonged period of vigorous economic growth, a bull market in stocks, and perhaps an explosion in the price of real assets.

Let us review the last three completed investment cycles.

Our story begins in early 1970, when for the first time in almost a decade vast numbers of Americans were feeling the chilling effects of a bona fide recession, either in the form of layoffs, short work weeks, forced salary cuts, or slow business. The stock market had been sagging for more than a year, and on January 30, the Dow closed at a five-year low. This was the first time since World War II that the mood of investors had become extremely pessimistic, and it meant that investors would be presented with a major opportunity to buy stocks within the next five months. In April, the North Vietnamese forces poured out of their long-standing border sanctuaries and moved into Cambodian territory. Only days later, President Nixon sent American troops into Cambodia, and a mass of Americans rose up against the President. College campuses from Maine to Oregon erupted with demonstrations and violence. As concern grew that the nation was becoming so divided that Nixon would be unable to govern, stocks on Wall Street collapsed in a bloody heap.

However, on June 30, 1970, five months had passed since investors had become extremely pessimistic. It was time to buy stocks. Although neither short- nor long-term rates had fallen into a fifteen-month low, we could expect an ebbing demand for credit to pull the props out from under interest rates. Investors who bought on that day would have gotten in on the ground floor of a new bull market. The Dow was at 683, which was only 8 percent above the low made five weeks earlier. However, indexes of growth and glamor stocks, such as the Glamor Stock Average kept by Edson Gould,[1] were to reach their lows four trading days later.

The investment climate turned friendly on September 21, when 90-Day T-Bills made a fifteen-month low, and this would provide the thrust to launch a recovery. It was no coincidence that the economy turned upward two months later, in November, and began an expansion that was to last three years. In February, 1971 investors got more good news. Long-term interest rates had also fallen into a fifteen-month low, and this suggested the friendly investment climate would be prolonged. Investors could now settle in for a nice long period of rising prices in investment markets.

When President Nixon, in a stunning turnaround, imposed a wage and price freeze on the economy in the summer of 1971, the stock market stumbled a bit. But according to our tools there was no hint of trouble. Both short- and long-term interest rates were quite low and inflation was still in a tolerable range. And sure enough, in a matter of a few months' time, stock prices came roaring back, as they do during a bull market. On April 5, 1972, the Dow closed at 954, and an observant market watcher would have noticed this was a two-year high. Optimism had returned. In November, the Dow sailed beyond the magic 1000 level, and one month

---

[1] Probably the foremost stock market technician during the 1970s.

later word came that prices were increasing at a feverish rate of 5.3 percent, indicating that inflation had
moved into high gear.

This was the first period of galloping prices in over
twenty years, and most investors were slow to grasp
the meaning of it. It meant that real assets, such as
gold, along with foreign currencies, would begin
breathtaking advances, while the stock market would
prove disappointing throughout the remainder of the
investment cycle. It was time to sell stocks. The Dow at
the time was 1027, and smart investors would have
taken their stock market profits—which, incidentally,
were 50 percent—and bought gold, which was trading
at $63 in London.[2] Three weeks later, on January 11,
1973, President Nixon lifted wage and price controls,
gambling that a voluntary program would be able to
contain inflation. On that very day, the Dow peaked at
1051—a high that was to stand for more than nine
years.

We were now in the stage of the investment cycle
that favors real assets. As the months wore on, President Nixon was implicated in Watergate; war broke out
in the Middle East, and OPEC slapped an embargo on
oil, beginning an energy crisis that was to send shock
waves throughout the Western world. All this time, inflation kept gathering momentum; the almighty dollar
cracked, and gold in London rose above $125 an
ounce. In November 1973, a recession began, and by
the end of the month, amid deepening economic
gloom, the Dow fell into a two-year low. But stocks
would not become a buy until a new investment cycle
began.

During the following eight months, the Nixon
presidency was coming unglued, and news from the inflation front kept getting worse. By mid-1974, inflation
was galloping along at a rate of 20.4 percent. But relief
was on the way. On July 12, 1974, word came that
long-term interest rates had made a seven-year high,

---

[2] Americans were not allowed to own gold at that time. But we can use the
price of gold as a proxy for real assets.

corroborating the seven-year high short-term interest rates had made back in July 1973. The investment climate had turned unfavorable, and this would soon put a brake on inflation. A red light was flashing, alerting investors that gold and other inflation hedges should be sold three weeks later, on August 2. On that date gold was $156 an ounce, and the profit to investors was 145 percent. The first investment cycle since 1970 was over. Our investors would have bought stocks five weeks after the bottom and sold just sixteen trading days before the high, and had they reinvested their stock profits into gold, they would have emerged from this cycle 267 percent richer.

During the following two months, while our investors sat safely on the sidelines, Americans were discovering the economy was in its deepest, most protracted business downturn since the Great Depression. In mid-September, under the weight of the bleakest economic statistics since World War II, the Dow fell into another five-year low. This suggested the awesome bear market, which by its end was to clip a numbing 45 percent from the value of stocks, was about over. Sure enough, three weeks later, at the weekly auction held on September 30, 90-Day T-Bills sank to their lowest level in fifteen months. The green light to buy was flashing. On the following day, the Dow was at the bargain-basement level of 604. Interestingly, the political cycle entered its favorable phase on that very day. Had short-term rates not fallen into a fifteen-month low, the buy signal would have been delayed only one day.

Three days later, investors were rewarded with a powerful stock market rally. Although the Dow was to come back and take out the low for one day in December, reaching 577, 5 percent below where stocks were bought, most other indexes held above their October lows. (Incidentally, this 5 percent temporary loss which was on paper only was the greatest investors were to suffer throughout the entire thirty-eight year period.)

In early 1975, as unemployment was reaching levels not seen in the adult life of most Americans, the

Dow exploded and by mid-February was back to 730. Although most investors were skeptical about the staying power of this baby bull market, to those familiar with this model there was no doubt an upward trend in stock prices had been established. In March, the economy turned up, and one month later, in mid-April, we got word that the sizzling inflation had finally moderated. For the rest of the year, it was clear sailing for stocks. On January 6, 1976, the Dow closed at 898, which was a two-year high, and you could have heard champagne corks popping on Wall Street. By mid-March, the Dow had surged beyond the 1000 level, and when the stock market reached an area of vulnerability in early October, the Dow was trading at 965. This meant we should be more cautious, but by no means was it time to get out. Long-term interest rates had made a fifteen-month low in February of 1976, pointing to a long period of fair weather ahead. The only question was whether the gains from here on would be in stocks or real assets.

As 1977 began, Wall Street was in a euphoric mood. Most analysts, encouraged by the low level of interest rates and the low P-E ratios most stocks were commanding, thought we were still in the early stages of a great bull market. Twelve hundred by Christmas did not appear an unrealistic expectation. However, they didn't reckon with another burst of inflation. Although inflation was cooling, the Wholesale Price Index was nowhere near a yearly low, and memories of the last rampaging inflation were still vivid. In November 1976, a new factor appeared on the inflation front. The Democrats, with Jimmy Carter in the saddle, had reclaimed the White House. Traditionally, the Democrats launch ambitious spending programs to fuel the economy. This, of course, usually ignites inflation—the only question being, how soon?[3]

When the Wholesale Price Index for February was released in early March 1977, it became evident that

[3] The Democrats took control of the White House four times in this century, and when reelection time rolled around, the rate of inflation was higher or clearly headed higher each time.

inflation was on the march again. We could expect another stampede into gold and other hard assets to begin soon. Time to make the switch from stocks to gold and other inflation hedges. Investors would still have gotten 965 on the Dow for their stocks—just 5 percent below the peak—and their gold would have cost $146 an ounce. Those who sold at that time would have pocketed 60 percent on stocks bought twenty-nine months earlier.

By October 1977 the Dow had fallen into a two-year low. But as we were in the inflationary part of the investment cycle, this was no time to buy stocks. The story for gold, however, was quite different. During the next three years inflation kept roaring down the tracks, picking up momentum, rewarding recklessness, punishing thrift, and destroying productive investment. For those who were invested in gold, foreign currencies, and other inflation hedges, it was very smooth sailing. When strife in Iran began disrupting critical petroleum supplies in late 1978, the price of oil skyrocketed and inflation began bubbling over. In early 1979, the rate of inflation reached double digits, and gold, much to most people's amazement, surpassed $250 an ounce—a glittering performance, but the best part of the rise was still to come. To be sure, the sign that time was running out on this inflation was given in September, when short-term interest rates reached a seven-year high, corroborating the seven-year high AAA Corporate Bonds made back in April. But an election was looming, the favorable phase of this political cycle ended. As 1979 drew to a close, events seemed to be racing out of control. Iran took over our embassy in Teheran, and barely two months later, Russian troops marched into Afghanistan—and interest rates reached levels never before dreamed of. Of course, gold and other precious metals were setting new records almost daily.

The investment climate turned unfavorable at the beginning of January 1980, and in that same month, the economy came to a screeching halt. Finally, the sign that inflation was winding down had been given. Three weeks later, on January 22, it was time to sell gold and other real assets. The signal was flashed one day after gold made its high of $850 an ounce, and wise investors would have gotten $737 an ounce, for a profit of 405 percent. By March, gold was back under $500. Those who parlayed their stock market profits into gold made 708 percent during this cycle.

The next favorable investment climate began when 90-Day T-Bills touched a fifteen-month low on May 12, 1980. As the stock market was already in a buy zone, it was all right to jump in on the following day when the Dow was at 816. To be sure, inflation had not yet moderated. But, as high rates of inflation are unlikely to be maintained early in a new investment cycle, this did not matter. In this case, inflation had not yet responded to the punitively high interest rates of late 1979 and early 1980. But it soon would.

In July, the economy turned up, and the stock market burst into a two-year high. Soon afterwards, both short- and long-term interest rates began rising at very disturbing paces. As long-term rates had not yet made a fifteen-month low, we could expect the recovery in the economy and stock market to soon fizzle out. In early December, long-term rates recorded new highs, and ten days later, their counterpart fell into step. The fate of this investment cycle was sealed. However, the stock market had not yet reached a caution zone. We could hold off selling until mid-April 1981, which was nine months after the Dow made a two-year high. In early January, Joe Granville, a prominent investment advisor who was on a hot streak and had a wide following, issued a sell signal, which sent stocks reeling. However, the stock market validated our model by coming back and making new highs. When smart investors sold on April 20, just one week before the actual peak, the Dow was at 1015, and they would have pocketed 24 percent in this unusually short investment cycle.

Investors who played these three cycles according to the model would have turned $10,000 into $368,000—more than a third of a million dollars, exclusive of dividends and interest earned on money markets when they were out of the stock market. Not bad for an eleven-year period of time during which the Dow showed hardly any net gain.

Since that time, one more cycle has begun. When did we get our buy signal? On August 3, 1982, with the Dow at 816, just seven days before the stock market began its most explosive rally in modern times. In the following weeks a newly awakened bull went ripping and snorting through Wall Street, thundering from one new high to another on record-shattering volume. On October 20, the Dow was once again back into a two-year high.

The caution zone began nine months later at 1227 on the Dow. It continued to the crash on October 19, 1987. This was an extended caution zone with much higher gains than usual. The stock market itself was being referred to as an "extended Bull market." However, a well defined sell signal appeared on September 9, 1987, with the Dow at 2549, when both the long-term and short-term interest rates reached a fifteen month high. We know now that cycles can be extended by periods of relative economic stability (see Chapter 13).

There have been five other investment cycles since World War II, and the stock market experienced a major bull market during each of them (see Table 13 and Chart 5). In the first cycle, we bought stocks on June 13, 1949, at 161 on the Dow, which, by the way, was the bottom day. Although the sale at 269 on the Dow came a year early, it was only 8 percent below the high of 293.

In the next cycle, the signal to buy stocks came at 261 on the Dow, six trading days after the low was made. The signal to sell was given on September 4, 1956, when the Dow was at 507, just 3 percent below the high made in April of that year. Actually, in August the Dow came within a tad (.1 Dow point) of that high. The sell signal came but one month after this secondary high.

The third buy signal at 435 on the Dow came almost ten weeks after the actual low—but the Dow was

Table 13   Stock Market Record 1946-1984

Exact Bottom	Dow	Buy Signal	Dow	Signal from Low %	Actual Top	Dow	Sell Signal	Dow	Signal from High %	Gain %
1. Jun. 13, 1949	161	Jun. 13, 1949	161	—	Jan. 5, 1953	293	Jan. 2, 1952	269	8	67
2. Sep. 14, 1953	255	Sep. 22, 1953	261	2	Apr. 6, 1956	521	Sep. 4, 1956	507	3	94
3. Oct. 22, 1957	419	Dec. 31, 1957	435	4	Dec. 13, 1961	734	Jan. 4, 1960	679	8	56
4. Jun. 26, 1962	535	Jun. 21, 1962	550	3	Feb. 9, 1966	995	Jan. 18, 1966	994	—	81
5. Oct. 7, 1966	744	Oct. 3, 1966	757	2	Dec. 3, 1968	985	Dec. 29, 1968	966	2	28
6. May 26, 1970	631	Jun. 30, 1970	683	8	Jan. 11, 1973	1051	Dec. 15, 1972	1072	2	50
7. Dec. 6, 1974	577	Oct. 1, 1974	604	5	Sep. 21, 1976	1014	Mar. 15, 1977	965	5	60
8. Feb. 28, 1978	742	May 13, 1980	816	10	Apr. 27, 1981	1024	Apr. 20, 1981	1015	1	24
9. Aug. 12, 1982	776	Aug. 3, 1982	816	5	Aug. 25, 1987	2722	Sep. 9, 1987	2549	6	212
10. Oct. 19, 1987[a]	1738	Jun. 19, 1989	2479	42						
		Average		8%			Average		4%	74%

[a] More than 25 percent break (See Chapter 13).

Chart 5   Dow Jones Industrial Average 1945-1984

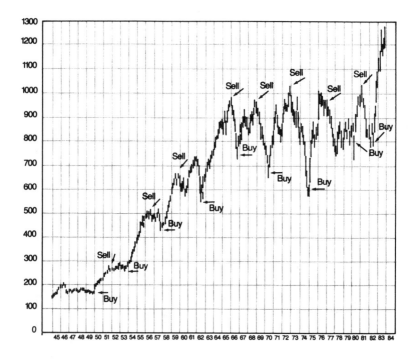

only 4 percent above the October low. Initially, it appeared that the sell signal at 679 on January 4, 1960, was given one day before the top. Following this peak, the stock market fell 17 percent, reaching a low of 566 in October of that year. However, a brisk rally began that took the Dow up to 734 in December 1961, just 8 percent above where smart investors sold.

During the fourth investment cycle, they bought stocks three days before the low was made and sold three weeks before the high. They would have paid 550, which was 3 percent above the low, and sold at 994, just one point less than the high of 995.

The fifth buy came at 757 on the Dow, just four days before the bottom. The sell sign was given ten trading days after the peak, coming on December 20, 1968, at 966. The actual top was on December 3rd, at 985 on the Dow.

Over all nine cycles, investors who followed this model would have bought and sold within an average of 6 percent of the exact bottoms and tops. Their average gain would have been 74 percent, and that was before dividends.

There are nine times that our investors were out of the stock market. While the Dow was shedding an average of more than 20 percent during these periods, leaving a trail of bloodied investors in its wake, those who applied these tools would have been sitting safely on the sidelines raking in the interest payments on savings, CDs, or money markets.

But this is only part of the story. The model has also allowed us to tell when inflation is likely to get out of hand. There were three episodes of galloping inflation during this period of time, and the model caught each of them. We would have bought gold and other tangibles near the beginning of those periods and sold close to the end. An investor who had followed the model in and out would have done much better than those who were married to gold, silver, or other inflation hedges.

There have been nine periods of sagging business, declining gross national product, and rising unemployment since 1946. The model sounded the alarm before eight of them began. The other signal came after a business setback actually started—but up until that time, the slowdown had been very mild. It was after the signal was given in July 1974 that the slump began to bite. The model would also have told business people that the economy was struggling to its feet shortly before each recovery began. The signal was given an average of five months before the economy turned upward.

What you have is a model that has an almost perfect fit with what actually occurred in the economic and financial landscape since World War II; a model that does not need reams of economic data, complex economic formulas, a basketful of technical indicators, or a computer. Nor do you have to plow through a mass of diverse and often conflicting facts. All you need is a newspaper, such as *The Wall Street Journal* and the weekly *U.S. Financial Data* bulletin published by the St. Louis Fed, and you are in business.[4]

To review guidelines:

A. The investment climate becomes favorable when either:
   1. short- or long-term interest rates fall to a fifteen-month low, or
   2. the favorable phase of a political cycle begins—on the first day of October two years before a presidential election.

B. The investment climate turns hostile when both short- and long-term interest rates make a seven-year high. (However, if this occurs during the favorable phase of the political cycle—from, say, October 1, 1978, to January 1, 1980— investors should wait until the election cycle is no longer favorable.)

C. A buy zone begins one week after the Dow closes into a two-year low.

---

[4] You might also want to subscribe to the *Federal Reserve* or the *Survey of Current Business Conditions*.

D. Extreme pessimism is registered when the Dow closes into a five-year low.

E. A caution zone begins nine months after the Dow closes into a two-year high.

F. An inflationary spiral begins when the rate of inflation reaches 5 percent and is the highest rate in a year—provided two years have passed since the last deflation has ended.

G. Inflation moderates when the rate of inflation falls to the lowest level in a year.

The rules for investing are:

A. Stocks
   1. are a buy when either:
      a. the investment climate is favorable and the stock market is in a buy zone, or
      b. five months after a level of extreme pessimism is reached.
   2. are a sale when:
      a. the stock market is in a caution zone and the investment climate turns unfriendly, or
      b. seven months after the investment climate has turned unfavorable, or
      c. an inflationary spiral begins.
   3. Once stocks are a sale, a new buying opportunity will not surface until another investment cycle begins.

B. Inflation hedges
   1. are a buy when an inflationary spiral begins and the investment climate is favorable.
   2. are a sale three weeks after the investment climate turns hostile.

Up until now, we have talked about the Dow and assumed that investors would have done as well as the average. But, of course, investors can try to beat the Dow, and that is the subject of the following chapter.

Chapter 6

Beating the Dow

There are usually three different phases to a bull market, and the marching band plays a different tune during each. There is a time when the stocks sensitive to interest rates march at the head of the parade, and a time when the stocks to own are those tied to the capital goods sector. During each bull market, there is a phase when the stocks of blue-chip companies such as General Motors, IBM, and Sears shine, and there is a phase when secondary stocks—the smaller companies usually found on the American Stock Exchange and the over-the-counter market—do significantly better than the overall market. There is a time when almost all stocks roar ahead and score big gains regardless of current earnings; but at other times, earnings play an important part. To outperform the Dow, we must recognize the phases of the market and tailor our portfolios to suit them.

The First Phase: This is a recovery period or the Discounting Phase. During this period a business recovery begins, and investors recognize it and quickly bid up share prices on the nation's stock exchanges. In Wall Street jargon, the market discounts an expected improvement in business earnings. And the stock market is able to get a lot of mileage out of these expected

69

earnings, because they stand in sharp contrast to the estimates put out by analysts in the depth of the recession. The recovery period usually lasts from nine to fifteen months, and it is generally the most exciting and profitable phase of a bull market. During this time, the bull market is indiscriminate. Most stocks roar out of the gate and stay on a fast track: stocks with poor earnings and stocks showing impressive earnings gains; stocks with low P-E ratios and stocks sporting high P-E ratios; stocks selling below book value and stocks at a premium to net worth. Consequently, it does not take a great deal of skill or stock market acumen to put in a good showing. Even poor stock pickers are likely to be racking up handsome profits and no doubt bragging about how brilliant they are. As investors recognize how easy it is to make money, euphoria begins to set in, and Wall Street analysts put on rose-colored glasses and wonder why they had been so cautious in making earnings projections. However, just as investors are getting into the party atmosphere and begin to think picking winning stocks is like shooting fish in a barrel, there is a change in the market's personality, and a new phase is about to begin.

The Second Phase: Following the recovery period, the nature of the bull shifts. From this point on, the stock market becomes very selective, and it is no long so easy to shake the money tree. The market stops betting on the come (future performance) and begins to respect companies that are achieving sizable earning gains. This adjustment time will not be smooth. Normally, there is a period of transition, which can be called the Discouragement Phase. During this second phase, the Dow usually experiences a minibreak, which squeezes our the foam and froth accumulated during the discounting period. This is a result of the overenthusiasm of the first phase, when share prices get ahead of themselves. In some cases, investors overcalculate the benefits of a business recovery. In other cases, ebullient Wall Street analysts project earnings estimates well beyond the companies' capabilities. When expectations are not met, investors become disappointed. During this transition period, there is an increasing number of unpleasant surprises, and this takes the wind out of investors' sails. However, once investors are sobered, the euphoria is replaced by a cautious optimism, and the bull regains its footings and resumes its upward charge.

The Third Phase: This phase usually begins at about the time the recovery broadens into a full-fledged expansion. At that time, factory-use rates are shooting up; this will precipitate a surge in capital goods spending, which will undergird the economy so that it takes on a self-feeding element. The third period is fed by a capital goods boom, and it can be called the Mature Phase. Although not nearly as exciting as the discounting period, it is nevertheless a time of solid stock market gains. Again, there is a new twist to the bull market. The stocks of the big, well-established companies, which had put in stellar performances, begin to falter. Their potential will have been recognized by both analysts and investors. Their prices will already reflect the maximum earnings gain likely to be achieved during the cycle. But not so with the secondary stocks. Many of these small companies will be growing at a faster clip than the economy in general, but because they are not closely followed by analysts and their names are not familiar to most investors, this favorable situation will not be reflected in the stocks. And it is these companies that normally lead the parade during the third phase.

Ordinarily, investors catch on to the character of a bull market just about the time that the bull is adopting a new personality. Strategies that had worked well during one part of a bull market become inappropriate

during a later phase. Obviously, the key to outperform-
ing the Dow is to recognize and stay in gear with the
phase of the bull market we are in. But how do we tell
when one phase ends and another begins? And which
stocks in particular are likely to shine during each
phase?

The first phase is the discounting phase, and it
can last up to fifteen months. For instance, the bull
market that began on December 6, 1974, with the Dow
at 577, ended fifteen months later. When the discounting phase came to an end on March 8, 1976 (March 6
was a Saturday), the Dow stood at 988, up a breathtaking 71 percent (Chart 6).

However, a discounting phase does not always last
that long. If short-term interest rates appear to be turning up before that time, it will bring the recovery period to a premature end. The sign that rates are
heading higher comes if nine months pass without a
new low in the rate for 90-Day T-Bills.[1] For instance,
the investment climate turned favorable on August 2,
1982, ten days before the Dow made its low. Short-
term interest rates continued to ratchet lower, reaching
7.429 percent on October 12, 1982.[2] But at that point
they reversed course and began to creep up. Nine
months later rates still hung above their October low
(see Table 14). When this discounting phase ended on
July 12, 1983, the Dow stood at 1198, up a whopping
54 percent from its low. The discounting phase lasts
until either the bull market is fifteen months old or
until nine months have passed since a bottom in
short-term interest rates—whichever comes first.

There have been seven other discounting phases
since World War II, and they are listed in Table 15.
Following the bull market that began in 1978, the Dow
made another two-year low before the investment climate turned favorable. In that case, the discounting period could last up until fifteen months from that low.

---

[1] Rates might fall to a new low later on, but they will no longer fuel an
across-the-board rise in stock prices.

[2] The weekly auction was held on Tuesday because government offices
were closed Monday in observance of Columbus Day.

Chart 6   Dow Jones Industrial Averages 1970-1977

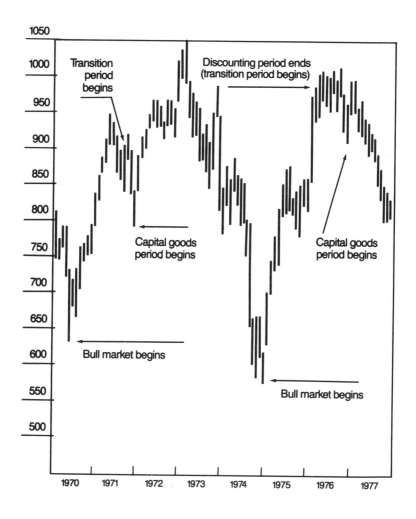

Table 14   90-Day T-Bills

	1981		1982		1983	
Jan 05	13.601%	Jan 04	11.658%	Jan 03	7.896%	
12	15.318	11	12.121	10	7.671	
19	15.595	18	12.505	17	7.619	
26	15.199	25	13.364	24	8.055	
				31	8.122	
Feb 02	14.657	Feb 01	13.850	Feb 07	8.252	
09	15.397	08	14.099	14	8.256	
16	15.464	15	14.740	21	7.888	
23	14.103	22	12.430	28	7.944	
Mar 02	14.463	Mar 01	12.450	Mar 07	8.205	
09	13.996	08	12.058	14	8.256	
16	12.758	15	12.909	21	8.434	
23	12.695	22	12.553	28	8.680	
30	12.501	29	13.399			
Apr 06	14.147	Apr 05	12.893	Apr 04	8.664	
13	13.783	12	12.849	11	8.165	
20	13.553	19	12.497	18	8.030	
27	14.190	26	12.469	25	8.150	
May 04	15.963	May 03	12.675	May 02	8.040	
11	16.433	10	12.248	09	8.140	
18	16.034	17	12.189	16	8.100	
25	16.750	24	11.480	23	8.460	
		31	11.520	30	8.650	
Jun 01	14.456	Jun 07	12.074	Jun 06	8.640	
08	14.982	14	12.248	13	8.730	
15	13.451	21	12.588	20	8.980	
22	14.337	28	13.269	27	9.090	
29	13.909					
Jul 06	14.400	Jul 05	12.806	Jul 04	9.100	9 months without
13	14.558	12	11.797	11	9.070	a new low
20	14.563	19	11.140	18	9.190	
27	15.065	26	10.559	25	9.130	
Aug 03	15.674	Aug 02	9.633	Aug 01	9.360	15-month
10	15.235	09	10.025	08	9.570	low
17	15.705	16	8.616	15	9.430	
24	15.832	23	7.748	22	9.180	
31	15.583	30	8.604	29	9.280	
Sep 07	15.611	Sep 06	8.565	Sep 05	9.210	
14	14.412	13	8.161	12	9.040	
21	14.198	20	7.849	21	8.990	
28	14.669	27	7.801	26	8.730	
Oct 05	14.206	Oct 04	8.102	Oct 03	8.720	
12	13.526	11	7.429 bottom	10	8.830	
19	13.613	18	7.437	17	8.630	
26	13.352	25	8.031	24	8.660	
				31	8.410	
Nov 02	12.675	Nov 01	7.813	Nov 07	8.830	
09	11.128	08	7.964	14	8.780	
16	10.693	15	8.446	21	8.810	
23	10.560	22	7.944	28	8.900	
30	10.400	29	8.280			
Dec 07	10.404	Dec 06	7.956	Dec 05	9.000	
14	11.101	13	7.995	12	8.930	
21	11.037	20	7.857	19	9.040	
28	11.690	27	7.975	26	8.940	

Table 15 First Phase

Bull Market Begins	Dow	1st Phase Ends	Months	Dow	% Gain from Low	% of Total Bull Market Gain
1. June 13, 1949	161	April 11, 1950	10	211	31	38
2. September 14, 1953	255	December 14, 1954	15	387	52	50
3. October 22, 1957	419	January 22, 1959	15	595	42	66
4. October 25, 1960[a]	566	July 31, 1961	9	705	25	30
5. October 7, 1966	744	January 8, 1968	15	908	22	68
6. May 26, 1970	631	August 26, 1971	15	906	44	66
7. December 6, 1974	577	March 8, 1976	15	988	71	94
8. April 21, 1980[b]	759	March 16, 1981	11	1002	32	92
9. August 12, 1983	776	July 12, 1983	11	1198	54	92
		Average	13		41	63
			Annualized		38%	

[a] The bull market actually began in June 1962, but the Dow made a twenty-two-month low in October 1960.
[b] Although the bull market actually began in February 1978, the Dow made another two-year low in April 1980.

Since 1946, the stock market has always begun a discounting phase at about the time the investment climate turns friendly. The driving force during this time is the steep decline in interest rates, which spur a business recovery. Once investors recognize the economy has embarked on the recovery road, they bid up stock prices. Interestingly, we began a discounting phase in 1960 after the climate turned friendly, even though a bona fide bull market did not begin. (That is, the Dow did not sink into a two-year low.) The Dow began a powerful advance in October 1960 at 566, and on July 31, 1961, which was nine months after the bottom in 90-Day T-Bills[3], was trading at 705—a gain of 25 percent. However, recovery periods that occur before the Dow falls into a two-year low are not likely to be followed by another phase unless the Dow falls into a two-year low.

During the first phase, investors clearly have the easiest time of it. The average gain for that phase in the years since World War II was 41 percent. On an annualized basis, this amounted to 38 percent. This accounts for 63 percent of the total bull market gains. Investors can do very well during this time simply by investing in a wide assortment of blue-chip stocks. However, the first phase is actually the easiest time to beat the Dow. This is because there are a variety of industries that are very sensitive to interest rates. Such industries as home building, building materials, manufactured housing, home furnishings, financial services, hotels and motels, apparel, specialty retailing, shoes, drug stores, recreations and leisure, transportation leasing, and publishing are usually the first to benefit from a new favorable investment climate. It is, in fact, the strong rebound of these industries that powers the economy out of recession.

---

[3] By the time both short- and long-term rates have fallen into fifteen-month lows, the stock market will usually be in a buy zone. If the Dow has not yet reached a two-year low by that time, we could nevertheless assume a recovery period will soon begin and buy immediately. In this case, we would have brought on August 22, 1960, the day after we got the word that long-term rates followed short-term rates into a fifteen-month low. Investors would have paid 630 on the Dow, and they would have pocketed 11 percent when they sold eleven months later at 705.

When the investment climate turns favorable, companies in these industries will usually still be reeling from the effects of the past period of high interest rates. They will appear loaded down with problems, and most investors will be shying away from these stocks. However, and this is very important, these problems are generally cyclical—that is, related to the contracting economy. Once interest rates have taken a dive, there will be a substantial improvement in the fortunes of these industries, and share prices will race ahead.

Table 16 contains a list of twenty of the leading companies in the industries that are traditionally interest-rate-sensitive. Gulf & Western is a large conglomerate with diversified holdings in several interest-sensitive areas. The other nineteen companies are either their industry's leader or else the most important factor in some area within the industry. For instance, Merrill Lynch is the acknowledged leader in the financial services industry. The largest firm in home building is U.S. Home. Two industries, home building and financial services, are extraordinarily interest-sensitive and three of the principal companies are included.

An investor who had plunked down an equal amount of money for each of these twenty stocks on August 3, 1982, when the last buy signal was flashed, and sold on July 12, 1983, when the discounting phase was over, would have pocketed 143 percent. This compares to a 47 percent gain on the Dow (see Table 17). Surely, you must feel that this is a special case—that we simply stacked the deck with the big winners after the fact. Yet had an investor bought these same twenty stocks during the previous four discounting phases, he or she would have consistently outperformed the Dow by almost four to one. The average return was 145 percent. In contrast, the average return on the Dow was only 37 percent.

As long as an investor is convinced that the problems of a given company are cyclical rather than the result of a long-term deterioration in the company's competitive position, stocks in these industries are the

Table 16   20 Interest-Rate-Sensitive Companies

1. Best Products	Specialty retailer	Largest catalog/ showroom merchandiser
2. Fleetwood	Manufactured housing	Largest in industry
3. General Cinema	Recreation	Largest theater chain
4. Gulf & Western	Conglomerate	Heavily involved in entertainment, financial services, and publishing
5. Holiday Inn	Hotels/motels	Operates the world's largest hotel network
6. E.F. Hutton	Financial services	Second largest securites broker
7. Kaufman & Broad	Home building	Largest California home builder
8. Levi Strauss	Apparel	Largest in industry
9. Levitz	Home furnishings	Leading low-price furniture retailer
10. Lomas & Nettleton Fin.	Financial services	Largest mortgage banker
11. Masco	Building materials	Largest producer of faucets
12. Melville	Shoes	Leading shoe retailer
13. Merrill Lynch	Financial services	Leading security broker
14. Mohasco	Home furnishings	Principal producer of carpet and rugs
15. Outboard Marine	Recreation	Largest maker of outboard engines
16. Pulte	Home building	Second largest
17. Ryder	Transportation leasing	Largest in industry
18. Time	Publishing	Leading publisher
19. U.S. Home	Home building	Largest in industry
20. Walgreen	Drug stores	Largest drugstore chain

ones to load up on when a buy signal is flashed. However, if some of these stocks are discounting earnings increases way beyond what past experience has shown is obtainable, it might be wise to hold off. Normally,

Table 17 Interest-Rate-Sensitive Firms during Last Five Bull Markets

	10/3/66–1/8/68	6/30/70–8/26/71	10/1/74–3/8/76	5/13/80–3/16/81	8/3/82–7/12/83
Best Products	a	a	697%	19%	121%
Fleetwood	500%	199%	212	42	290
General Cinema	152	180	250	56	79
Gulf & Western	196	132	197	2	129
Holiday Inn	212	82	134	66	94
E. F. Hutton	a	a	447	107	146
Kaufman & Broad	376	131	289	59	184
Levi Strauss	a	a	193	30	114
Levitz	a	135	253	29	209
Lomas & Nettleton Fin.	63	118	109	50	95
Masco	63	78	171	49	91
Melville	181	81	231	46	87
Merrill Lynch	a	a	306	72	332
Mohasco	54	129	85	62	108
Outboard Marine	84	228	113	71	75
Pulte	a	a	160	143	238
Ryder	129	87	128	81	85
Time	18	92	110	64	142
U.S. Home	a	292	186	164	136
Walgreen	139	65	39	59	99
Average	167%	136%	215%	64%	143%
Dow Average	20%	33%	64%	23%	47%
Average 6 Cycles	145%				
Dow 6 Cycles	37%				

a Not listed.

once this phase ends, these stocks should be sold. Much of the earnings improvement they are likely to achieve will have been already discounted, and their performance during the remainder of the bull market is often lackluster to downright poor. In general, we should be able to beat the Dow hands down during the discounting phase by packing our portfolios with companies in the interest-rate-sensitive industries.

The second phase follows on the heels of the recovery period and usually lasts until the business recovery blossoms into a full-fledged economic expansion. This generally occurs about nine months after long-term interest rates first touched a fifteen-month low. But there is also another requirement. The transition period will last until the bull market is at least eighteen months old. The second phase follows the recovery period, and it will last until the bull is at least eighteen months old and, in addition, nine months have passed since AAA Corporate rates first sank into a fifteen-month low. Both must occur.

A transition phase began on March 6, 1976 when the Dow stood at 988. Although the bull market turned eighteen months old in early June of that year, long-term interest rates have touched a fifteen-month low on February 6, just four months earlier (see Table 18). When nine months were up on November 8, 1976 (the seventh was a Saturday), the Dow was trading at 933, down 5 percent from its level when this second phase began eight months earlier (Chart 6). If the AAA Corporate Bond rate does not fall into a fifteen-month low, the stock market will remain in this second phase throughout the remainder of the bull market. For instance, the transition that began on January 8, 1968, when the Dow was trading at 908, lasted until the bull ended in December of that year. There have been seven other transition periods, and they are listed in Table 19.[4]

---

[4] Actually, the transition period beginning in July 1961 started before the bull market began. However, during this phase the Dow touched a two-year low and the bull officially began. The second phase would last until the bull was eighteen months old.

Table 18   AAA Corporate Bond Rates

	1974		1975		1976	
Week Ended		Week Ended		Week Ended		
Jan 05	7.73%	Jan 04	8.93%	Jan 03	8.66%	
12	7.77	11	8.91	10	8.63	
19	7.85	18	8.84	17	8.60	
26	7.88	25	8.78	24	8.58	
				31	8.57	
Feb 02	7.87	Feb 01	8.74	Feb 07	8.56	15-month
09	7.82	08	8.68	14	8.57	low
16	7.85	15	8.63	21	8.56	
23	7.87	22	8.58	28	8.51	
Mar 02	7.87	Mar 01	8.57	Mar 06	8.55	
09	7.92	08	8.59	13	8.55	
16	7.99	15	8.61	20	8.54	
23	8.05	22	8.69	27	8.50	
30	8.11	29	8.78			
Apr 06	8.17	Apr 05	8.87	Apr 03	8.46	
13	8.25	12	8.94	10	8.42	
20	8.26	19	8.95	17	8.36	
27	8.28	26	8.97	24	8.36	
May 04	8.34	May 03	9.01	May 01	8.41	
11	8.38	10	8.96	08	8.48	
18	8.36	17	8.88	15	8.56	
25	8.38	24	8.85	22	8.62	
		31	8.89	29	8.65	
Jun 01	8.39	Jun 07	8.85	Jun 05	8.63	
08	8.40	14	8.76	12	8.63	
15	8.40	21	8.73	19	8.61	
22	8.49	28	8.75	26	8.60	
29	8.57					
Jul 06	8.62	Jul 05	8.82	Jul 03	8.63	
13	8.66	12	8.84	10	8.57	
20	8.71	19	8.82	17	8.53	
27	8.77	26	8.85	24	8.55	
				31	8.55	
Aug 03	8.86	Aug 02	8.86	Aug 07	8.51	
10	8.93	09	8.93	14	8.48	
17	8.98	16	8.95	21	8.42	
24	9.03	23	8.96	28	8.43	
31	9.07	30	8.96			
Sep 07	9.13	Sep 06	8.93	Sep 04	8.41	
14	9.20	13	8.94	11	8.38	
21	9.29	20	8.98	18	8.39	
28	9.32	27	8.94	25	8.36	
Oct 05	9.37	Oct 04	8.96	Oct 02	8.37	
12	9.38	11	8.93	09	8.33	
19	9.29	18	8.86	16	8.30	
26	9.19	25	8.81	23	8.31	
				30	8.33	

Table continues

Table 18   AAA Corporate Bond Rates (continued)

1974		1975		1976		
Nov 02	9.09	Nov 01	8.77	Nov 06	8.30	9 months
09	8.99	08	8.76	13	8.31	later
16	8.89	15	8.75	20	8.27	
23	8.84	22	8.81	27	8.17	
30	8.84	29	8.81			
Dec 07	8.90	Dec 06	8.83	Dec 04	8.09	
14	8.87	13	8.86	11	8.01	
21	8.85	20	8.81	18	8.00	
28	8.90	27	8.72	24	7.96	
				31	7.91	

This transition period is the most treacherous time during a bull market. During this time, the fuel derived from declining interest rates usually runs out, and worries about the durability of the economic recovery surface. Investors become skittish, and the Dow is likely to suffer a substantial setback. For instance, the Dow fell 9 percent during the first two months of the transition phase that began in January 1968. During the most recent transition period, beginning in July 1983, the Dow fell by more than 10 percent. Eight transition periods lasted three months or more (in 1981, the bull ended one month into the discouragement phase), and the average drop in the market from high to low was 12 percent. From the beginning to the end of the second phase, the average gain on the Dow was a puny 1 percent (1.5 when annualized).

During the transition period, stock selection becomes very important. Investors should become more discriminating and focus on those stocks where a substantial improvement in earnings is noted. However,

Table 19 Second Phase

Begins	Dow	Ends	Months	Dow	Gain/Loss	% Down from Bull Market High at Low of Second Phase
1. April 11, 1950	211	December 13, 1950	8	228	8%	14
2. December 14, 1954	387	March 14, 1955	3	391	1%	7
3. December 22, 1959	595	April 22, 1959	3	625	5%	4
4. July 31, 1961	705	December 26, 1963	29	760	8%	27
5. January 8, 1968	908	December 21, 1968	11	966	6%	13
6. August 26, 1971	906	November 26, 1971	3	816	(10%)	16
7. March 8, 1976	988	November 8, 1976	8	933	(6%)	8
8. March 16, 1981	1002	April 20, 1981	1	1015	1%	8 [a]
9. July 12, 1983	1215	February 13, 1984	7	1150	4%	11
		Average	8		1%	12%
		Annualized			1.5%	

[a] Was only one month.

Table 20   10 Stable Growth Companies

1.	AT&T	Utility	Largest company
2.	Avon	Cosmetics	Largest company
3.	Beatrice Foods	Food processing	Largest company in industry
4.	Coca-Cola	Soft Drinks	Largest company
5.	General Foods	Food processing	Leading producer of packaged goods
6.	McDonald's	Fast food	Largest in industry
7.	Philip Morris	Tobacco	Largest cigarette producer
8.	Ralston Purina	Food processing	Largest producer of dog and cat food
9.	Sears	General retailing	Industry leader
10.	Tampax	Toiletries	Leading producer of tampons for female hygiene

there is one group of stocks that usually does significantly better than the overall market during this period. These are the stable growth companies, which have relatively predictable earnings. They can be found in industries such as tobacco, cosmetics, toiletries, soft drinks, food processing, fast foods, general retailing, and utilities. Table 20 contains a list of ten of the leading companies in the stable growth industries. While the Dow was shedding 10 percent during the discouragement phase that began in August 1971, this ten-stock portfolio held relatively stable, giving up only 2 percent. Over the last six transition periods, this list of ten stocks has an average gain of 11 percent, which stands in sharp contrast to the 4 percent average return on the Dow. (See Table 20a.)

However, this is the one period during a bull market when the trend is not clearly up, so it would probably be wise to hedge your bets against a drop in prices. An investor could to this by shorting some other stocks

Table 20a Stable Growth Companies during Last Six Bull Markets

	7/31/61– 12/26/63	1/8/68– 12/20/68	8/26/71– 11/26/71	3/8/76– 11/8/76	3/16/81– 4/20/81	7/12/83– 2/13/84
AT&T	38%	(2%)	(3%)	10%	6%	2%
Avon	108	2	0	16	4	(22)
Beatrice Foods	42	33	(9)	11	4	15
Coca-Cola	50	14	1	(12)	(4)	3
General Foods	35	17	(5)	0	0	5
McDonald's	[a]	53	9	(13)	13	(2)
Philip Morris	0	14	(14)	12	5	20
Ralston Purina	10	13	3	3	(2)	22
Sears	54	8	0	(4)	12	(11)
Tampax	55	14	2	(5)	5	(10)
Average	44%	20%	(2%)	2%	4%	2%
Dow Average	38%	6%	(10%)	(6%)	1%	(4%)
Average 6 Cycles	11%					
Dow 6 Cycles	4%					

[a] Not listed.

that appear to be weak and not in a stable growth industry. Or he might buy puts on the S&P 100s.[5]

The third phase, when capital goods prosper, begins when the bull is eighteen months old and, in addition, nine months have passed since long-term interest rates first touched a fifteen-month low. It will last until we get a final sell signal. A capital goods period began on November 26, 1971, when the bull turned eighteen months old. This was also more than nine months after AAA Corporate Bonds had made a fifteen-month low, and the Dow stood at 816, 10 percent below its level when the transition phase began. This capital goods phase lasted until an inflationary spiral surfaced on December 15, 1972, and put an end to the bull market. The Dow on that later date was 1027, 26 percent higher than when this phase began.

There have been six other mature phases and they are listed in Table 21.[6] The average gain during this time was 32 percent and when annualized it comes to 21 percent (before dividends.) Although secondary stocks are generally favored during this phase, there is also still one area where the large, well-known companies are likely to outpace the Dow. These are the industries that will benefit from a capital goods boom. Industries that manufacture machinery, machine tools, construction machinery, aerospace, aluminum, auto equipment, farm equipment, and other equipment typically benefit when consumer-related businesses begin to buy equipment and add new plants in earnest. The industrial technology sector, which includes computers, micro-electronics and precision instruments also puts in a stellar performance during this time.

Table 22 contains a list of twenty companies, each of which is the most prominent in some area of a capi-

---

[5] A put is an option that gives an investor the right to sell at a fixed price for a specific period. An investor pays a premium for this right, which is the cost of the put. Say the investor paid $200 to purchase a July 1984 put on the Standard & Poor's 100 with the right to sell at 140. If the actual S&P index falls to 120 before the put expires, the investor can exercise and pocket the difference between 140 and 120, which would be about $2,000.

[6] Twice long-term rates failed to reach a fifteen-month low. Consequently, there was no capital goods phase.

Table 21   Third Phase

	Begins	Dow	Ends	Months	Dow	Gain/Loss
1.	December 13, 1950	228	January 2, 1952	13	269	18%
2.	March 14, 1955	391	September 4, 1956	18	507	30%
3.	April 22, 1959	625	January 4, 1960	9	679	9%
4.	December 26, 1963	760	January 18, 1966	25	994	31%
5.	November 26, 1971	816	December 15, 1972	13	1027	26%
6.	November 8, 1976	933	March 15, 1977	4	965	3%
7.	February 13, 1984	1210	September 9, 1987	42	2549	110%
			Average	18		32%
					Annualized	21%

Table 22   20 Capital Goods Companies

1. Alcoa	Aluminum	Industry leader
2. Avnet	Electronics	Leading distributor of electronic components
3. Black & Decker	Machine tools	Largest maker of portable power tools
4. Boeing	Aerospace	Largest in industry
5. Caterpillar Tractor	Construction machinery	Largest in industry
6. Cincinnati Milicron	Machine tools	Largest manufacturer of machine tools
7. Cummins Engine	Machinery	Largest maker of high-speed diesel engines
8. Deere	Farm equipment	Industry leader
9. Eastman Kodak	Precision instruments	Largest producer of photographic products
10. Hewlett-Packard	Precision instruments	Leading manufacturer of precision electronic equipment
11. Intel	Electronics	Semiconductor technological leader
12. IBM	Computers	Acknowledged industry leader
13. Midland-Ross	Machinery	Largest manufacturer of industrial heating furnaces
14. Motorola	Electronics	Dominant manufacturer of commercial communication equipment
15. Perkin-Elmer	Precision instruments	Largest manufacturer of specialized analytical instruments
16. Stanley Works	Machine tools	Largest manufacturer of hand tools
17. Tektronix	Precision instruments	Largest manufacturer of cathode ray oscilloscopes
18. Texas Instruments	Electronics	Leading producer of semiconductor products
19. Timken	Auto equipment	Leading producer of roller bearings
20. Xerox	Office equipment	Leading manufacturer of copy/duplicating equipment and supplies

tal goods-type industry. Because the microelectronic revolution is changing the face of the American economy and society, four leading companies have been included. Four firms in the precision instrument industry, which play an important role in a high-technology economy, were also included. This portfolio of twenty companies increased by 58 percent in the capital goods period that began in November 1971 (Table 22a). In contrast, the gain in the Dow during that period was only 26 percent. Over the last four capital goods periods (including the one that began in November 1971) this portfolio experienced an average increase of 46 percent, as opposed to 17 percent for the Dow.

In the third phase, investors should seek out those companies that business turns to in order to satisfy its appetite for capital goods. If these companies and industries are not facing any unusual long-term problems, they are the ones to stuff portfolios with during the third phase. They should handily outperform the Dow. If both long- and short-term interest rates make a seven-year high during the third phase before a final sell signal is given,[7] the capital goods boom begins to fade. In this case, investors should become very careful and begin to trim the stocks that are performing poorly.

Had investors followed the model in and out of the stock market during the five and a half investment cycles beginning in 1962, the average gain would have been 47 percent. If however, they have also geared their portfolios to the phases of the market, the average return shoots up to 188 percent, four times the profit had they stuck to a portfolio of Dow stocks (Table 23). During the 1970-1981 period, a starting capital investment of $10,000 would have grown to about $2,564,000—a notable improvement from the $368,000 obtained by sticking with the Dow.

To beat the Dow, then, an investor must first check and see what phase of the bull market we are in and then look for the stocks that fit the phase. But in a

---

[7] This would be because either we are in the favorable period of an election cycle or the stock market is still in a buy zone.

Table 22a Capital Goods Companies during Last Four Bull Markets

	4/22/59– 1/4/60	12/26/63– 1/18/66	11/26/71– 12/15/72	11/8/76– 3/15/77
Alcoa	23%	19%	41%	15%
Avnet	a	37	30	13
Black & Decker	29	96	58	(1)
Boeing	(23)	326	79	6
Caterpillar Tractor	6	108	71	1
Cincinnati Milicron	(4)	70	30	24
Cummins Engine	4	33	15	28
Deere	(19)	67	118	(2)
Eastman Kodak	22	100	70	(11)
Hewlett-Packard	10	87	92	(7)
Intel	a	a	162	(2)
IBM	14	23	33	10
Midland-Ross	26	76	11	25
Motorola	102	221	81	(4)
Perkin-Elmer	21	78	64	(11)
Stanley Works	25	115	28	11
Tektronix	a	82	70	1
Texas Instruments	45	242	60	(18)
Timken	20	36	10	10
Xerox	8	158	36	(14)
Average	18%	104%	58%	42%
Dow	9%	31%	26%	3%
Average 4 Cycles	46%			
Dow 4 Cycles	17%			

[a] Not listed.

dynamic economy like ours, industries have life cycles of their own; after a reasonably long period of fast growth, they mature and lose their zip. Investors should investigate to make sure that these pace-setting industries are not developing arteriosclerosis. An example: although the steel industry is usually sensitive to

Table 23 Total Return during Last Six Bull Markets

Investment Cycle Beginning In	Discounting Phase % Gain	Discouragement Phase % Gain	Mature Phase % Gain	Total Gain	Dow	Outperformed Dow
1962	—	44	104	194	81	2.4/1
1966	167	20	—	220	28	7.8/1
1970	136	(2)	58	265	50	5.3/1
1974	215	2	4	234	60	3.9/1
1980	64	4	—	70	24	2.9/1
1982	143	2	110	255	212	1.2/1
Average				206%	75%	3.9/1

capital goods spending, it does not always put on a stellar performance during a third phase because it is an ailing industry. For that reason it was not included in our capital goods portfolio. Investors should keep an eye on the health of these industries, period.

To recap: There are three phases to a bull market. The discounting phase comes first, and lasts until the bull market is fifteen months old or until nine months have passed without a new low in short-term interest rates—whichever comes first. The star performers during that time are stocks in those industries that will benefit from a sharp fall in interest rates. The second phase is usually a period of transition, wherein the stock market pauses to catch its breath, and it lasts until either the third phase begins or the bull market is over. During this time, it pays an investor to be cautious and stick with high-quality stable growth companies. The third phase is the captial goods phase, and it only begins when the bull market is both eighteen months old and nine months have passed since long-term interest rates turned favorable, and it lasts until the final sell signal is given. This phase generally favors the late bloomers, those companies tied to capital spending and the industrial-technology sector.

Let us now look at ways to profit when an inflationary spiral breaks out.

Chapter 7

Two New Ways to Profit from an Inflationary Spiral

The traditional way to hedge against inflation is to load up on gold, silver commodities, and foreign currencies. Yet many investors view these liquid inflation hedges as too speculative, preferring the less volatile types of assets such as real estate. But real estate is a notoriously illiquid asset and therefore not well suited for an inflationary spiral, which usually lasts for a relatively short period of time. It takes time to unload a home or a building and the costs associated with buying and selling are fairly steep. Commissions, legal fees, and points on a mortgage typically run about 12 percent of the purchase price or more. An investor who bought a house for $100,000 and sold it for $112,000 would be saddled with a sales commission of approximately $6,700, and legal fees for the purchase and sale might amount to about $2,100. Add in points on a mortgage (say, three points on a $90,000 mortgage, which would be $2,700) and other associated closing costs, and you are easily up to $12,000. To recover the investor's costs, real estate must usually appreciate by at least 12 percent, and that generally takes a while. Consequently, real estate is essentially a long-term investment.

We have two suggestions for those who want a conservative way to invest and profit during a period of runaway inflation. The first is a commodity fund. Most funds have provisions that call for closing out the fund and returning the remaining assets to the investor if more that one-half the original investment is lost. This, of course, will protect investors from a major pitfall of commodity trading, the possibility of losing more than you invested. Even in a worst-case situation, investors should be able to get back 40 to 45 percent of their investment as long as the principals are reputable.

The majority of commodity funds are technically oriented. That is, their buy and sell decisions are made on the basis of trend-following methods, such as moving averages.[1] For example, after running a computer study of price trends during the past five years or so, a fund manager might decide that the best time to buy has been when a five-day moving average crossed over a twenty-five-day moving average. The manager will then use this method to invest in a diversified portfolio of commodities—some may have as many as thirty positions at one time. The basic idea of a diversified trend-following system is to milk those commodities that display a powerful trend while holding losses on trendless commodities to a minimum. The profits generated by a major move in a commodity are usually enormous, well able to offset the losses on a batch of trendless commodities and still provide investors with a handsome return.

However, there is an important assumption behind this approach. At least one, and preferably two, out of ten commodities must experience a major price adjustment. Unless this occurs, it is doubtful that enough profits will be generated to make up for the countless small losses. Certainly there have been a lot of big moves during the past twelve years, and most commodity funds have been quite profitable. But this last twelve years were not necessarily typical of what an investor can expect; most of that period was a time of sizzling inflation, and in general, dynamic price ad-

---

[1] In contrast, a fund using the fundamental approach would draw conclusions based upon an analysis of the economic factors which affect supply and demand.

justments are a function of galloping inflation. Had these funds been operating in the period from 1952 to 1965, a time when there was virtually no inflation, they probably would have been losers. During that time, there simply were not very many big profit moves.   Trading systems based on catching the *big move* would have been buried under an avalanche of small losses.

A commodity fund makes sense when we get a sign that we are in for a run of inflation. As long as investors choose a fund with reputable management[2] and a decent long-term record, and don't forget to get out when inflation cools, they should do well. Many of these funds, in fact, made well over 100 percent annually during past periods of runaway inflation. And it is important to select a fund that bases its decisions on technical considerations—there is no guarantee that a fundamental-type fund will catch even a fair portion of the dramatic price adjustments that occur at that time.

The second suggestion for conservative investors in times of inflation is to buy condominium apartments in buildings still under construction. In most cases, a developer will open a sales office and offer apartments for sale just prior to or after breaking ground. An investor can put down 10 percent (in some cases, 20 percent) of the sale price and reserve an apartment at a guaranteed price. During times of rapid inflation, the builder will usually raise the price several times before the project is completed. When the building is completed, investors can "flip" their investment—sell their apartment and buy another in a new building going up. There are several advantages to flipping. First, because there is no mortgage, there is no negative carry. In times of inflation, the cost of a mortgage and other expenses is frequently greater than what the apartment brings in rent, leading to an out-of-pocket loss. However, by buying condos under construction, investors do not have to incur a mortgage or other expenses until the building is complete. Nor do

---

[2] Preferably, the fund should be backed by a legitimate brokerage firm.

they have to find a renter. The second advantage is that most contracts give the investor the right to forfeit the 10 percent down payment and not close on the apartment. This means if there has been a big break in the real estate market, the flipper will be limiting the loss to 10 percent of the purchase price. Third, it is usually much easier to sell condominium apartments than it is to sell a house: when the building is complete, developers will advertise in order to bring in a lot of traffic. Remember, they are not trying to sell one house, but perhaps one hundred or more apartments. It will be easy to unload an apartment at this time by offering it at slightly less than what the others are going for.

The profits that can be made on these apartments during inflationary times are often enormous. During the late 1970s it was not uncommon for a condo that was originally offered at $100,000 to be going for $150,000 by the time the building was completed eighteen months later. A $10,000 down payment would have reaped a profit of about $38,500 after allowing for a 6 percent sales commission and 1 percent legal fees on the purchase and sale ($9,000 and $2,500)—not bad!

Flipping is probably the simplest way to make a short-term investment in residential real estate, as it insures the investor a degree of liquidity. An investor should make sure the developer has a reputation for doing a good job. Also, it is usually better to buy in an area where there are other completed apartment buildings. The neighborhood will then have developed amenities, and people will be drawn to be near friends who have bought in the area. If an investor can find a building that is more that a year away from completion, and three-quarters of the apartments have already been spoken for, better yet. There will be fewer apartments for sale when the building is completed, and when someone wishes to buy in, the investor will be holding the ace.

When inflation rears it head, then, investors can consider a commodity fund and/or a condo under construction. These two vehicles provide a low-risk opportunity to participate in an inflationary spiral.

Now back to the model. As you have seen, it has worked astonishingly well during the last thirty-eight years. But before you become totally convinced that you have the answer to investment timing, let us alert you to a potential problem. Models, you see, work well as long as the environment they measure—the underlying economic and financial background that most people take for granted—stays intact. However, when the environment changes there is usually trouble, and in the past, this has been the downfall of most models constructed by professionals. In the next chapter, we are going to show you how to deal with this problem.

Chapter 8

When the Environment Changes

Our model for investment timing has called all the twists and turns in the economy and investment markets since World War II with almost pinpoint accuracy. However, the investment battlefield is cluttered with the debris of models that worked reasonably well for a long period of time but lost their effectiveness when the environment changed. If we hope to surmount this pitfall, we must be able to adjust the model to fit the overall environment we are dealing in.

There are basically two types of overall environments. One is characterized by a long secular rise in both prices and interest rates. It has an inflationary bias. A secular movement in prices is a long-term trend that spans a decade or more. The other environment is characterized by a long secular decline in prices and interest rates. The bias in these times is deflationary. And since the dawn of the Industrial Revolution, the American economy has operated within the framework of one or the other of these environments.

Since 1946, we have been in an environment that has had an inflationary bias. Beneath the ups and downs in prices and interest rates, there was a pronounced secular trend pointing up. The Wholesale Price Index, which began this period at about 56, had reached a level of 306 by the end of 1983, a gain of more than 445 percent. During this span, there were only two temporary respites from this pattern of rising prices—a 7.9 percent falloff in 1948-49 and a 6.2 percent slide during 1951-53 (see Chart 7). AAA Corporate Bond rates, which were 2.46 percent when the environment began, marched steadily upward reaching 15.85 percent in September 1981. Throughout the trend to higher and higher rates, each break held above the previous low. For instance, the low of 7.88 percent made in early 1977 was higher than the previous bottom of 7.05 percent made in 1972. (See Chart 8.) An environment with an inflationary bias is typically a time of rapid and sustained economic growth. Recessions are usually brief and mild affairs, and each succeeding economic expansion easily surpasses the peak recorded during the previous business expansion. It is a time of glittering economic opportunities, and business, it seems, can do no wrong. It is also a time when it is easy for investors to shake the money tree. The rising tide of prosperity produces excess cash, which spills over into investment markets. Most forms of investment from the stock market to real estate, from commodities to antiques, from art to gold, experiences a powerful secular uptrend in prices.

The past thirty-eight years were, of course, a time of rapid economic growth. Of the nine contractions, only two, those of 1973-75 and 1981-82, could be considered even moderately deep and prolonged. The Dow began its march at 161 in 1949 and reached 1287 in late 1983—a gain of about 700 percent. Gold, which languished at a fixed price of $35 an ounce for years, touched $850—a mind-boggling rise of 2330 percent. The Dow Jones Commodities Futures Index went from about 37 (adjusted) to 239—a rise of 545 percent. The price of real estate went off the charts. Homes, which in some areas were selling for under $10,000 when the period began in the late 1940s, were going for well over $100,000 by late 1983. The story for other tangibles was much the same: price explosions of mammoth proportions. To be sure, the upward course of prices in investment markets was marred by setbacks from time to time. However, these jolts were not severe. Within a

Chart 7   Wholesale Price Index 1914-1984

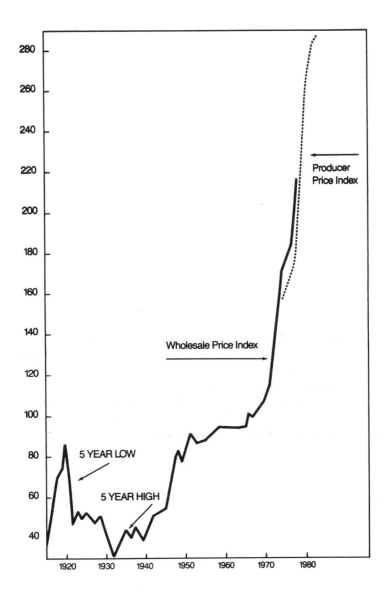

Chart 8   AAA Corporate Bond Rates 1914-1984

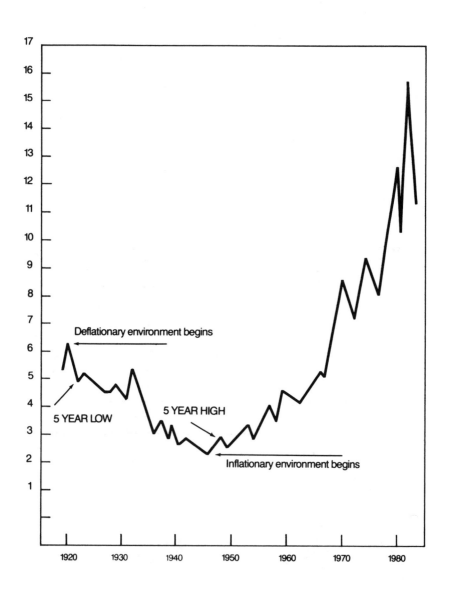

very short period of time, there was a recovery that brought prices back into a new high. In fact, the only investment that did poorly in this period was long-term bonds, which continued to sag as interest rates ratcheted upward.

At other times, however, a deflationary bias has held sway. The economy operated with the framework of a long-term decline in prices and interest rates. In general, these have been periods of hard times. Economic contractions are often accompanied by brutally severe unemployment. Business firms fight to keep market share, and the survival of many firms, big and small, becomes increasingly uncertain. During these times, the economy cannot seem to get back on the fast growth track, and growth opportunities fade. Most notable is the bottomless tumble that nearly every form of investment, from real estate to commodities, from stocks to antiques, experiences. The foundation of these markets, which are built during times when prices are on the upward slope, cracks, and profits that may have taken a generation to build go down the drain, leaving a trail of bewildered and shattered investors. During such times, it is no longer glamorous to take risks.

This environment last prevailed in the American economy from 1920 until 1946. The Wholesale Price Index, which stood at 86.2 in May 1920, fell to 30.8 by early 1933—a decline of 65 percent (Chart 7). The decline in long-term interest rates was even more protracted. From a peak of 6.38 percent in 1920, AAA Corporate Bond rates began a lengthy retreat that did not end until they reached 2.46 in May 1946—a slide of more than 60 percent (Chart 8). During this period, there were five economic contractions,[1] and three of them were very deep and prolonged: industrial production fell more than 30 percent. In contrast, the largest falloff in industrial production in the present inflation-

---

[1] Although 1945 was officially designated a recession, most economists consider the picture distorted by the special circumstances surrounding the transition from a wartime to a peacetime economy, and as such, do not consider this a bona fide recession.

ary environment was 15 percent, during the 1973-75 recession.

Bear markets during deflationary periods are usually very steep. The stock market suffered a staggering 89 percent loss between 1929 and 1932. In the course of three years, an investment of $1,000 shrank to $110. Then in 1937, just after investors caught their breath, the stock market went into another sickening slide that did not end until the Dow had lost 52 percent of its value. The least severe bear market of that deflationary period, the 45 percent break in 1920-21, equaled the 1973-74 break, which was by far the worst during the present inflationary environment (Chart 9). Buyers of real estate, art, antiques, and other investments became scarce, and these markets also suffered chilling declines. Real estate was off more than 25 percent during this period. To say the least, deflationary environments are not favorable times for investors. There were, however, some opportunities for profits. Long-term bonds, those of high quality, did very well as interest rates stayed on a downhill track. Investment markets often staged very substantial rallies after having been battered down to bargain levels. For instance, after reaching a low of 41 in 1932, the Dow rebounded to 194 in 1937—a rise of more than 350 percent.

The chief characteristic of an inflationary environment is a pronounced pattern of rising long-term interest rates, much like the one that has occurred since 1946. A secular downtrend in long-term rates, such as occurred between 1920 and 1946, is the telltale sign that we are in a deflationary environment (Chart 8). Wholesale prices, on the other hand, do not give so accurate a reading of the environment. This is because they often bottom out and begin to rebound well before an inflationary environment begins. For instance, during the last deflationary environment, wholesale prices made their low in 1933, thirteen years before interest rates reached their nadir. Thus, long term-interest rates provide the best guide as to the overall environment. The last deflationary environment began when AAA Corporate rates peaked in June 1920 and lasted

Chart 9   Dow Jones Industrial Average 1914-1949

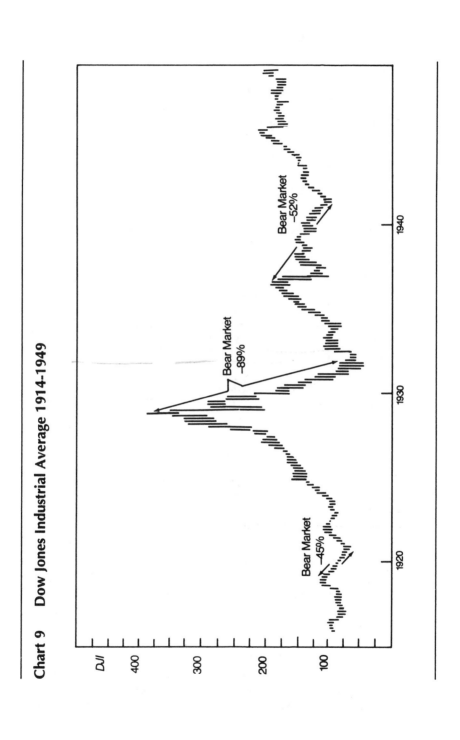

until April 1946, at which time long-term rates touched bottom and the present inflationary environment began. This pattern of secular trends in the long-term interest rates also prevailed before 1920. For instance, long-term interest rates peaked in 1869 and ushered in an environment of secularly falling prices, which continued until rates bottomed in 1899. And the following twenty-one years until 1920 were clearly a time of secularly rising prices (see Chart 10).

Since 1946, we have been in an overall environment characterized by an inflationary bias. Most of us have known no other. We have grown up within this framework and have adapted to it. Of course, we take its existence for granted. Yet if history is any guide, somewhere along the line the overall environment will once again shift to one with a deflationary tilt.

How do we recognize a shift in the overall environment? When both long-term interest rates (AAA Corporate Bonds) and the Producer Price Index (the raw number) make a five-year low, one confirming the other, we can conclude that the pattern of an inflationary environment has been shattered. For instance, the Wholesale Price Index made a five-year low in December 1921. And when long-term rates followed suit in July 1922, we could have recognized the onset of the last deflationary environment (see Table 24 and Appendix B). The sign that a deflationary period has ended would be a five-year high in both long-term interest rates and producer prices. It would indicate that long-term rates had made a secular bottom. The current inflationary environment would have been spotted as early as December of 1947. At that time, long-term interest rates made a five-year high, confirming the five-year high wholesale prices had made back in December 1935. In both cases, we would have been able to spot an emerging new environment about two years after it had actually begun.

Of all the errors that investors and would-be investors make, perhaps the greatest is that they take their overall environment for granted. They expect what they have seen and experienced in the recent

Chart 10   Long-Term Rates[*] 1865-1920

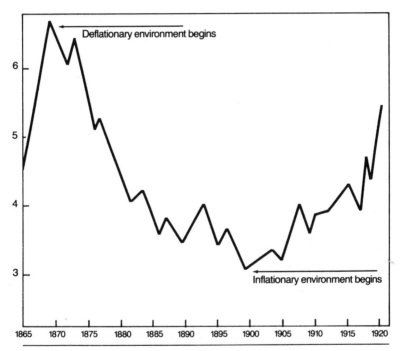

*Adjusted Average of High Grade Railroad Bond Yields

source: Frederick R. Macaulay, *The Movement of Interest Rates, Bond Yields and Stock Prices in the United States Since 1856*

Table 24 Wholesale Price Index 1913-1948 (1967 = 100)

Year	Ann. Avg.	Jan.	Feb.	Mar.	Apr.	May	June	July	Aug.	Sept.	Oct.	Nov.	Dec.
1913	36.0	36.3	36.0	36.0	35.9	35.5	35.5	35.9	35.9	36.4	36.4	36.2	35.6
1914	35.2	35.4	35.2	35.1	34.9	34.8	34.8	34.7	35.9	36.2	35.1	34.9	34.7
1915	35.8	35.2	35.4	35.2	35.4	35.5	35.2	35.7	35.4	35.2	36.2	36.9	38.2
1916	44.1	39.7	40.4	41.5	42.1	42.5	42.8	43.0	43.9	44.9	46.9	50.2	51.2
1917	60.6	52.7	53.9	55.5	58.9	62.2	63.0	63.4	64.4	63.7	63.1	63.3	63.4
1918	67.6	64.5	63.2	65.1	66.2	66.1	66.5	68.0	69.3	71.0	70.3	70.3	70.3
1919	71.4	69.3	67.0	67.7	68.6	69.7	69.9	72.8	74.5	72.8	73.0	74.6	77.7
1920	79.6	81.3	81.1	81.8	85.4	86.2	85.9	85.6	83.2	80.1	74.4	68.8	62.2
1921	50.3	58.8	54.1	52.9	51.0	49.6	48.2	48.2	48.3	48.2	48.5	48.5	48.0
1922	49.9	47.1	48.0	47.9	48.1	49.6	49.7	51.3	50.9	51.2	51.4	51.8	51.9
1923	51.9	52.6	53.3	53.9	53.5	52.5	51.7	50.8	50.5	51.5	51.3	50.8	50.6
1924	50.5	51.4	51.5	50.8	50.1	49.5	49.0	49.3	50.0	50.0	50.6	51.1	52.4
1925	53.3	53.1	53.6	53.7	52.5	52.4	53.1	53.8	53.5	53.3	53.4	53.9	53.3
1926	51.6	53.2	52.6	51.9	51.7	51.8	51.8	51.3	51.1	51.5	51.3	50.8	50.5
1927	49.3	49.2	49.8	49.5	48.9	48.4	48.5	48.6	49.1	49.7	49.9	49.7	49.7
1928	50.0	49.7	49.5	49.3	49.9	50.3	50.0	50.2	50.3	50.9	50.0	49.5	49.5
1929	49.1	49.5	49.2	49.6	49.3	48.8	49.1	49.8	49.7	49.6	49.0	48.2	48.1
1930	44.6	47.7	47.1	46.5	46.5	45.8	44.8	43.4	43.4	43.5	42.8	41.9	41.0
1931	37.6	40.3	39.6	39.2	38.5	37.8	37.2	37.1	37.2	36.8	36.3	36.2	35.4
1932	33.6	34.8	34.2	34.0	33.8	33.3	33.0	33.3	33.6	33.7	33.3	32.9	32.3
1933	34.0	31.4	30.8	31.0	31.1	32.4	33.5	35.5	35.9	36.5	36.8	36.7	36.5
1934	38.6	37.2	37.9	38.0	37.9	38.0	38.5	38.5	39.4	40.0	39.4	39.5	39.7
1935	41.3	40.6	41.0	40.9	41.3	41.4	41.2	40.9	41.5	41.6	41.5	41.6	41.8

Year	Ann. Avg.	Jan.	Feb.	Mar.	Apr.	May	June	July	Aug.	Sept.	Oct.	Nov.	Dec.
1936	41.7	41.6	41.6	41.0	41.1	40.5	40.9	41.5	42.0	42.0	42.0	42.5	43.4
1937	44.5	44.3	44.5	45.2	45.4	45.1	45.0	45.4	45.1	45.1	44.0	43.0	42.1
1938	40.5	41.8	41.2	41.1	40.5	40.3	40.4	40.6	40.2	40.4	40.1	40.0	39.8
1939	39.8	39.7	39.7	39.6	39.3	39.3	39.0	38.9	38.6	40.8	40.9	40.8	40.9
1940	40.5	40.9	40.6	40.4	40.5	40.4	40.0	40.1	40.0	40.2	40.6	41.0	41.3
1941	45.1	41.7	41.6	42.0	43.0	43.8	45.0	45.8	46.6	47.4	47.7	47.7	48.4
1942	50.9	49.5	49.9	50.3	50.9	51.0	50.9	50.9	51.1	51.5	51.6	51.7	52.0
1943	53.3	52.5	52.9	53.3	53.5	53.6	53.5	53.3	53.2	53.2	53.2	53.1	53.3
1944	53.6	53.3	53.4	53.5	53.5	53.6	53.8	53.7	53.5	53.6	53.7	53.8	54.0
1945	54.6	54.1	54.2	54.3	54.5	54.7	54.8	54.7	54.5	54.3	54.6	55.0	55.2
1946	62.3	55.2	55.5	56.2	56.8	57.2	58.2	64.4	66.5	64.0	69.2	72.1	72.7
1947	76.5	73.2	73.9	75.7	75.2	74.8	74.8	75.6	76.6	78.1	79.1	79.9	81.4
1948	82.8	82.9	81.3	81.3	82.0	82.4	83.0	83.7	84.3	84.2	83.3	83.1	82.6

past to continue. But when an epic upheaval does occur, investors who felt they were playing it safe by betting on the time-tested rules of the past are unable to understand what hit them. Hadn't they played by the rules? Yes, but by the wrong rules. When the environment changes, the old rules and strategies become inappropriate and must be replaced by new ones.

If history repeats itself, we will come face-to-face with an environment vastly different from the one we know today. In that case, what do we do? For the answer, read the next chapter.

Chapter 9

The Other Environment: Deflation

When the environment tilts to deflation, we enter an economic and investment world very different from the last one we have known. And it is not as kind to investors and businessmen as the one in which prices and interest rates are on an upward slope. The length and nastiness of the breaks in most investment markets will surprise most people. Fortunately, we can adjust the model and track the turns in the economy, the stock market, and inflation just as effectively during deflation as during an environment with an inflationary bias. Basically, there are three important differences between the environments, along with one new rule.

The most important variation is that an investment climate turns sour more easily. It does not take very much of a rise in interest rates to bring the economy to a screeching halt and send the stock market into a nosedive; a fifteen month high in both short- and long-term interest rates will usually do the trick. But to make sure business people have been dissuaded from borrowing, the rally in AAA Corporate rates should also be at least equivalent to 7 percent of the bottom rate. If you glance at Table 25, you can see that the bottom rate registered in January 1937 was 3.08, or 308 basis points. (A basis point is equal to one hundredth of a percentage point.) Seven percent of that

Table 25   AAA Corporate Bond Rates

1935		1936		1937		
Week Ended		Week Ended		Week Ended		
Jan 05	3.80%	Jan 04	3.42%	Jan 02	3.10%	
12	3.78	11	3.39	09	3.08	
19	3.78	18	3.37	16	3.08	bottom
26	3.76	25	3.35	23	3.08	
				30	3.13	
Feb 02	3.74	Feb 01	3.35	Feb 06	3.17	
09	3.73	08	3.34	13	3.20	
16	3.70	15	3.32	20	3.26	
23	3.68	22	3.31	27	3.23	
		29	3.32			
Mar 02	3.66	Mar 07	3.30	Mar 06	3.24	
09	3.65	14	3.30	13	3.29	
16	3.68	21	3.30	20	3.34	rise of
23	3.67	28	3.29	27	3.37	7%
30	3.67					
Apr 06	3.68	Apr 04	3.28	Apr 03	3.38	
13	3.66	11	3.27	10	3.44	15-month
20	3.65	18	3.29	17	3.43	high
27	3.65	25	3.30	24	3.39	
May 04	3.65	May 02	3.31	May 01	3.40	
11	3.64	09	3.29	08	3.36	
18	3.66	16	3.29	15	3.34	
25	3.65	23	3.26	22	3.33	
		30	3.25	29	3.30	
Jun 01	3.64	Jun 06	3.24	Jun 05	3.30	
08	3.64	13	3.24	12	3.27	
15	3.62	20	3.25	19	3.27	
22	3.60	27	3.24	26	3.27	
29	3.59					
Jul 06	3.57	Jul 04	3.24	Jul 03	3.29	
13	3.55	11	3.22	10	3.27	
20	3.56	18	3.22	17	3.25	
27	3.56	25	3.23	24	3.25	
				31	3.23	
Aug 03	3.56	Aug 01	3.23	Aug 07	3.22	
10	3.57	08	3.22	14	3.21	
17	3.59	15	3.22	21	3.24	
24	3.62	22	3.21	28	3.26	
31	3.64	29	3.21			
Sep 07	3.63	Sep 05	3.19	Sep 04	3.26	
14	3.60	12	3.18	11	3.28	
21	3.59	19	3.17	18	3.29	
28	3.58	26	3.17	25	3.28	
Oct 05	3.56	Oct 03	3.19	Oct 02	3.29	
12	3.54	10	3.19	09	3.28	
19	3.53	17	3.19	16	3.28	
36	3.51	24	3.18	23	3.29	
		31	3.18	30	3.27	

Table 25   AAA Corporate Bond Rates   (continued)

1935		1936		1937	
Nov 02	3.49	Nov 07	3.17	Nov 06	3.23
09	3.48	14	3.15	13	3.24
16	3.47	21	3.14	20	3.24
23	3.47	28	3.13	27	3.25
30	3.47				
Dec 07	3.46	Dec 05	3.11	Dec 04	3.24
14	3.44	12	3.10	11	3.22
21	3.45	19	3.09	18	3.22
28	3.43	26	3.11	25	3.20

figure is 22 basis points (figures are rounded to the next highest number), or a rise to 3.30 or more, which was reached in the week ending March 20 when the rate registered 3.34.[1]

Fifteen-month highs and lows in short- and long-term interest rates are listed in Tables 26 and 27. Prior to 1946, the market for Treasury issues was almost nonexistent, so 90-Day Prime Banker's Acceptances, which played an important role in the Federal Reserve Bank operations at that time, have been substituted as the proxy for short-term interest rates. Also, prior to 1934 AAA Corporate Bond rates were available only on a monthly basis.

A favorable investment climate was launched on July 8, 1932, when the rate on a 90-Day Prime Banker's Acceptances sank to a fifteen-month low. Long-term rates followed suit six months later, indicating that investors could now look forward to a long period of fair weather. However, in March 1933, just as the economy was struggling to its feet following the most awesome

[1] This was still short of a fifteen-month high in AAA rates.

Table 26   90-Day Prime Banker's Acceptances

15-Month Low	15-Month High
July 1, 1921	April 27, 1923[a]
May 9, 1924	September 11, 1925
November 22, 1929	October 23, 1931
July 8, 1932	March 24, 1933[a]
April 20, 1934	July 31, 1936

Note: The dates are for the following Friday, when the figure was made available to investors.

[a] Fell back into a fifteen-month low before long-term rates confirmed.

depression in the life of the American economy, short-term interest rates flared up to a fifteen-month high (see Appendix C). But this was not enough to derail the economic recovery or the bull market in stocks. As long as the AAA Corporate rate did not also register a fifteen-month high, the climate would remain friendly to investors. And in April 1934, 90-Day Prime Banker's Acceptances slipped back into a fifteen-month low, and the interest rate threat receded. There would be no further hint of trouble on the interest rate front until late

Table 27   AAA Corporate Bonds

15-Month Low	15-Month High
September 2, 1921	September 6, 1929
May 2, 1930	November 6, 1931
February 3, 1933	April 16, 1937
October 21, 1938	October 6, 1939[a]
January 19, 1940	October 3, 1947

Note: The dates are for the following Friday, when the figure was made available to investors.

[a] Fell back into a fifteen-month low before long-term rates confirmed.

July 1936, when short-term rates again reached a fifteen-month high. This time long-term rates followed
suit. We got word of that on April 16, 1937, when the
AAA rate reached 3.44. As this rate was also up more
than the equivalent of 7 percent of the bottom rate, it
was curtains for this favorable investment climate.

There were three other favorable investment climates during the last deflationary environment, and
they are listed in Table 28. Surprisingly, investment climates that surfaced during this environment lasted
much longer than those during the present environment of securely rising prices. Their average length was
seventy-two months; the average during inflationary
times was thirty-seven months. This longevity was
probably due to the elevated level of pessimism preval-
ant during deflationary times, when people become so
cautious that it takes longer for the economy and stock
market to develop the types of excesses that usually
render them vulnerable.

The second major difference in the model's rules
during deflation is that the stock market swings from a
five-year low to a five-year high during these times. Because of the secular downward pressure on prices, an
up-phase in the investment cycle will not begin until
extreme pessimism has been recorded. The stock market enters a buy zone one week after the Dow falls into
a five-year low. However, in this treacherous environment, the stock market does not automatically become
a buy five months after extreme pessimism has been
recorded. The investment climate must also turn
friendly before investors are given the green light to
buy. On the flip side of the coin, there is more room to
rally before a mood of optimism surfaces. A caution
zone begins nine months after the Dow closes into a
five-year high. And the yellow light keeps flashing
until the Dow retreats into a five- year low once more.

The Dow recorded a five-year low on April 14,
1942, and one week later, the average stood at 97.
This buy zone began just one week before the Dow
touched bottom, and by the time the Dow made a five-
year high on January 3, 1945, investors were way

Table 28 Investment Climate

Turns Favorable	Turns Unfavorable	Length in Months	Economy Turned Up	Months after Climate Turned Favorable	Business Contraction Began	Months after Climate Turned Unfavorable
July 1, 1921	September 6, 1929	98	August 1921 [d]	1	August 1929	[e]
November 22, 1929	January 1, 1932[b]	26			—	
July 8, 1932	April 16, 1937	57	March 1933	8	May 1937	1
October 1, 1938[a]	January 9, 1948[c]	107	June 1938	[f]	November 1948	10
Average		72				

[a] Began favorable period of the political cycle.
[b] Extended until the favorable period of the election cycle ended.
[c] Due to turn unfavorable on January 1, 1948, but in December 1947 the environment shifted to one with an inflationary bias.
[d] Recovery impeded by a massive deflation.
[e] Contraction began one month before climate turned unfavorable.
[f] Expansion began four months before climate turned favorable.

ahead of the game. When the yellow light flashed nine months later, the Dow stood at 183. Investors who had had the courage to buy in April 1942 were rewarded with a return of 89 percent. There were two other times during the last deflationary environment that extreme pessimism was recorded. Both times, the stock market was substantially higher by the time a caution zone was reached. All three buy and caution zones are listed in Table 29; see also Chart 11. The average profit to investors who bought one week after a five-year low and sold when the yellow light first flashed was 80 percent.

During an environment of secularly declining prices, a flare-up in the price level becomes self-accelerating only when the stock market is in a caution zone. This is the third and last variation in the rules. In order for inflation to get up a head of steam, businessmen and consumers must adopt an expansive attitude toward spending and borrowing. This will not occur until about nine months after the Dow has made a five-year high. The economy will not be vulnerable to an inflationary spiral until sentiment turns optimistic. On the other hand, if the Dow falls into a five-year low while an inflationary spiral is in progress, it means businessmen and consumers will soon become cautious in their spending and borrowing habits, and inflation is about to wind down.

A friendly investment climate began in October 1938, and about two and a half years later, in mid-May 1941, the rate of inflation had reached 6.2 percent and was gaining momentum (see Table 30). Although the stock market was in a caution zone, two years had not passed since the Wholesale Price Index made its last yearly low in August 1939. We had to wait until mid-August 1941 before we got the sign that an inflationary spiral was beginning. The upward pressure on prices would last until the Dow fell into a five-year low in April 1942. This sign of extreme pessimism in the stock market warned that the demand for goods and services would soon fall apart and that time was running out on this inflationary episode. During that eight-month

Table 29   Buy and Caution Zones

5-Year Low	Dow 1 Week Later	% from Actual Low on Dow	5-Year High	Dow 9 Months Later	Gain	Time Elapsed (months)
June 20, 1921	67	5%	November 18, 1924	142	112%	50
May 20, 1931	130	68%	July 14, 1936	181	39%	71
April 14, 1942	97	5%	January 3, 1945	183	89%	42
			Average		80%	54

Chart 11   Dow Jones Industrial Average 1914-1949

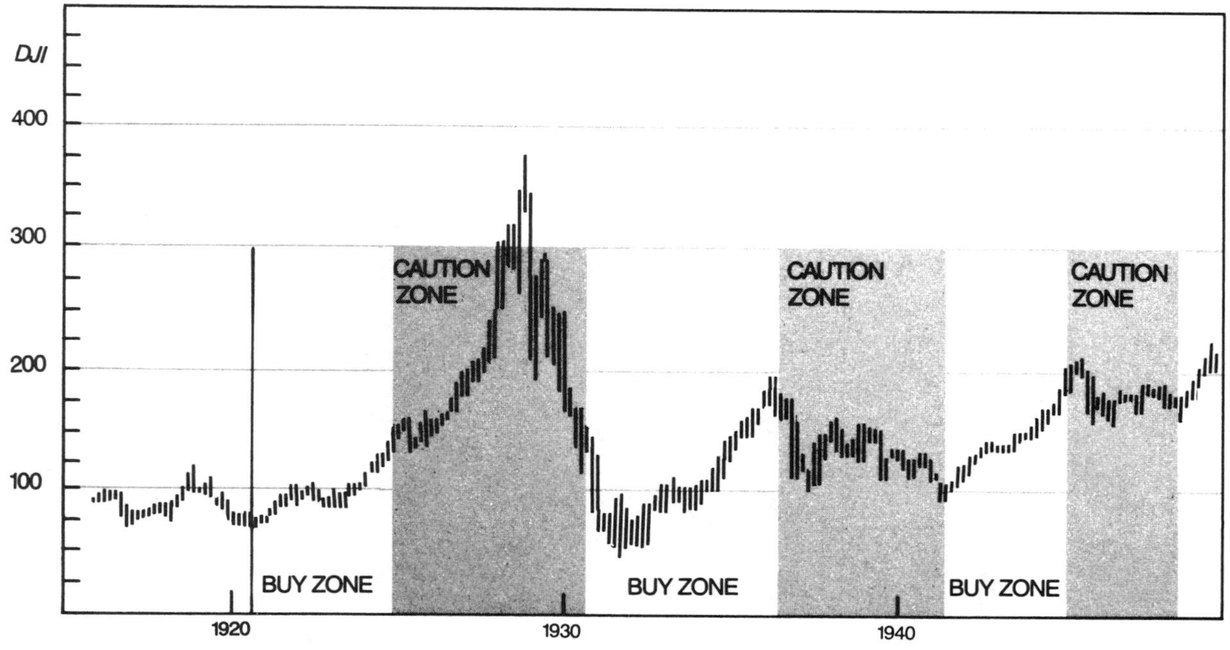

Table 30   Rates of Inflation

Year	Jan.	Feb.	Mar.	Apr.	May	Jun.	Jul.	Aug.	Sep.	Oct.	Nov.	Dec.
1914	(2.5)	(2.2)	(2.5)	(2.8)	(2.0)	(2.2)	(2.2)	0	(0.6)	(3.6)	(3.6)	(2.5)
1915	(0.6)	+0.6	0.3	1.4	2.0	1.1	2.9	(1.4)	(1.8)	3.1	5.7	10.1
1916	12.8	14.2	17.9	18.9	19.7	21.6	20.7	24.0	27.6	29.6	36.0	34.0
1917	32.7	33.4	33.7	39.9	46.4	47.2	47.4	46.7	41.9	34.5	26.1	23.8
1918	22.4	17.3	17.3	12.4	6.3	5.6	7.3	7.6	11.5	11.4	11.1	10.9
1919	7.4	6.0	4.0	3.6	5.4	5.1	7.1	7.5	2.5	3.8	6.9	10.5
1920	17.3	21.0	20.8	24.5	23.7	22.9	17.6	11.7	10.0	1.9	(7.8)	(20.0)
1921	(27.7)	(33.3)	(35.3)	(40.3)	(42.5)	(43.9)	(43.7)	(41.9)	(39.8)	(34.8)	(29.5)	(22.8)
1922	(19.9)	(11.3)	(9.5)	(5.7)	0	+3.1	6.4	5.4	6.2	6.0	6.8	8.1
1923	11.7	11.0	12.5	11.2	5.8	4.0	(1.0)	(0.8)	+0.6	(0.2)	(1.9)	(2.5)
1924	(2.3)	(3.4)	(5.8)	(6.4)	(5.7)	(5.2)	(3.0)	(1.0)	(2.9)	(1.4)	+0.6	3.6
1925	3.3	4.1	5.7	4.8	5.9	8.4	9.1	7.0	6.6	5.5	5.5	1.7
1926	0.2	(1.9)	(3.4)	(1.5)	(1.1)	(2.4)	(4.6)	(4.5)	(3.4)	(3.9)	(5.8)	(5.3)
1927	(7.5)	(5.3)	(4.6)	(5.4)	(6.6)	(6.4)	(5.3)	(3.9)	(3.5)	(2.7)	(2.2)	(1.6)
1928	+1.0	(0.6)	(0.4)	+2.0	3.9	3.1	3.3	2.4	2.4	0.2	(0.4)	(0.4)
1929	(0.4)	(0.6)	+0.6	(1.2)	(3.0)	(1.8)	(0.8)	(1.2)	(2.6)	(2.0)	(2.6)	(2.8)
1930	(3.6)	(4.3)	(6.3)	(5.7)	(6.1)	(8.8)	(12.9)	(12.7)	(12.3)	(12.7)	(13.1)	(13.8)
1931	(15.5)	(15.9)	(15.7)	(17.2)	(17.5)	(17.0)	(14.5)	(14.3)	(15.4)	(15.2)	(13.6)	(13.7)
1932	(13.6)	(13.6)	(13.3)	(12.2)	(11.9)	(11.3)	(10.2)	(9.7)	(8.4)	(8.3)	(9.4)	(8.8)
1933	(9.8)	(9.9)	(8.8)	(8.0)	(2.7)	+1.5	6.6	6.8	8.3	10.5	11.6	13.0
1934	18.5	23.1	22.6	21.9	17.3	14.9	8.5	9.7	9.6	7.1	7.6	8.8
1935	9.1	8.2	7.6	9.0	8.9	7.0	6.2	5.3	4.0	5.3	5.3	5.3
1936	2.5	1.5	0.2	(0.5)	(2.2)	(3.2)	+1.5	1.2	1.0	1.2	2.2	2.4
1937	6.5	7.0	10.2	10.5	11.4	10.0	9.4	7.4	7.4	4.8	1.2	(3.0)

Year	Jan.	Feb.	Mar.	Apr.	May	Jun.	Jul.	Aug.	Sep.	Oct.	Nov.	Dec.
1938	(5.6)	(6.3)	(9.1)	(10.8)	(10.6)	(10.2)	(10.6)	(10.9)	(10.4)	(8.9)	(7.0)	(5.5)
1939	(5.0)	(4.8)	(3.6)	(3.0)	(2.5)	(3.5)	(4.2)	(4.0)	+1.0	2.0	2.0	2.8
1940	3.0	2.3	2.0	3.1	2.8	2.6	3.1	3.6	(1.5)	(0.7)	+0.5	1.0
1941	2.0	2.5	4.0	6.2	8.4	12.5	14.2	16.5	17.9	17.5	16.3	17.2
1942	18.7	20.0	19.8	18.4	16.4	13.1	11.1	9.7	8.6	8.2	8.4	7.4
1943	6.1	6.0	6.0	5.1	5.1	5.1	4.7	4.1	3.3	3.1	2.7	2.5
1944	1.9	0.9	0.4	0.0	0.0	0.6	0.8	0.6	0.8	0.9	1.3	1.3
1945	1.5	1.5	2.2	1.9	1.9	1.9	1.9	1.9	1.3	1.7	2.2	2.2
1946	2.0	2.4	2.7	4.2	4.6	6.2	17.7	22.0	17.9	26.7	31.1	31.7

period, cash wheat rose from 89 cents to $1.00, for a gain of 12 percent. There was one other inflationary spiral during this time. (See Table 31.)

During an environment of secularly falling prices, we can also slip into a deflationary spiral. This occurs when producer prices are falling at an annual rate of 5 percent or more, and the rate of falloff is the most in twelve months—but only if people are susceptible to inflationary expectations. Deflationary expectations cannot take hold until two years have passed since the high of the last inflationary trend. During a deflationary period, an inflationary trend is certainly not equivalent to an inflationary spiral; it is merely a mild upturn in inflation, expressed as a one-year high in the Producers Price Index, interrupting the secular deflationary environment. This rule is actually the exact converse for that of an inflationary spiral during an environment of secularly rising prices. A deflationary spiral remains in effect until the rate of deflation registers the lowest reading in twelve months.

A deflationary spiral began on September 15, 1930. Although word came in April of that year that prices were tumbling at better than a 5 percent rate, it was not until September that two years had passed since the last inflationary trend had ended. At that

---

Table 31   Inflationary Spiral

	Begins	Runs Out of Gas	Gain/Loss
	August 15, 1941	April 21, 1942	
Wholesale Price Index	46.6	50.9	9%
Cash Wheat	.89[a]	1.00	12%
Dow	124	97	(22%)
	July 15, 1946	January 30, 1948b	
Wholesale Price Index	64.4	82.9	29%
Cash Wheat	1.87[a]	2.81	50%
Dow	200	174	(13%)

[a] Average monthly prices received by farmers.
[b] Rules for an inflationary environment.

time, we could conclude that the deflationary forces had become self-feeding. This massive deflation lasted until mid-April 1932, when we got news that the rate of deflation had registered its lowest reading in a year. During that seventeen-month period, the Wholesale Price Index fell more than 22 percent and investment markets virtually collapsed, putting an end to the hopes and dreams of hundreds of thousands of investors. The Dow fell from 236 to 64, a numbing drop of 73 percent. Cash wheat, which averaged about 70 cents[2] in September 1930, had fallen to an average of 35 cents by August 1931, a decline of 50 percent. The story in real estate, tangibles, or most any other asset was much the same: merciless slaughters. The Dow fell into a five year-low in May 1931, but unlike similar drops in this century, share prices did not turn up within five months. The difference was a deflationary spiral that darkened expectations and ripped apart confidence. The stock market continued its dismal slide throughout the whole of this deflationary spiral and finally came to rest in early July 1932, just eleven weeks after the massive deflation abated. This was the only time an economic rebound did not follow on the heels of a friendly investment climate.

What happens is that when the economy is trapped in a deflationary spiral, consumers delay purchases in the hope that goods will become less expensive later on. In addition, because prices normally fall much faster than wages, profit margins are pinched. Naturally, there is a reluctance on the part of business to expand, and the economy is apt to go into free fall.

During a deflationary spiral, an investor should hold cash.[3] The only acceptable exception to holding cash is to invest in long-term bonds: buy only those of the highest quality. It does not matter if there are bargains or if the investment climate has turned favorable.

[2] Monthly average received by farmers.

[3] Although many banks failed in the thirties, this would not have created a problem to followers of the model, as they would have already shifted back into stocks before the massive run on the banks began. Today, with the advent of the Federal Deposit Insurance Corporation, bank safety is hardly an issue, at least until a level of $100,000 is exceeded.

Investment of all kinds should be shunned—and Shunned should be spelled with a capital *S*.

To review the rules for a deflationary environment:

A. Stocks are a buy when one week has passed since the Dow made a five-year low and the investment climate is also favorable. (Exception: a deflationary spiral.)

B. Stocks are a sale when either:
   1. the investment climate turns unfavorable (that is, both short- and long-term interest rates have made a fifteen-month high, and in addition, long-term rates have rallied the equivalent of 7 percent from the low).
      a. If the stock market is in a caution zone (a caution zone begins nine months after the Dow registers a five-year high), stocks are a sale immediately.
      b. If the stock market has not yet reached a caution zone, investors can wait up to seven months before selling.
   2. an inflationary spiral begins. (An inflationary spiral can only occur when the stock market is in a caution zone.)
   3. a deflationary spiral begins. (A deflationary spiral begins when producer prices are falling at an annual rate of 5 percent or more and the rate of falloff is the largest in twelve months—but only if two years have passed since the last mild inflation has ended.)

Let's see how these rules worked during the 1920 to 1946 deflationary period.

The first buy signal came on July 5, 1921, just after we received word that short-term interest rates had made a fifteen-month low; the Dow, which had made a two-year low back in November 1920, stood at 67. It was not necessary to wait for a five-year low in the Dow, as it was not yet evident that a deflationary environment had begun. Yet in this case it would have made no difference. The Dow actually did slip into a five-year low on June 20, 1921, two weeks before the buy signal flashed. Although the outlook was grim and most investors were pessimistic, this proved to be an ideal time to buy stocks. Investors would have gotten in on the ground floor, just before the greatest bull market of all time was getting under way. The stock market was to climb relentlessly upward for eight years, barely pausing to catch its breath.

In July 1922, long-term bonds descended into a five-year low, and as the Wholesale Price Index had already reached that level seven months earlier, it indicated we were now operating in a deflationary environment. Although this would not disturb our investment posture, it did mean the rules had changed. Although a bull market was in progress, it would now be easier to shoot down both the economy and the stock market. Recession struck in 1923. However, the stock market had not reached a caution zone and the investment climate remained favorable. The signs still pointed up, and investors could feel confident that the upward trend of stock prices would continue intact. Sure enough, the Dow did not even react to a two-year low.

On November 18, 1924, the Dow made a five-year high, and nine months later, a yellow light began to flash. But not to worry. The investment climate was still favorable and there was no hint of any trouble on the inflation front. In late 1927, the American public, inflamed by year after year of Coolidge prosperity, discovered the stock market. During the next year and a half, this bull market roared and snorted through Wall Street, thundering from one record high to another. By mid-1929, all the old markers by which the price of stocks were measured had long since been passed, and many otherwise intelligent people continued to speculate in stocks about which they knew little, in belief that a new era of prosperity has dawned. To them it was inconceivable that the stock market had anywhere to go but up. Of course, the speculative public would have no idea that the green light had turned to red on

September 6, 1929. But on that date, the model signaled that during the month of August long-term rates were 7 percent above their previous low rate. As the stock market was in a caution zone, a red light flashed. Stocks were to be sold the very next trading day when the Dow stood at 377, which was only four days after and 1 percent below its peak. An investor following the model would have bought within 6 percent of the low and sold 1 percent below the high of the greatest bull market of all time (see Table 32 and Chart 12).

There is often a steep rise in stocks at the beginning of a deflationary environment. This is because money flows out of real assets—inflation hedges—that have prospered during inflationary times and into financial assets—that is, stocks and bonds.

According to the model, an investor would have been safely on the sidelines during the crash of October 1929. The investment climate turned friendly in November 1929, but stocks did not fall into a buy zone. Consequently, investors should still have been in cash in mid-September of 1930, when a deflationary spiral was signaled, derailing hopes for a recovery. This could have been a time for aggressive investors to go short, as nothing usually withstands the merciless onslaught that occurs during a massive deflation. Under the crushing weight of a collapsing price level, the economy sank into a black hole, and one by one, investment markets peeled off into steep nosedives, which bewildered the majority of investors who had known nothing but continued price increases.

In early 1931, the Dow made a five-year low, and to most Wall Streeters, stock prices looked very cheap. But we were still in a deflationary spiral, so the model said stay out (or be short). As the economic crisis deepened during the following year, not a week went by without some prominent figure proclaiming a bottom was in sight. But they were dead wrong. During that long, excruciating year, the investment climate turned hostile again in early January 1932, putting further pressure on the economy, and the Dow shed another 65 percent.

Table 32 Stock Market Record 1920-1946

Exact Bottom	Dow	Bought	Dow	% from the Bottom	Actual Top	Dow	Sold	Dow	% from the Top	Gain
1. August 24, 1921	63	July 5, 1921	67	6	September 3, 1929	381	September 7, 1929	377	1	463%
2. July 8, 1932	41	July 9, 1932	41	1	March 10, 1937	194	April 17, 1937	180	7	339%
3. April 28, 1942	92	April 21, 1942	97	5	May 29, 1946	212	July 15, 1046	200	6	106%
		Average		4.0%				Average	4.7	303%

Chart 12 Dow Jones Industrial Average 1914-1949

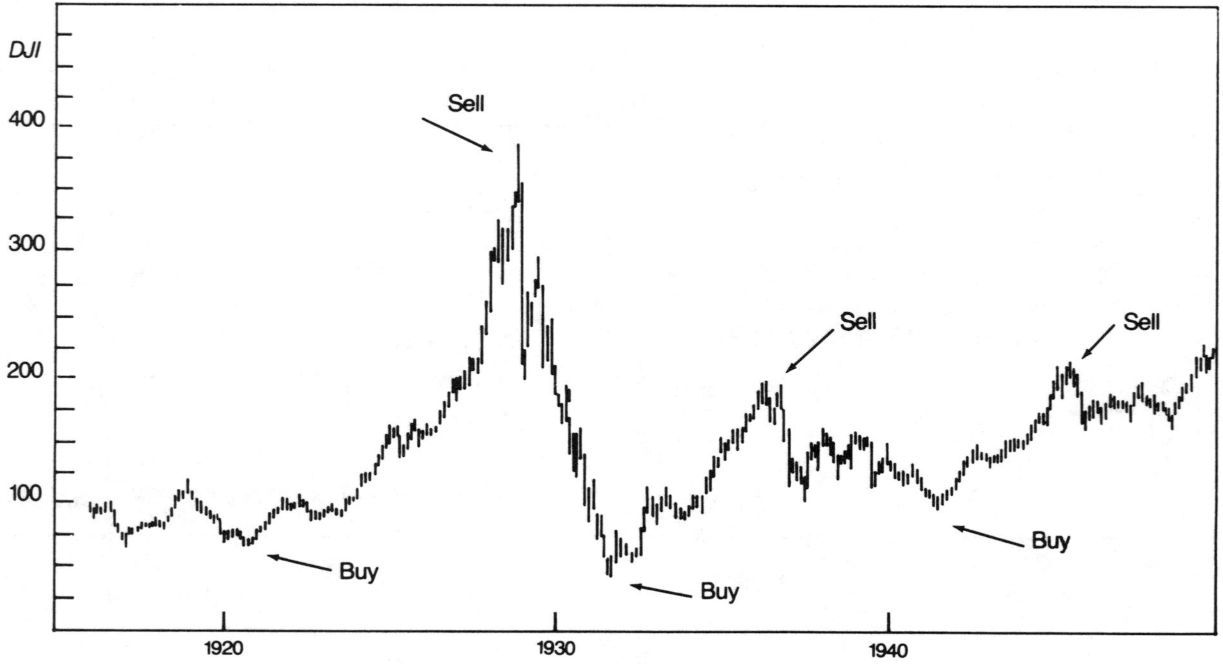

The first hint that the clock was ticking away on the great bear market came in mid-April 1932 when the Wholesale Price Index for March was released and showed the lowest rate of price decline in a year. Although the news that the deflationary spiral had finally run its course was cause for cheer, it was not yet time to buy, as the investment climate was still unfriendly. The stock market continued to slide—but only for eleven more weeks. When the Dow reached 41 on July 8, not many people would have believed the greatest stock market slide in our history was over and stock prices were poised to begin their most explosive rally of the century. Yet on that very day the investment climate turned favorable. The model beeped out the message to whomever was listening—BUY stocks. Investors who listened bought one day after the end of the bloodiest bear market of all time, while the Dow was just 1 percent above its low. By mid-1933, the forces of recovery had gained the upper hand, and the Dow was back over 100 and on its way up to 194. According to the model, there was no reason to sell until after the stock market reached a caution zone. The yellow light began flashing on April 14, 1937, and two days later, the investment climate turned hostile, sounding the alarm that time had run out on the recovery in business and the stock market. When investors sold on April 17, the Dow stood at 180, just 7 percent below its high. Soon after, another stock market plunge followed. By March 1938, the Dow had sunk to 98—down a chilling 45 percent from where the indication to sell was given.

Another friendly investment climate began on October 1, 1938, but it was too early to buy: the stock market had not yet registered a five-year low. However, investors were given a brief opportunity to profit from an inflationary spiral. In mid-August, 1941, two years after the last yearly low in the Wholesale Price Index, inflation, at the most recent reading, was roaring down the track at a 14.2 percent rate and gaining momentum. As there was a yellow light flashing in the stock market, it was time to load up on inflation hedges.

But in April 1942, the Dow fell into a five-year low and put a brake on this inflation. Yet during that eight-month span, prices of tangibles and commodities pushed higher. Cash wheat, for instance, which began this period at 89 cents[4] was trading at $1.00—a gain of 12 percent—when we got the signal to unload.

When the stock market fell into a five-year low in April 1942, the mood of pessimism was at its most pervasive level in this century. The lighting-like Japanese victories in the early part of the war had shattered confidence. No one, or practically no one, was interested in the stock market: average daily volume on the New York Stock Exchange fell to the lowest level since 1914, and a membership on the Exchange, which had sold for more that $500,000 in 1929, went for only $17,000. Yet on April 21, with the Dow trading at 97, our model flashed the word to buy stocks. Investors who heeded this signal would have bought exactly one week before the bottom day and would have stood pat until an inflationary sprial was signaled in mid-July 1946. Investors would have gotten 200 on the Dow, and again boosted their net worth by more than 100 percent.

Inflation moved into high gear in July 1946, and investors were presented with another opportunity to buy real assets. The sign to sell would not appear until January 30, 1948. In this case, it became evident that the environment had shifted to one of secularly rising prices before the investment climate had turned sour.[5] Therefore, it was necessary to switch to the rules for an environment with an inflationary bias. That is, both short- and long-term rates had to register a seven-year high before the sign to dump inflation hedges flashed. When investors sold in late January 1948, they would have gotten top dollar. Cash wheat bought at $1.87[6] in

---

[4] Average monthly price received by farmers.

[5] Although long-term rates had followed short-term rates into a fifteen-month high on October 3, 1947, the election cycle was in a favorable phase, and as a result, the investment climate was due to turn sour on January 1, 1948.

[6] Average monthly price received by farmers.

July 1946 would have fetched $2.18 in January 1948. And cash soybeans, which cost investors $2.31, would have brought $4.31—a gain of 78 percent.

The record, as we can see in Table 32, is every bit as good for stocks during this time as during an inflationary environment. Three forays into the stock market would have produced an average profit of—would you believe?—303 percent. All of the signals came within seven weeks and 7 percent of the actual bottom or top. Not bad for one of the most treacherous periods in American financial history. Furthermore, businesspeople who followed this model would have been warned to expect a slow-down in economic activity just before the two deepest contractions of this century. Another warning came in early November 1931, when the investment climate turned unfavorable in the midst of a business contraction. Sure enough, that business slump proved to be the deepest and bloodiest and most prolonged in American history. Although two recessions during the last deflationary period—those of 1923 and 1926[7]—were not signaled by a turn in the investment climate, neither was accompanied by a big spill in stock prices. In fact, the stock market did not even make a two-year low.

Now let us review the entire sixty-three year record.

---

[7] The contraction of 1926, was probably the shallowest on record. According to many economists of that time, if you didn't look closely, you might have missed it.

Chapter 10
The Amazing Record

The American Economy and its financial markets are subject to a recurring series of investment cycles that go from boom to bust and back again. Yet most traditional economists and Wall Street forecasters have been unable to spot these turns. Fortunately, investors can monitor these trends by keeping their eyes on four indicators. They are:

1. Interest rates, both the weekly auction rate of 90-Day-T-Bills and the weekly average of Prime AAA Bonds;
2. The four-year political cycle;
3. The Producers Price Index; and
4. The level of the Dow Jones Industrial Average.

The first two give investors a reading on the investment climate. This climate is the most important factor affecting the economy, the stock market and other investment markets.

When the climate is friendly, it is usually smooth sailing for investors. There have been thirteen favorable climates since 1921 and twelve foreshadowed a period of sustained economic growth along with a major bull market in stocks. Only one friendly climate aborted before it promoted a vigorous economic recovery along with a period of rising stock prices, and that was because a deflationary spiral had begun. But we never got a buy signal, and no harm was done.

On the other hand, the onset of a hostile investment climate warns that a powerful brake is being applied to the economy and the stock market is being set up for a steep nosedive. Investors should take this warning seriously. Since 1921 there have been thirteen times that the climate turned hostile, and twelve of those times the economy sank into recession within nineteen months' time[1], and the odds turned heavily against investors. In all thirteen cases, the stock market suffered a substantial setback and was unable to struggle to its feet until the Dow had sunk into a buy zone.

The Producers Price Index can be used to measure inflation or deflation. An inflationary spiral destroys confidence in the dollar and causes investors to flee from common stocks and seek refuge in real assets. There were four periods of galloping inflation and each rang down the curtain on the stock market and played a tune that had investors in gold, silver, commodities and other tangibles tapping their toes. Investors should also become concerned if they spot a deflationary spiral. During a massive deflation, money increases in value, and this deals a crushing blow to the prosperity of investors in stocks, gold, real estate and other tangibles. All investments, with the lone exception of bonds, should be shunned.

Market watchers can get a fix on the mood of other investors by keeping an eye on the level of the Dow. A group of stock market observers called "technicians" believe that a trend, once set in motion, will not reverse course until a large number of players become believers and bet that the trend will go on and on indefinitely. That is, bear markets last until the public has become pessimistic, and bull markets do not become vulnerable to a major selloff until investors have turned overly optimistic. To track that sentiment, technical analysts have devised a host of indicators such as the short interest ratio, odd lot sales, and the cash posi-

---

[1] In 1967, actually a minirecession.

tion of mutual funds. However, an investor can get a more accurate reading on market sentiment without the confusion of having to interpret a basketful of technical indicators by watching for a two-year high or low on the Dow, or five-year highs and lows during deflationary times. Each and every bull market since 1946 began after the Dow had retreated to a two- year low. The three bull markets during the last deflationary environment began after the Dow had sunk into a five-year low. The record book also makes it plain that those who sold after stocks reached a high-risk zone would have been cashing in during periods of optimism and high prices.

Each indicator used by itself would have produced above-average returns; the average gain during the twelve buy zones was 45 percent. Profits generated during friendly investment climates were even better, averaging 90 percent. But when used in concert, these tools provide a model that has tracked the economy, the stock market and other investment markets with uncanny accuracy.

The test of any model is how well it performed during a past period—the longer the time span, the better. Let us examine the record from 1921 through 1989.

The model would have alerted investors to all the major tops and bottoms in the stock market within an average of 6 percent of the exact turning points (Table 33). There were thirteen buys,[2] and ten came within 6 percent of the actual bottom. Eight were also within two weeks of the low. And there was hardly any sweat. Only five of the thirteen buys showed even a paper loss; the worst being 6 percent in 1921. But the best part is that investors would have escaped each and every bear market during the sixty-nine year period. All twelve sell signals were flashed within 8 percent of the top. Six actually came within 3 percent of the peak. Each time, the investor would have been able to repurchase stocks at levels considerably below the prior

---

[2] Including the buy in August 1982.

Table 33 Stock Market Record

Buy Signal	Dow	Signal from Low %	Sell Signal	Dow	Signal from High %	Gain (%)	$1,000 Becomes
1. July 5, 1921	67	6	September 7, 1929	377	1	463	$ 5,630
2. July 9, 1932	41	1	April 17, 1937	180	7	339	24,716
3. April 21, 1942	97	5	July 15, 1946	200	6	106	50,914
4. June 13, 1949	161	—	January 2, 1952	269	8	67	85,024
5. September 22, 1953	261	2	September 4, 1956	507	3	94	164,948
6. December 31, 1957	435	4	January 4, 1060	679	8	56	257,318
7. June 21, 1962	550	3	January 18, 1966	994	—	81	465,747
8. October 3, 1966	757	2	December 20, 1968	966	2	28	596,156
9. June 30, 1970	683	8	December 15, 1972	1027	2	50	894,234
10. October 1, 1974	604	5	March 15, 1977	965	5	60	1,430,774
11. May 13, 1980	816	10	April 20, 1981	1015	1	24	1,774,160
12. August 3, 1982	816	5	September 9, 1987	2549	6	212	5,535,380
13. June 19, 1989	2479	42					
Average		7.2			4.2	132%[a]	

[a] Average of the first twelve buys; the June 1989 buy is not included.

sale; remarkable enough, this held true following the smaller breaks of 1953 and 1957.

The record, of course, was perfect as far as profitability. All twelve buys were profitable—the average gain being 132 percent before dividends.[3] A $1,000 investment in a portfolio of Dow stocks in 1921 held through thick and thin would have been worth approximately $41,000 in March, 1990. But, what if grandfather had bought and sold according to this model? Why, then the family would have been worth an incredible $5,975,000 in early March, 1990—this does not include dividends. And if Grandfather had been able to scrape together $100,000 back then, the grandchildren would be rubbing elbows with the Rockefellers and the DuPonts.

Of course, this assumes investors did as well as the Dow. But as we saw earlier, investors could have geared their portfolios to the phases of a bull market and outperformed the Dow by a staggering four to one. Investors who began in late 1966 with $1,000 and followed the model in and out of the market at the major turning points would have had portfolios worth approximately $6,750 in January 1984.[4] However, had those same investors tailored their portfolios to the phases of the market, they would have been sitting on a nest egg of approximately $165,000 at the beginning of 1984.

This model has also guided investors in and out of inflation hedges near the beginning and end of each inflationary spiral. Investors who have an itch to own hard assets could have been spared a lot of grief had they played only when inflation was galloping ahead. At other times, it was wise to ignore hard assets, as cash could have been employed more advantageously elsewhere. For instance, gold investors would have been out of the market from August 1974 until mid-March 1977; during that period, gold skidded and slid almost 50 percent from its peak while the stock market

[3] The thirteenth buy, which took place in June 1989, has not yet been closed out.

[4] Only stock market profits are included. Gold is ignored.

boomed. In early 1977, when the signal flashed that inflation hedges were on the march again, gold was still 6 percent below its August 1974 price.[5] In addition, these indicators sounded the alarm before each post-World War II recession[6] and foreshadowed all nine business recoveries. Business people should take note, as these major turns in the economy from expansion to contraction and from recession to recovery have the greatest impact on the bottom line of the balance sheet.

If there is a shortcoming to this model, it was a failure to alert business people to three recessions that began in the 1920-1946 period. But two of these recessions appear to have been statistical flukes. The 1926 recession was largely attributable to a shutdown of the Ford Motor Company, which at that time was the largest producer of automobiles. (Henry Ford closed down his plant to allow a changeover from the Model T to an updated Model A.) It was by far the shallowest peacetime recession on record. Unemployment never got above 4.1 percent, and it is estimated that from peak to trough, GNP actually increased by .3 percent. There was no evidence of concern on Wall Street. Throughout the whole of that recession, the Dow climbed from one new all-time high to another. In fact, many economists at the time proclaimed there was no slump. The eight month recession in 1945 was the result of a transition from a wartime to a peacetime economy. People were not thrown out of work, and the stock market didn't even pause to acknowledge the statistical slowdown in business.

Actually, the business contraction of 1923 was the only bona fide recession not preceded by a hostile investment climate. But is was also the only true recession that did not send the stock market reeling into a two-year low. The recession of 1923 appears to have been the result of a transition from an inflationary to a

---

[5] Investors sold at $156 in August 1974, and in mid-March 1977, gold was trading at $146.

[6] Actually, the 1974 signal was given just before the recession turned nasty.

noninflationary environment. By the time an inflationary environment ends, people have become thoroughly fed up with the rapid increase in prices. During the transition period, any hint that inflation is about to return will throw a scare into the public and the authorities. When the rate of inflation shot up to 11.7 in January 1923, the Fed became concerned and tightened up. The result was to tip the economy into recession. Although prices were rising at a double-digit clip, and there was wide-spread fear that another bout of inflation was starting, the model did *not* give a signal that an inflationary spiral was about to begin. This was because two years had not passed since the last deflationary trends had ended. Sure enough, this flare-up proved to be brief. By July 1923, inflationary momentum had turned down.

Throughout a sixty-three year span marked by wars, recessions, assassinations and crises of various sorts, this model has produced an almost perfect record. The message to investors is clear: keep your eyes on these indicators. Most of the headline-grabbing news can in fact be ignored. The three questions investors *should* keep asking are:

1. Is the investment climate friendly?
2. Are we in a price spiral—inflationary or deflationary?
3. Is the stock market in a buy or caution zone?

Investors should also watch to see whether we are in the discounting, the discouragement, or the mature phase of a bull market.

But what if the parameters assigned to these tools bend somewhat in the future? Slightly different yardsticks would have had only a minimal effect on our results. For instance, say we considered a nine-month (rather than a fifteen-month) low in either long- or short-term rates as the sign the investment climate had turned friendly. The average stock market profit would only have slipped back to 117 percent. Had we taken swings in the Dow from a one-and-a-half-year high to a one-and-a-half-year low as signs of investor optimism and pessimism, the average profit would still have been 112 percent. Or, had we used 3 percent instead of 5 percent as the flash point where an inflationary spiral is ignited, the average profit would have been reduced by less than 1 percent. The important points to keep in mind are the following: a significant change in the rate of interest will have a major impact on the economy and investment markets; when the government stimulates the economy in order to get re-elected, investment markets will respond; when inflation moves into high gear, real assets soar, and the stock market will be left behind; a big swing in the level of the Dow provides the best reading as to when pessimism or optimism takes hold. These indicators measure the vital signs in the American economy, and it behooves investors to pay attention.

One other important consideration; investors should keep tabs on whether the overall environment is one of secular inflation or deflation. The overall environment becomes inflationary when both AAA Corporate Bond rates and producer prices turn up and make a five-year high; a five-year low in both long-term interest rates and producer prices indicates the environment has acquired a deflationary tilt. Investors who heed these signs should be able to detect a shift in the environment within two years after it actually occurs.

These indicators we have devised can also be used to measure other factors at work in the economy. In the following two chapters, we will show you how to spot when interest rates are primed to move up or down, and as an interesting sidelight, how to predict the winning party of the next presidential election.

Chapter 11
When to Buy and Sell Bonds

Each new investment cycle begins following a sharp fall in interest rates and lasts until rates have experienced a big raise. Investors can take advantage of this rhythmic alteration in rates, from low to high and back again to low; the obvious strategy is to buy bonds just before interest rates hit the skids (when rates fall, the price of the underlying bond rises) and sell bonds, even going short,[1] just before interest rates shoot up. (When interest rates rise, the prices of the underlying bonds falls.) Simple! But to do this, investors must first pinpoint when rates are ready to plummet and when they are about to shoot up—and any economist will tell you this is no easy matter.

Actually, two fundamental factors affect the direction of interest rates. The first is the posture of the Fed—whether it is being stingy or expansive with money supply growth. When the Fed adopts an easy-money policy, the banking system will be bursting with lending power, and it is easier for interest rates to fall. On the other hand, a tight monetary posture saps

---

[1] The Chicago Board of Trade and the Chicago Mercantile Exchange provide futures contracts on bonds and T-Bills. Investors can profit from rising interest rates by selling a futures contract short.

the banking system of funds and puts upward pressure on interest rates. But to predict the direction of interest rates, we need to know more than if the Fed is following an easy- or tight-money course; we must also be able to get a handle on the demand for credit, to know whether it is increasing or drying up. Yet measuring these two factors is very difficult. Most economists, in fact, throw up their hands. However, we can get a reading on the demand and supply of credit by using the tools we've already talked about.

The best reading on the Fed's posture can be gotten by watching the rate of inflation. *Whenever* inflation reaches 2.5 percent or more and is gaining momentum, even if it hasn't been two years since the last downtrend in the price index, you can bet the Fed will become wary of fanning the fires of inflation and begin to tug on the reins of money supply. On the other side of the coin, don't count on the Fed to pursue an expansionary monetary policy until inflation has lost momentum—that is, until the rate of inflation has fallen to its lowest level in twelve months.

The most reliable measure of the demand for credit is probably the level of the Dow, *whenever* the Dow reaches a two-year high, it suggests that confidence in the recovery has grown, and businessmen and consumers are about to adopt a free-spending mentality. This surely means a ballooning demand for credit. For the purpose of bonds it is necessary to wait nine months. On the other hand, the demand for credit usually does not fall apart until after the Dow registers a two-year low. That is the indication that businesspeople and consumers have become pessimistic about the outlook for the economy and will back away from spending and borrowing.

When both fundamental factors point up, we have reached the point in the investment cycle where interest rates are about to shoot up. That is, when inflation reaches 2.5 percent or more and the stock market is also in a two-year high, it suggests that the banking system will become unable to provide the funds necessary to accommodate the mushrooming demand for credit, and interest rates will be driven through the roof. This, of course, is the time for investors to short bonds. (See Table 34.) In general, this upward pressure on rates will last until both fundamental factors turn down. When the rate of inflation has lost momentum and the Dow has fallen into a two-year low, we can expect the Fed to be pumping money into an economy that doesn't need more liquidity, and the stage will be set for a sharp drop in rates. This, of course, is the surest time to buy bonds. (See Table 35.)

However, during an inflationary environment, there is a secular bias toward higher interest rates, and as a result, the decline in interest rates does not usually continue until the two fundamentals affecting interest rates turn up again. Normally, rates fall for only a brief period of time, and then once the economy begins to rebound, they begin to creep back up. Yet we can count on the decline in rates to last until signs of an economic recovery are visible. This is because once the Fed decides to wet-nurse an ailing economy back to health, it provides sufficient money growth to keep interest rates falling until it is assured that the recovery is in place.

The most reliable indicator that the economy has struggled to its feet is the stock market. Generally, the economy regains its footing within seven months of a stock market bottom, as you can see in Table 36. (The longest time between a stock market bottom and the beginning of an economic recovery was eight months in 1954.) Once seven months have passed since the Dow has made its low, the "sure" part of the interest rate decline is over. Usually the Fed becomes convinced that the economy has found the path to a more moderate pace, and interest rates will not sink much lower. This of course, is the time to dump our bonds.

To summarize: When inflation heats up to 2.5 percent or more and the stock market make a two-year high, we reach the point in the investment cycle where interest rates shoot up. This upward pressure on rates generally lasts until both fundamentals affecting interest rates turn down. When the Dow has fallen into a

Table 34   Selling Bonds Short

Investment Cycle Begins	Dow 2-Year High	Rate of Inflation Hits 2.5% and Gaining Momentum	Time to Sell Bonds[a]
1. June 13, 1949	November 18, 1949	August 15, 1950	August 16, 1950
2. September 22, 1953	February 4, 1954	April 15, 1956	April 16, 1956
3. December 31, 1957	September 15, 1958	—	—
4. June 21, 1962	September 5, 1963	July 15, 1965	July 16, 1965
5. October 2, 1966	October 3, 1968	April 15, 1968	October 4, 1968
6. June 30, 1970	April 5, 1972	September 15, 1971	April 6, 1972
7. October 1, 1974	January 7, 1976	March 15, 1977	March 16, 1977
8. May 13, 1980	July 17, 1980	[b]	July 18, 1980
9. August 3, 1982	October 20, 1982		

[a] Day after both fundamental factors had turned up.
[b] Already at that level when the investment cycle began.

Table 35 Buying Bonds

Interest Rates Poised to Take Off	Dow 2-Year Low	Inflation Loses Momentum	Time to Buy Bonds[a]
1. July 16, 1946	June 6, 1949	August 15, 1947	June 7, 1949
2. August 16, 1950	September 14, 1953	October 15, 1951	September 15, 1953
3. April 16, 1956	October 17, 1957	June 15, 1957	October 18, 1957
4. [b]	June 14, 1962	[c]	June 15, 1962
5. July 16, 1965	August 16, 1966	December 15, 1966	December 16, 1966
6. October 4, 1968	July 25, 1969	June 15, 1970	June 16, 1970
7. April 6, 1972	November 27, 1973	April 15, 1975	April 16, 1975
8. March 16, 1977	April 21, 1980	—	—
9. July 18, 1980	June 17, 1982	December 15, 1980	June 18, 1982

[a] Day after both fundamental signs have turned down.

[b] No sign that interest rates were poised to take off during the cycle that began in December 1957.

[c] Inflation had never gained momentum during this cycle.

Table 36   Economic Recovery

Stock Market Bottom (Dow)	Economic Recovery Begins	Months After Stock Market Bottom
June 1949	October 1949	4
September 1953	May 1954	8
October 1957	April 1958	6
October 1960[a]	February 1961	5
October 1966	April 1967[b]	6
May 1970	November 1970	6
December 1974	March 1975	3
April 1980	July 1980	2
August 1982	November 1982	3

[a] Although not a two-year low in Dow, was a stock market bottom that held for more than a year.

[b] Estimated.

[c] Actually, a year and a half low, but held for more than two years.

two-year low and inflation has lost momentum, it means rates are ready to take a plunge. Normally, we can expect this fall in interest rates to continue until the Dow has gone seven months without making a new low. The time beginning seven months after a low in the stock market and lasting until both fundamentals are pointing up is a gray area wherein rates usually, but not necessarily edge up. During that time, the future direction of interest rates is essentially indeterminant.

When an investment cycle began in mid-May 1980, inflation was still galloping ahead at 14.7 percent rate and gaining momentum.[2] Two months later, on July 17, the Dow closed into a two-year high, and as both fundamental factors were now pointing up, we had the signal that interest rates were about to take off.

---

[2] Although we had a sign that inflation was running out of gas in January 1980, inflation had not yet lost momentum, and until that occurred, we would still be vulnerable to upward pressure on interest rates.

During the week ending July 18 the rate on AAA Corporate Bonds averaged 11.09 percent. (In this chapter, the focus will be on the long-term rate, as it is the more important of the two rates.) During the following weeks, as the economy was snapping back from a sharp recession, long-term interest rates soared. By the end of November, they had reached 13.03 percent, another seven-year high. A few weeks later, December 15 to be exact, the sign that inflation had lost momentum was given, and many respected economists put their reputations on the line by predicting that interest rates would soon follow inflation down. But they were overlooking the fact that credit demands would also have to ease before interest rates were ready to take the plunge. And we would not get an indication of that until the Dow fell into a two-year low. In the following months, corporate rates continued on up past all previous markers, tarnishing the credibility of many economists; the rates continued to rise until they reached the unheard-of level of 15.85 percent.

On June 17, 1982, the Dow finally fell into a two-year low, flashing the signal that the demand for credit was about to dry up and interest rates were poised to fall. The rate on AAA Corporates during the week ending June 18 averaged 14.79 percent—a staggering 340 basis point higher than when the sign that interest rates were pointing up was given. Within days, interest rates began to slip. In mid-August, Drs. Henry Kaufman and Albert Wojnilower, two prominent Wall Street forecasters who had been holding out for higher rates, threw in the towel, and rates nosedived. When we looked up in March 1983, which was seven months after the Dow made its low, the rate on AAA Bonds averaged 11.79, a whopping 300 basis point below their level nine months earlier.

Let's see how an investor using this knowledge to trade T-Bond futures on the Chicago Board of Trade would have fared.[3] An investor would have sold a June 1982 contract at the close on July 18, 1980 at 7816. This was one day after receiving the word that interest rates were poised to rally. Unfortunately, the price of this contract immediately rallied, and three days later closed at 7913. the investor was out over $900 on paper. But that was the extent of the paper losses. On the following day, this T-Bond contract began a down-hill slide that would continue until it reached 5608 during September 1981. During the following nine months, rates bumped along the bottom.

The time to cover bond shorts was on June 18, 1982, the day after the sign that interest rates were about to tumble flashed. We would have paid 5910, and the profit after a commission charge was roughly $19,100. The investor would also have gone long (bought) a March 1983 contract at 6003 in order to take advantage of the expected fall in rates. A few days later, this contract closed at 5929, and investors were out 6/32—a loss of $187.50. But once again, this was the extent of paper losses. By early March 1983, this contract had soared to 7826. And when investors sold on March 18, 1983,[4] they would have gotten 7608, representing a profit of $16,081.25—after a $75 commission charge. (The three-year profit on $4,000 margin totaled more than $35,000.)

The two fundamentals affecting interest rates turned up during six of the seven other completed investment cycles that began after 1946. Each time, a significant rise in interest rates followed. As we can see in

---

[3] For a "good faith" margin deposit of about $4,000 or less, and investor can buy or sell a T-Bond contract consisting of a packet of twenty-year government bonds with aa face value of $100,000. Presumably, delivery is to be made or taken on the date the contract expires, which can be as far as two and a half years into the future. (Actually, very few trades, result in making or taking delivery. The overwhelming majority are closed out [longs sell out and shorts buy in] well before the contract expires.) The price of these contracts reflects the quotes of the underlying bond, and is expressed in thirty-seconds of a point, such as 61 3/32. Each thirty-second is worth $31.25, and a move of a full point—say, from 61 3/32 to 62 3/32—changes the value of a contract by $1,000. To wipe out an investor's equity completely would take an adverse move of four full points.

[4] Markets were closed on March 12 and 13.

Table 37, interest rates were much higher by the time we got the sign that rates were ready to plummet (see Chart 13). As in our example, investors who had bet on these rises in interest rates would have had to sweat out only minimal paper losses. Just two were more than one basis point—a 20-basis point loss on the sale made in April 1972, and another 20-basis-point loss on the March 1977 sale. Seven other buys were also indicated, and each was quite profitable. On the average, these buys came at the equivalent of 4 percent of the top rate. Only one paper loss totaled more than nine basis points—a 31-basis-point loss in 1982. (See Table 38.)

As you have probably noticed, it was more profitable to have been a seller than a buyer of bonds. The profit on shorting bonds was on average equivalent to 36 percent of the rate when the signal flashed. On the other hand, the profit on bond purchases was on average only equivalent to 9 percent of the rate when the signal was given. This difference is no doubt due to the strong upward bias prevalent during an inflationary environment.

During a deflationary environment, the story is somewhat different. The best indication of a shift in the demand for credit will now be a five-year high or low on the Dow. A five-year low, on the other hand, indicates that businesspeople and consumers will be very cautious in their spending and borrowing habits, and naturally, the demand for credit will fall apart. Also, in this environment of securely falling prices, a 2.5 percent rate of inflation is not enough to rattle teeth at the Fed and cause them to tighten up. To frighten authorities at the Fed into hitting the monetary brakes, it takes a breakout of an inflationary spiral. As long as we are not in a full-blown inflationary spiral, we can count on the Fed to take an accommodating monetary stance.

The time to buy bonds is when both fundamentals point down. Because of a strong bias toward lower interest rates during this environment, the downward pressure on rates will last until the two fundamentals

Table 37 Inflationary Environment: Upward Pressure on Rates

AAA Rate at Cyclical Low	Time to Sell Bonds	AAA Rate	% from Low	Subsequent Low in Rates	Interest Rates Ready to Fall	AAA Rate	Gain (Basis Points)	From Rate When Signal Given
2.57	August 16, 1950	2.61	2	—	September 15, 1953	3.31	70	26%
2.85	April 16, 1956 [a]	3.27	15	3.26	October 18, 1957	4.07	80	25%
3.55								
4.19	July 16, 1965	4.48	7	4.47	December 16, 1966	5.38	90	20%
5.00	October 4, 1968	6.02	20	—	June 16, 1970	8.55	253	42%
7.05	April 6, 1972	7.25	3	7.05	April 16, 1975	8.95	170	23%
7.88	March 16, 1977	8.09	3	7.89	June 18, 1982 [b]	14.79	670	83%
10.34	July 18, 1980	11.09	8	—	June 18, 1982	14.79	360	33%
	Average		8%					36%

[a] No signal given.
[b] There was no sign to cover shorts before the 1980 break in interest rates. Consequently, investors remained short until June of 1982.

Chart 13   AAA Corporate Bond Rates 1945-1984

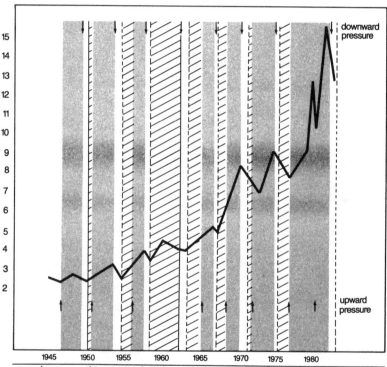

upward pressure on interest rates shaded
indeterminate areas are represented by diagonal lines

Table 38 Inflationary Environment: Downward Pressure on Rates

AAA Rate at Cyclical High	Time to Buy Bonds	AAA Rate	% from High	Subsequent High in Rates	7 Months after Dow Low	AAA Rate	Gain (Basis Points)	From Rate When Signal Given
2.90	June 7, 1949	2.71	7	—	January 13, 1950	2.57	+ 14	5%
3.42	September 15, 1953	3.31	3	—	April 14, 1954	2.85	+ 46	14%
4.14	October 18, 1957	4.07	2	4.13	May 22, 1958	3.57	+ 50	12%
4.61	June 15, 1962	4.28	7	4.37	January 26, 1963	4.21	+ 7	2%
5.52	December 16, 1966	5.38	3	5.40	May 7, 1967	5.19	+ 19	4%
8.60	June 16, 1970	8.55	1	8.60	December 26, 1970	7.48	+107	13%
9.38	April 16, 1975	8.95	5	9.01	July 6, 1975	8.84	+ 11	1%
13.00	—	—	—	—	—	—	—	—
15.85	June 18, 1982	14.79	7	15.10	March 12, 1963	11.79	+300	20%
	Average		4%					9%

turn up again. The only time bonds should be sold (and perhaps shorted) during a generally deflationary environment is when the Dow is in a five-year high, and in addition, an inflationary spiral has begun. Unless both fundamentals indicate upward pressure on the cost of credit, the uptrend in interest rates that normally occurs at the end of each investment climate is likely to be very feeble and not worth pursuing.

The first bond purchase was indicated on November 16, 1920. As it was not yet evident that a deflationary environment had begun, investors were still playing by the rules for an inflationary environment. Therefore, these bonds would have been sold on March 25, 1922, which was seven months after the bottom in the stock market, for a profit of about 85 basis points. In July 1922, long-term rates made a five-year low, and it became clear that the environment had shifted to one with a deflationary bias. As the Dow was not yet in a five-year high nor was inflation in high gear, investors were presented with a golden opportunity to buy long-term bonds. AAA rates, which averaged 5.00 during the month of July, continued to fall for *nineteen years* before both fundamentals pointed up again. To be sure, investors had to sit through three rallies that were equivalent to more than 10 percent of the bottom rate.[5] But none were preceded by a turn in both fundamentals, and within a short period of time, rates sank back into new lows. The time to sell these bonds was in mid-August 1941, when we received word that inflation had moved into high gear. (The Dow, which had reached a caution zone in April 1938, had not yet retreated into a five-year low.) The rate on AAA Corporate Bonds was 2.75 and investors were ahead a whopping 251 basis points. (See Table 39 and Chart 14.)

Investors could also have reversed course and gone short on that date to take advantage of the expected rise in rates. Soon thereafter, the Dow slipped into a five-year low, and one fundamental was pointing

---

[5] At one point investors had a paper loss of 41 basis points.

Table 39 Deflationary Environment: Downward Pressure on Rates

AAA Rate at Cyclical High	Time to Buy Bonds	AAA Rate	% from High	Subsequent High in Rates	Both Fundamentals Turn Up	AAA Rate	Gain (Basis Points)	From Rate When Signal Given
6.38	November 16, 1920[a]	6.08	5	6.26	March 24, 1922[b]	5.23	85	14%
5.22	July 1922	5.00	4	5.41	August 16, 1941	2.75	225	45%
2.87	August 16, 1942	2.81	2	2.82	July 16, 1946	2.49	32	11%
	Average	4%						23%

[a] Bought following a two-year low on the Dow and loss of inflationary momentum, as it was not yet clear that the environment had turned deflationary.

[b] Seven months after stock market low.

Chart 14   AAA Corporate Bond Rates 1919-1949

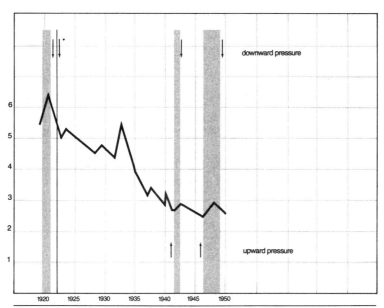

upward pressure on interest rates shaded
*environment turns deflationary; downward pressure begins

down. The other fundamental fell into step in mid-August 1942, when it became clear that inflation had lost momentum. The AAA Corporate rate was at 2.81, and after pocketing a profit of 6 basis points, it was back to the long side again. (See Table 40.) Investors would have held these bonds for almost four years, and when they sold in July 1946, they were 32 basis points richer.

Another short sale was called for on July 16, 1946. In this case, the environment shifted before the Dow fell into a five-year low, and investors were to switch to the rules of an inflationary environment. And when both fundamentals turned down again on June 7, 1949 investors were ahead 22 basis points. During this environment it was much more profitable to have been a buyer than a seller of bonds. The profit made from the three bond purchases was on average equivalent to 23 percent of the rate when the signal was flashed. On the other hand, the two short sales would have produced a profit equivalent to 5 percent of the rate when the signal was given. This is almost exactly the reverse of what occurred during an inflationary environment.

As you can see, these signpoints would have enabled investors to catch the bulk of most major moves in interest rates since 1920. Significant rises in the rates of interest usually come after the two fundamentals affecting interest rates point up. There was only one time that long-term interest rates rallied more than the equivalent of 25 percent of the bottom rate without the two fundamentals indicating upward pressure on rates. That was during the investment cycle that began in late 1957, and that interest rate rally was one of the mildest since World War II. Also, during this sixty-three year span, only once did investors fail to have adequate warning before long-term interest rates plunged by more than the equivalent of 10 percent of the top rate. That occurred in early 1980, and that drop no doubt was due to the imposition of credit controls. However, unlike most interest rate falls, the decline did not continue until seven months had passed since the Dow reached its low: rates touched bottom two months after the low in the Dow and then

Table 40   Deflationary Environment: Upward Pressure on Rates

AAA Rate at Cyclical Low	Time to Sell Bonds	AAA Rate	% from Low	Subsequent Low in Rates	Both Fundamentals Turn Down	AAA Rate	Gain (Basis Points)	From Rate When Signal Given
2.71	August 16, 1941	2.75	2	2.72	August 16, 1942	2.81	6	2%
2.46	July 16, 1946	2.49	1	—	June 7, 1949	2.71	22	9%
	Average		1.5%					5%

romped upwards—reaching a new high by early winter. Unless they had been very nimble, bond buyers would have been trapped. This certainly was the one interest rate fall well worth missing.

The same indicators used to call the turns in the stocks and tangibles market can be used to measure the dominant forces affecting interest rates. In this case, we use the level of Dow to get a reading on the demand for credit, and the rate of inflation as a guide to whether the Fed is likely to pursue a tight or easy monetary policy.

Now let us jump over to the political arena and see how part of the model can be used to predict presidential elections.

Chapter 12

Predicting Presidential Elections

The most important barometer as to the health of the economy is the rate of interest. Interestingly, we can also get a reading on which party is likely to win a presidential election by checking out the long-term rates about a year before voters go the polls—say, on November 15. The reason we look at the long-term rates is because they are the best reflection of what it costs people to finance a new home, what corporations must pay to finance new factories, or what farmers pay when they borrow to buy tractors and machinery.

When long-term rates are low on November 15 twelve months before a presidential election, business people, farmers and consumers have access to cheap credit during the following year. It will be relatively easy to buy cars, washing machines, video players, homes, factories, machinery, tractors, or what have you. And it's a pretty safe bet that on election day the economy will be pulsating with energy; factories will be humming, job opportunities will be plentiful, and from Fifth Avenue in New York to Rodeo Drive in Los Angeles, the nation's shops will be teeming with activity. People will be content with their lot, and the president—and his party—will be popular. In times like these, the populace will allow the chief executive a lot of leeway before they take him to task for any slipups.

On the other hand, when long-term rates are high on that crucial day a year before the election, it will be expensive to finance new cars, homes, or other consumer durables. During the following year, consumers will keep their purse strings tied, jobs will become harder to find, the economy will lose its zip, and a wave of discontent is likely to sweep across the land—the mood of the country will be bitter on election day. This, of course usually spells trouble for the party controlling the White House, especially if the challenging party nominates a candidate who can attract independent voters and induce moderates of the governing party to follow a new direction.

But what is a high rate, and what is a low rate of interest? We can apply the same yardstick used in Chapter 2 as a guide to turns in the investment climate. Long-term rates will be considered high from the time they make a seven-year high until they fall back into another fifteen month low.[1] (See Table 41.) For example, AAA Corporate Bond rates made a seven-year high in April 1979 and on November 15, 1979, were even higher. This probably sealed the fate of the Carter presidency. Long-term rates will be considered low from the time they make a fifteen-month low until a subsequent seven-year high is made. AAA Corporate rates made a fifteen-month low in January 1971, and on November 15, 1971, they were still near their low. This meant that Nixon was headed for an easy win in the 1972 election. Since 1919, there have been seven elections preceded by high interest rates a year earlier—1920, 1932, 1952, 1968, 1976 and 1980—and each time the ins were thrown out as the voters chose to go along with a candidate who offered a different approach (See Table 42).

During the eight years prior to the 1920 election, the Democrats controlled the White House. That period had begun with high hopes that Woodrow Wilson would lead a moral crusade to reform America and the world. However, by the end of Wilson's second term,

---

[1] The same yardstick will apply in both environments.

Table 41   Long-Term Interest Rates

Low	High
	July 1917[a]–August 1921
August 1921–October 1931	October 1931–January 1933
January 1933–January 1948	January 1948–January 1949
January 1949–June 1951	June 1951–February 1954
February 1954–August 1956	August 1956–January 1958
January 1958–January 1958	January 1959–August 1960
August 1960–December 1965	December 1965–January 1971
January 1971–July 1974	July 1974–February 1976
February 1976–April 1979	April 1979–August 1982
August 1982	[b]

[a] Based on High Grade Railroad Bonds.
[b] Rates have not achieved a new 7 year high.

an outbreak of lawlessness, strikes and protests had tried the patience of the American people, and the nation became tired of noble causes. More important, by 1920,[2] the economy was in a very deep recession. It was hardly surprising that the county changed horses and elected the Republican Warren Harding, who promised a return to "normalcy."

The 1932 election was conducted in the midst of the Great Depression. The national output had fallen by nearly half, unemployment was approaching 25 percent, the rash of bankruptcies appeared endless, and the nation's banking system was trembling. When high interest rates have led to a business contraction prior to the election, economic hardship is evident. The voters will be displeased with the governing party for having lost control over the economy. The challenging candidate is able to make headway simply by promising to get the economy working again. In early November of

[2] The records for AAA Corporate Bonds only go back to 1919. However, prior to that period, we can get a good indication of long-term rates by looking at High Grade Railroad Bonds, and those rates went into a seven-year high in July 1917 and remained high until well after that election (see Appendix A).

1932, voters in droves deserted Herbert Hoover and the Grand Old Party. Franklin Delano Roosevelt, who promised voters a "new deal," was elected president and began the Democrats' reign as the dominant political party.

In 1952, Americans lost patience with the Korean War, which had bogged down into a military stalemate. Revelations of scandal and treason by members of the Truman administration also soured the public on the Democrats. It was hardly surprising that the voters decided it was time for a change and chose General Dwight D. Eisenhower, a Republican who promised to end the war in Korea, and to chart the country's course. In this case, the discontent seemed to center on a noneconomic factor, the frustrating war in Korea. But it appears that even when heads of state are experiencing difficulty in some "noneconomic" area, they will still be able to command the loyalty of the majority *as long as long-term interest rates remain low.* However, should the cost of credit shoot up, that support melts away. The high cost of money hurts Americans in the pocketbook, and the resulting frustrations are transferred to the problem with which the administration is having the greatest difficulty. The majority of voters holds the president accountable for fouling up. The major point is that the level of long-term interest rates is the barometer by which we can measure the satisfaction or discontent of the populace.[3]

An election was again held in the midst of a recession in 1960, and John F. Kennedy, promising "to get the economy moving again," edged out Richard Nixon, who carried the standard for the Republicans. The fact that long-term interest rates reached levels that could be considered low three months before the election may have helped to make for a very close election.

---

[3] High interest rates might actually be the result of unpopular policies. When it senses a growing displeasure with some noneconomic policy, an administration is likely to push harder on the economic front in order to maintain popular support. Excessive stimulus is applied to the economy, and soon drives up interest rates. This in turn spreads the dissatisfaction until confidence in the regime is lost.

In 1968, the disillusionment with American involvement in Vietnam was evident, and the voters wanted a change of direction. The Democrats were thrown out, and Richard Nixon, who said he had a plan to end the war, eked out a victory. The closeness of this race was probably due to the fact that Republicans chose Nixon, who was the loser of the 1960 election, to head their ticket. A defeat in a prior presidential election tends to tarnish a candidate's image as a leader. His abilities and ideas have already been scrutinized by the electorate and found wanting. The voters are not disposed to follow a loser in a new direction. Since the Civil War, whenever a loser has run again, his proportion of the popular vote has fallen.[4] The 1968 election proved to be no exception. Nixon's share of the popular vote fell to 43.4 percent from 49.5 percent eight years earlier. However, because many dissatisfied voters threw in their lot with George Wallace, a third-party candidate, Nixon won.

In 1976, Gerald Ford was laboring under the still-lingering effect of Watergate and the memory of the 1973-75 recession, which had been the deepest and most protracted since the Great Depression. But far more important was the fact that long-term interest rates did not fall into a fifteen-month low until February of 1976. This would prove to be too late by three months, and Jimmy Carter, a Democrat who promised to restore trust in government, rode into the White House. However, the belated fall in interest rates helped keep the contest close.

Again in 1980, the country was in a slump during an election year, and Ronald Reagan scored a sweeping

---

[4] During the previous hundred years, four losers have tried again. Grover Cleveland got 48.7 percent of the vote in loseing the election of 1888. In 1892 he got only 46.1 percent of the vote, but that was enough to beat Benjamin Harrison, as a third-party candidate had siphoned off 8 percent of the vote. William Jennings Bryan ran three times, and his percentage of the popular vote shrank from 46.8 percent in 1896 to 45.5 percent in 1900, and finally to 43.1 percent in 1908. Thomas Dewey received 45.9 percent of the popular vote in 1944; four year later his vote slipped to 45.1 percent. Adlai Stevenson also had two stabs at the presidency, and his share of the popular vote fell from 44.4 percent in 1952 to 42 percent in 1956.

victory over incumbent Jimmy Carter. Everything, it seemed, was going wrong for Carter during the election year; besides the recession during the early part of the year, there were the hostages in Iran, Senator Kennedy's attacks in the primaries, double-digit inflation, and Mr. Carter's own perceived ineptitude. But it is quite likely that no one factor, probably not even all of them together, contributed as much to Carter's defeat as the fact that just prior to the election long-term interest rates reached double-digit levels for the first time in the nation's history. This proved to be the poorest showing for a reigning party since World War II.

In each of these seven elections, the incumbent political party was a victim of the high long-term interest rates that had affected the economy a year before the election. Twice, in 1960 and 1976, long-term interest rates fell after the critical date but before the election, and both times the incumbent part put up a strong fight, receiving 49 and 48 percent of the vote respectively. On the other hand, when interest rates were high on the crucial date and stayed that way throughout the election year, it was clear that the reigning party was heading for a crushing defeat. In each of these five elections, the ins were unable to capture as much as 45 percent of the vote.

Eleven elections took place against a background of low long-term interest rates—1924, 1928, 1936, 1940, 1956, 1964, 1972, 1984 and 1988—and each was smooth sailing for the incumbent party (see Table 42). The voters were obviously delighted with the ins and gave them a huge vote of confidence.

In 1924, Calvin Coolidge, a Republican, kept the White House with a 54 percent of the popular vote. Herbert Hoover carried the standard for the GOP in 1928 and trounced Al Smith by capturing over 58 percent of the vote. In 1936, the country reelected Franklin Delano Roosevelt in a landslide. He ran up the largest percentage of the popular vote to that time— 60.8 percent. Again in 1940 and 1944, Roosevelt won reelection with respectable pluralities, especially consid-

Table 42 Presidential Elections and Interest Rates

Election of	Interest Rates November 15 1 Year Earlier	Incumbent Party	%	Challenging Party	%	Plurality
1920	High	Cox (D)	34.1	*Harding (R)*	60.4	26.3%
1924	Low	*Coolidge (R)*	54.0	Davis (D)[a]	28.2	25.8%
1928	Low	*Hoover (R)*	58.1	Smith (D)	40.8	17.3%
1932	High	Hoover (R)	39.7	*Roosevelt (D)*	57.4	17.7%
1936	Low	*Roosevelt (D)*	60.8	Landon (D)	36.5	24.3%
1940	Low	*Roosevelt (D)*	54.7	Wilkie (R)	44.8	9.9%
1944	Low	*Roosevelt (D)*	53.4	Dewey (R)	45.9	7.5%
1948	Low	*Truman (D)*	49.6	Dewey (R)[b]	45.1	4.5%
1952	High	Stevenson (D)	44.4	*Eisenhower (R)*	55.1	10.7%
1956	Low	*Eisenhower (R)*	57.4	Stevenson (D)	42.0	15.4%
1960	High	Nixon (R)	49.5	*Kennedy (D)*	49.7	0.2%
1964	Low	*Johnson (D)*	61.1	Goldwater (R)	38.5	22.6%
1968	High	Humphrey (D)	42.7	*Nixon (R)[c]*	43.4	0.7%
1972	Low	*Nixon (R)*	60.7	McGovern (D)	37.5	23.2%
1976	High	Ford (R)	48.3	*Carter (D)*	50.4	2.1%
1980	High	Carter (D)	41.9	*Reagan (R)*	51.8	9.9%
1984	Low	*Reagan (R)*	58.8	Mondale (D)	40.6	18.2%
1988	Low	*Bush (R)*	53.4	Dukakis (D)	45.7	7.4%

Note: Winners in Italic.

[a] LaFollette ran as a Progressive and gathered over 16% of the vote.
[b] Thurmond and Henry Wallace combined got nearly 5% of the vote.
[c] George Wallace got about 13% of the vote.

ering that he had defied tradition by not stepping aside after two terms in the White House.

In 1948, the prospects for the Democrats keeping the White House appeared bleak. Opinion polls showed that the incumbent, Harry Truman, was very unpopular with the voters, and the pollsters along with nearly everyone else, thought Tom Dewey would be a shoo-in. To make matters worse, the Democrats were splintered by defections from both the left and right wings of the party. Strom Thurmond, running at the head of the States Rights party, was attacking in the southern states, a traditional source of Democratic strength. And Henry Wallace, running under the banner of Progressive party, threatened to cut heavily into the liberal vote. But in November 1948, Truman surprised everyone and pulled off the most stunning political upset in the nation's history. Although he failed to capture a majority of the votes cast, Truman beat Dewey by a margin of 4.5 percent of the popular vote. The outcome would not have been a surprise to those people who noted that on November 15, 1947, long-term interest rates were low. However, barely seven weeks later, in early January of 1948, long-term interest rates made a seven-year high. This would seem to indicate a very tight race—and so it proved; Truman had the narrowest margin of victory ever for a governing party when interest rates were low (Truman's prospects for victory also were given a boost when the GOP chose Dewey, who had lost the 1944 election, to lead them).

In the election of 1956, Eisenhower received a resounding vote of confidence from the American people, who obviously were quite pleased with the course he had charted. He rolled up 57 percent of the vote. Although interest rates shot up and made a seven-year high ten weeks before the election, there was not enough time to undermine Eisenhower's popularity. Besides, the Democrats had chosen Adlai Stevenson, the loser in the 1952 election, to head their ticket. In 1964, the Democrats kept the White House as Lyndon Johnson snared 61 percent of the vote. Johnson's huge landslide might at first glance appear to be due to the fact that he was running against Barry Goldwater, who, as a candidate from the right wing of the Republican party, was out of tune with independents and more moderate Republicans. But when long-term interest rates are low, opposition parties are more likely to nominate candidates representing an extreme faction of the party. People in the center of that party are relatively content and not much interested in toppling the current administration. Their support for politicians of their own party is likely to be only lukewarm. In this setting, it is easy for a minority group to capture the party. In 1924 and 1928, for instance, the Democrats nominated candidates who were out of step with large elements of their own party.[5] And again, in 1972, they were to nominate a left-of-center candidate.

The election of 1972 followed the usual script. In November 1971, long-term rates were low, and one year later, Richard Nixon buried George McGovern in one of the biggest landslides ever, garnering over 60 percent of the popular vote. When Nixon instituted wage, price and interest rate controls in 1971, thereby preventing long-term interest rates, which had reached favorable levels in December of 1970, from rising, he may have unwittingly ensured reelection.

When Ronald Reagan ascended to the Presidency he vowed to control inflation and bring interest rates down. AAA Corporate Bonds had an interest rate of 15.85 percent in October of 1981. By November of 1983 rates had been down to 11.29 percent. This made election to a second term almost a given. Reagan continued to battle inflation and high interest rates after his successful election to a second term in 1984. This effectively made the economic issue rather neutral for

---

[5] In 1924, the Democrats nominated John Davis, a conservative lawyer with ties to Wall Street. This alienated labor and western liberals who took a walk from the Democratic party and voted for the Progressive party. The Democratic candidate in 1928 was Al Smith, who as a Catholic and Tammanyite (the corrupt machine that ran the city of New York), was anathema to the South, which was one of the party's traditional power bases.

George Bush in the 1988 election. Corporate bond rates were hovering around 10 percent in late 1987.

It is clear that when interest rates are low a year before the election, it will be difficult to oust the ins. In fact, the challenging party was never able to attract as much as 46 percent of the popular vote. (Twice—in 1948 and 1956—interest rates became high during the election year—but both times the situation was clouded by the fact that the outs decided to go with a loser. Perhaps a more attractive candidate could have tightened the race, especially in 1948.)

The message is clear; the two most important factors that bear on an election are the level of long-term interest rates on the fifteenth of November, a year before the election, and the attractiveness of the challenging candidate. Of the two, it appears that the level of interest rates is more important. While other factors such as political scandals or foreign involvements, may play a role, the level of long-term interest rates has called the tune in each of the past eighteen elections.[6]

---

[6] If the economy is still in recession twelve months before election time, the ins will probably have a difficult time of it even if long-term interest rates have been battered down to a fifteen-month low. Had interest rates shot up during October 1931, it is hard to believe that Hoover would have been reelected.

Chapter 13
Looking Back

Strategic Investment Timing (SIT) was published in the fall of 1984, shortly before the American people gave Ronald Reagan and his controversial laissez faire supply side economic policies a resounding vote of confidence. What followed was a golden era for stocks and bonds. As inflation went down for the count, interest rates tumbled, the economy plodded ahead and despite a queasy feeling that everything was not quite right—surely the buildup of gargantuan budget and trade deficits would soon bring the economy to its knees—the value of financial assets soared into uncharted territory. Spurred on by mounds of cash and an insatiable appetite for takeovers and stock repurchases, the Dow in a relentless climb cracked barrier after barrier. When a sharp plunge in bond prices during the spring of 1987 uncoupled stocks from the bolstering effect of falling interest rates, no one seemed to pay attention. Share prices barely paused to catch their breath before zooming off the charts.

In August, 1987, as champagne corks were popping in celebration of the fifth anniversary of the Reagan Bull Market, the Dow reached the dizzying height of 2722. Prices were selling at twenty-two times profits—a post-World War II record. Dividend yields on Industrial stocks had shrunk to less than two-and-one-half percent—levels never before seen. Surely, it should have been obvious to any alert observer that stocks were overvalued and ripe for a fall.

Yet, what in hindsight seems apparent was missed by most investors in late 1987. This is because the mood on Wall Street had become positively giddy. A gambling mentality had taken over. High-stakes financial maneuvering was generally accepted as a short-cut to wealth. Investors were buying options on options snapping up paper backed by paper backed by paper. In this euphoric atmosphere traditional standards of value were sneered at.

One day before the top of this bull market was achieved, an article entitled "Why The Bull Is Such A Long Distance Runner": appeared in *Business Week*.

> This market has rocketed nearly 800 points so far this year—a 41% rise, that is the best in more than 50 years. Better yet, there is plenty of evidence that the bulls' strength is far from spent . . .
>
> True, the market may look out of line using traditional measures of stock value. But yesterday's yardsticks may not be appropriate for today's market. For example, dividend yields are low because companies are using their cash to repurchase shares rather than raise dividends. What many pros are missing is that the market is playing catchup. For years it was undervalued. Consider this: if the stock market had only kept up with 1/2 the rise in Gross National Product, since 1966, the Dow would stand at 3000.

Investors thought this bull was not near the end of its charge. The familiar refrain heard on Wall Street was "The fat lady hasn't sung yet." Nervous investors were reassuring themselves and each other with an analogy to opera. The message: bull markets don't end until Wall Street is invaded by hordes of wild-eyed optimists willing to pay any price to "join in." Therefore, as long as speculative activity had not reached such a fever pitch, no need to worry.[1]

---

[1] Interestingly, there was a logical inconsistency. It was O.K. to discard traditional ideas of value, such as "stock prices are thought too high when the dividend yield dips below 3%." However, the idea that this bull market could come unraveled before there were clear-cut signs of over-optimism was derided.

The investing public believed this! The Dow was on its way to 3600 as Robert Prechter, the leading technical guru of the 1980s had long since predicted. And those who didn't get on board this once-in-a-lifetime bull surely would be left hanging far behind in the race for riches.

Yet, barely eight weeks later, investors from London to Hong Kong were stunned by the most spectacular global stock market crash ever. After sliding for seven weeks, the Dow, on October 19, 1987, took a chilling spill of more than 500 points. In a single day more than one-fifth of the value of equity holdings was wiped out: vanished into a black hole. Nobody had witnessed anything like it ever before. The world financial system teetered on the brink of the abyss, threatening to bring down with it the entire international economy before pulling back. Many investors who had rushed in seeking easy money had been ruined.

The numbing collapse in share prices sent shock waves that were felt from Wall Street to Rodeo Drive. It left the investing public in a confused and badly demoralized state. From the vantage point of early 1988, it surely looked as if the Republicans would be thrown out of the White House and the policies which had proven so successful from the point of view of economic stability and wealth creation would be discarded. Interestingly enough, the interest rate rule for predicting the election a year in advance laid out in *SIT* called for the Republicans to retain the White House—*picking the winner for the eighteenth time in a row*. No wonder it took fifteen months and many false starts and further dashed hopes to retrace what had been lost in a single day. However, it was not until long-term interest rates took another spill in June 1989 that the Dow's upward crawl turned into a charge.

How well did the Strategic Investment Timer do during this period? In late September, 1987, Yale Hirsch's October issue of *Smart Money*, which had been tracking the "Stoken System," printed this front page article:

STOKEN SYSTEM GIVES SELL SIGNAL CAPPING A
5-YEAR BLUE CHIP BASH . . . his September 9th
sell with the Dow at 2549 . . . was (the) first signal
since his buy on August 3, 1982, with the Dow at
816. The gain on the long side was a whopping
212% . . .

SIT sounded the alarm within 6 percent of the bull
market's high water mark and investors who listened
retreated safely to the sidelines—parking their money
in T-Bills or the like—and watched while the Dow
plunged a chilling 32 percent from the point at which
they had sold. Perhaps the fat lady hadn't completed
her song, but, without doubt, a portly female had
promenaded to center stage and was belting out a tune
that Strategic Timers heard just before the curtain fell.

To be sure, several people have written the author
stating that they missed the signal and wanted to
know how it was arrived at. The confusion resulted
mainly because the rules in *SIT* change depending
upon whether the environment has an inflationary
bias or a deflationary cast. And detecting these once-in-
a-generation shifts in environment can be tricky. As we
said earlier, the most important factor to keep your eye
on is the long-term interest rate: When this long-term
rate falls to a five year low, it is the telltale sign the
environment has shifted to one favoring deflation. This
happened in July, 1985, and provided solid evidence
that the inflationary environment, which had been in
existence since 1946, had dissipated.

I also recommended using the Producer Price
Index as a confirming indicator and suggested that it,
too, should fall to a five-year low. However, the more I
pondered this second requirement, the less important I
felt it was. The post-World War II evolution to a Key-
nesian economy, with Washington ready and willing
to inject enormous amounts of cash into the economy
in order to shore up demand, has left in its wake a
structural bias toward inflation. Therefore it seemed
quite unlikely that the massive fall-offs in the price in-
dices experienced sixty years ago would be repeated.

In April, 1986, the Producer Price Index fell to a
two-year low for the first time since the early 1960s.

This convinced me that we were now operating in an environment that had a deflationary bias. I shared this thought with Yale Hirsch, who was fascinated with what he termed the "Stoken System" and had decided to monitor it in *Smart Money*.

All that was now needed to derail this bull market were rises in both long- and short-term interest rates to fifteen-month highs. I did not give much credence to the fact that we were about to enter a favorable phase in the political cycle. This was because the stock market and the economy had soared during the whole of 1985-86, totally ignoring the *down* phase of this election cycle . . . without a cooling period (i.e. a stock market slump) early in a new administration's reign. It becomes questionable whether it will be able to provide the stimulus necessary to keep the stock market and economy on an upward course prior to the next election.[2]

In the spring of 1987, under the impact of a resurging economy and a turn-up in commodity prices, long-term bonds collapsed and that rate went soaring to a fifteen-month high. But 90-day T-Bills did not follow suit until the weekly auction of September 9th. Sure enough, bright and early the next morning, Yale Hirsch, who doesn't let anything slip by him, was on the phone asking me, "Is this it?" "Yes Yale," I replied, and two weeks later the October issue of *Smart Money* was in the mail and the rest is history.

So far, so good. The problem is that after the crash, share prices got up off the floor and began a recovery which has taken them to new highs—and during all this time those who strictly followed the Stoken System sat on their hands. This is because during deflationary times Strategic Timers are not supposed to buy until stocks sink into a five-year low. Although the Dow's fall of 36 percent was the second steepest break since 1945, it was only able to erase a

---

[2] Since 1936, Wall Street had greeted every new administration with a bear market during the first two years of their watch. The softening in the financial and economic structure provided politicians the leeway to pump up the economy before the following election.

year and a half of the previous up move—well short of a five-year low.

I think that due to the altered structure of the economy we have shifted to a disinflationary environment rather than a deflationary one. We are experiencing a long period of relative price stability wherein the inflation built into the economy during the preceding inflationary period is gradually squeezed out, in contrast to a period of falling prices.

The question is, What parameters do we use in a disinflationary environment? Since we don't have any model to go by, it makes sense to be more flexible in the use of the indicators. Periods of relative price stability such as the present usually provide a very favorable overall climate for stocks. Consequently, I would be more liberal in defining a buy zone. Steep falls in the Dow, say 25 percent or more, are probably enough to drop stocks to a level where investors can think of buying—even if the Dow has not fallen to a 2-year low. Certainly following the panic of October, 1987, wherein the Dow shed a numbing 500 points in a single day and reached a level of more than 36 percent below its August high water mark, it would not be outrageous to consider stocks in a buying zone. (Actually the Dow fell to a 1-1/2 year low—not far from a 2-year low.)

So far it seems that a disinflationary period has a strong resemblance to a deflationary environment and therefore I would suggest using these rules in monitoring the interest rate and inflation indicators. When long-term rates fell to a 15-month low on June 19, 1989, the signal to buy should have flashed. Investors would have gotten back in the market at 2479 on the Dow.[3] Although well above the October, 1987 low it was still about 3 percent and a great deal of grief *below* the point at which strategic investors had sold.

---

[3] Although the Producer Price Index was still accelerating by more than a 5 percent rate, no need to worry. As we saw earlier, a fifteen-month interest rate low is also a good indication that inflation will soon moderate. Also, during the present environment, stocks must also reach a caution zone before the existence of an inflationary spiral is signaled.

Since 1984, there have been two interest rate signals and both were followed by significant stock market moves. The stock market meltdown in October, 1987, followed directly on the heels of an interest rate sell signal. And the mid-June, 1989, buy signal lit another fire under the Dow, which so far has propelled stocks back into new all time highs.

On the other hand, investors should be wary of acting on an inflation signal during a noninflationary period unless stocks are in a caution zone. This is because when stocks enter a caution zone it indicates relative optimism which is a necessary ingredient to fuel a galloping inflation.

During this new type environment it may prove easier to push stocks off a cliff. Therefore, once stocks make a new 5-year high, I don't think it would hurt to cut back somewhat—perhaps to a one-half position— especially if we get a hint that the fundamentals are souring, such as one interest rate making a 65-week high, or inflation heating up to a rate of, say, 3 percent.

To sum up: During the present period, I would suggest more flexibility in the use of the indicators. Investors should consider each indicator by itself and try to make some allowance for what it is telling us.

Chapter 14

A Glimpse of the Future

January 1990: the Dow celebrated entry into the 1990s by achieving another all-time high on the first business day of the new year—2810, up a whopping 56.95 points in a single day. The buy signal from mid-June of 1989 was truly of value.

As discussed in Chapter 13, the economic tone of disinflation may require some cautious flexibility in the use of indicators. Disinflation may become a tightrope with inflation on one side and deflation on the other. Most investors well understand the economic effects of inflation, but the conditions of deflation can be somewhat illusive.

If a deflationary environment emerges, how long is it likely to last? The last such environment lasted twenty-six years, and the one before that survived for thirty years. However, before you set your sights on a long period of declining prices, we should alert you to the fact than an important structural change has taken place in our economy following the 1930s.

Prior to the 1930s, economists thought that the key to material progress was savings. They would be channeled into productive investment, and this in turn would lead to a vast expansion in the supply of goods. There was no need to worry about demand. According to the economic theory of that day, the production process would automatically return to workers and entrepreneurs the purchasing power needed to buy the goods produced. In the words of the French economists Jean-Baptiste Say, "Supply creates its own demand." And Say's "law of markets" dominated the thinking of nineteenth-century economists.

To be sure, classical economists recognized that a surge of savings or hoarding could create a shortfall in spending, and throw supply and demand out of balance. But they believed such imbalances would be temporary. They thought that a market economy, left to its own devices, had an automatic adjusting mechanism. When demand was inadequate to clear the market, prices were slashed, and consumers dipped into their savings to take advantage of the bargain. Before you knew it there was a shortage of goods, and the engines of production would be revved up again. In this scheme of things, there could never be a serious and continuing shortage of purchasing power in a capitalist economy. Supply and demand were in balance.

The economic system of the nineteenth century was also characterized by a belief in free markets. It was taken as an article of faith that individuals should be allowed the widest measure of freedom to pursue their own ends. Workers shared this faith in free markets. Although they bore the brunt of the periodic crises this system produced, they accepted this state of affairs as being in tune with nature, which, they acknowledged, was also harsh at times. Surely, it did not go unnoticed that this type of economy, even with its ups and downs, had given the masses a higher standard of living and a greater measure of economic security than any the world had ever known. Lunch pails were, in fact, becoming fuller.

Western governments of that time practiced a form of supply-side economics. Their aim was to encourage the growth of supplies. To accomplish this end, they restricted their role in the economy so as not to interfere with the free play of market forces. The only acceptable government intrusion into the economy during that time was in providing the stable monetary framework thought to be essential to induce people to save.

Yet in spite of general prosperity, there was a serious flaw with laissez-faire economics. Every so often, productive capacity so outstripped the ability to consume that it became necessary to eliminate the excess capacity that developed. When this occurred, a fall in prices would not bring the economy into balance; the economy would instead spin downward farther and farther out of control, leaving in its wake a dominolike pattern of bankruptcies and a nightmare of unemployment. These upheavals were not temporary. Rather, they lingered and were accompanied by long periods of declining prices—in short, deflationary environments.

This of course is what happened in the 1930s. The Great Depression was so terrifying and prolonged that it seemed to defy all the laws of economics. It dragged on and on, and economists thought the self-adjusting mechanism of the economy had broken down and the engines of production had stalled permanently. For more than a decade, there was never a year that unemployment fell below 15 percent, and the threat of violence hung in the air, imperiling the very system of capitalism itself. It was the British economist, John Maynard Keynes who stepped forward to save the day. According to Keynes, Say's law was mistaken: supply did not always create its own demand. The level of demand could become insufficient to soak up the supply of goods, and an economy could wallow in this state of affairs for a disturbingly long period of time. But Keynes had a solution: the government could correct the flaw by shifting its priority from the supply to the demand side of the equation, Instead of concerning itself with incentives to encourage the growth of supply, they would concentrate on managing demand. That is, when individuals wouldn't spend, the government ought to step into the breach and inject purchasing power into the economy. This would offset the falloff in personal consumption and stop an economic setback from spiraling into a depression. Simple but logical.

The idea created a profound change in the direction and emphasis in economics and led to a far-reaching restructuring of the economy. Governments throughout the Western world began to manipulate the level of demand, creating purchasing power via unemployment insurance, social security, welfare and cheap credit to home and car buyers, so as to ensure a high level of prosperity. For a long while it worked, or so it seemed. The period since World War II has been the most prosperous the world has ever seen. Recessions were brief, mild and infrequent. Each time the economy began to stall, governments would swoop down and increase spending, and shortly thereafter, the economy righted itself and roared back to new high levels.

No wonder the Keynesians thought they had led us into a new era of economic enlightenment. They believed that they had solved the core problem of economics, balancing the supply of goods with demand, and as a result, rapid economic growth could now be continuous. According to this new economic theory, the government would provide the spark to the economy by fueling purchasing power, and industry would fall into step, gearing up to satisfy the ballooning demand. We would be blessed with an outpouring of goods every bit as plentiful as in a laissez-faire economy. Economic theory had come full circle: *it was now taken for granted that demand created its own supply.*

However, economic history shows that it is harder to achieve a balance between supply and demand than economists like to think. The Keynesians were able to cure the malady of insufficient demand and thus block the possibility of a self-feeding contraction, but only at the price of creating another instability—a chronic tendency toward rising prices. In order to generate larger and larger amounts of purchasing power, money and credit were channeled into consumption. There was a falloff in the level of savings, and consequently a shortfall in new investment in plant and equipment. It became impossible to generate the supply increases necessary to accommodate the growing demand. The result: periodically, the spending power of the nation would dwarf the productive capacity of the economy,

producing a period of protracted and poisonous inflation, such as that in the 1970s.

The economic system of capitalism is inherently
unstable. This instability may result from a tendency of
supplies to grow faster than demand or from a propen-
sity for demand to outpace the buildup of supplies. In
either case, the instability is soon recognized. The government then uses its power to correct the imbalance.
It adopts policies directed at strengthening the weaker
side.[1] Because of its immense power, the government
alters the division of strength in the tug of war between supply and demand. The weaker side of the
equation becomes the stronger.

In pre-Keynesian economics, the government focused on the supply side, and as a result, productive
capacity grew faster than spending power. This instability vented itself in long, sickening depressions, and
there was a tendency for prices to fall. When the government shifted its priorities to the demand side, the
spending power of the nation outstripped the expansion in productive capacity. Demand dwarfed supply,
and in order to induce industry to expand to meet the
growing demand, *prices had to rise.* Simple Economics
101.

We are left with a structural bias toward inflation
and it is no wonder that the inflationary environment
that began in 1946 lasted thirty-five years—well beyond the length of previous ones. But of course, this
problem has been recognized. With a flourish of trum-
pets and a roll of drums, Reaganomics arrived on the
scene in 1980. Its aim: to revitalize the productive
power of the nation. It sought to do this by getting the
government out of the economy and reimposing the
incentives of the marketplace. Essentially, Reaganomics
is an attempt to return to good old-laissez-faire capitalism, a.k.a. supply-side economics.

But we cannot be fooled. There is no turning back.
The world in which laissez-faire economics flourished

---

[1] In the eighteenth century, the chief problem was thought to be an inability to generate a sufficient amount of new investment, while in the Great
Depression the great problem was an insufficiency of demand.

has passed on to the ages. The 1930s were a major turning point in Western society. The structural change in the economy precipitated an important change in the climate of opinion. People recognized that by giving the reins of the economy to government, they could have a new type of capitalism: capitalism with a heart, capitalism that brings with it the promise of economic stability and social justice. People would not have to suffer through long bouts of hard times, nor would they have to arbitrarily accept the verdict of an often cruel and impersonal marketplace. Their faith in free markets was replaced by a belief that government *could* and *should* steer and shape the economy. Since the 1930s, any presidential aspirant, whether Democrat or Republican, has had to promise prosperity if he or she hopes to reach the White House. If this promise is broken, the voters will show no mercy at re-election time.

The current flirtation with supply-side economics is not based on a newly acquired faith in free markets. It does not mean that we have become receptive to the idea of sending millions of workers to unemployment lines so as to maintain a stable price level. Reaganomics was able to capture the imagination of the American public only because it was presented as virtually painless therapy; Ronald Reagan promised an easy transition from an inflationary to a noninflationary economy. But a change in the government's priorities to the supply side will surely set the economy up for a classic nineteenth-century-type bust—that is, an inadequacy of demand, which will trigger an unbargained-for period of hardship. When the American people recognize that the price of a return to supply-side economics is the restoration of an economy that experiences periodic bouts of economic misery, they will turn their backs on this type of solution to inflation and send the Republicans packing. The most likely outcome is a demand that the experiment of government intrusion into the economy be carried to its natural conclusion. This means fashioning additional structural changes, such as indexing and partial wage controls, so as to limit the fury of inflation. In return for near-total control over the economy, the government will be forced to expand its promise to "no depression and no loss of purchasing power." [2]

The result will be a continuing bias to inflation. Inflationary environments will last much longer than deflationary environments. Very likely, the next deflationary environment will be fairly short. The 60 percent falloff in wholesale prices experienced during the last deflationary environment most likely will not be repeated.

To sum up: the odds favor a turn to a deflationary environment in the not-too-distant future, if it has not already begun. But that deflationary environment will probably be considerably shorter than those of the past. Soon after long-term rates fall the equivalent of one-half the high rate, we can begin to prepare for a return to an inflationary environment.

Now let us devise a strategy to take advantage of the shifts in the investment cycle.

---

[2] Beacause a move to greater government control is likely to follow a severe recession that reduces pressure on resources, there will be a foundation to tolerate a demand-side economy for a while. Keynesianism was implemented on the heels of the depression of the 1930s, and as a result, it took more than a generation before its inflationary potential was realized.

Chapter 15

Theory: The Way the Economy Works

Our model makes the assumption that changes in the rate of interest are the mechanism by which the economy adjusts. But is it? Let us see if the economy operates the way the model assumes it to.

An important fundamental change takes place in the market-place for money during a business slump. As production slows, inventories are liquidated, capital spending is postponed, and the demand for money is reduced. At the same time, people begin setting aside more of their paychecks in anticipation of rainy days ahead. The result: an excess of lendable funds, which drives down the cost of money (interest rates).

But once the return on savings has a substantial fall and borrowing costs tumble, people stop adding to their savings, and some are encouraged to step up their spending. Still others, perhaps the more daring, take notice of the skimpier return on their savings and shift a portion of this money into the stock market, which has fallen to a level where it now offers a rate of return competitive with that on bonds, money market funds and bank certificates of deposit. Prices on the country's stock exchanges rebound, and this increases the wealth of large segments of the population, thereby boosting their buying power. The downward spiral in both business and the stock market is checked.

Although the upturn in spending is not torrential, its impact is considerable. During the slump, business typically puts itself on a healthier footing: inventories are cut, unproductive workers laid off, and tattered balance sheets repaired. Leaner and more productive business firms are able to operate on lower budgets. As a result, a modest uptick in spending produces a tidal wave of profits. Savvy investors recognize this explosion in corporate earnings and shift greater portions of their savings into the stock market. This, of course, fuels the upward march of stock prices, which in turn enhances purchasing power even more. Business confidence returns, and consequently, firms increase depleted inventories, and hire more workers . . . jobs become easier to find, pay scales rise, and this leads to an increase in consumer confidence, followed by a surge in consumer spending . . . business responds by reactivating idled plant and machinery, laying in more inventory, and hiring additional workers . . . the expansion takes on a life of its own.

In its early stages, the recovery in both the economy and the stock market has a healthy glow to it. The past recession has left its mark on a goodly number of business people, bankers, investors and workers. Perhaps they have lost money or a job. Then again, they may not have. But surely, they cannot help but notice the pain inflicted on neighbors, coworkers and many other participants in the American economy. Consequently, they develop a sense of caution and are not likely to be so quick to revert back to their former free-spending ways. Because of this new-found conservatism, the early stage of the recovery is generally stable and sound. The rebound in interest rates and prices is held in check. But after a while, the expansion picks up an enormous head of steam and spills over into practically every industry and every sector in the country. It becomes clear to even the most casual observer that a boom is occurring, and euphoria takes hold and flows through the business community. In this giddy atmosphere, business people, workers and investors begin to act recklessly. Production is expanded in anticipation of even greater increases in consumer demand, workers begin to spend larger and larger portions of their paychecks and forget about saving for a rainy day, and investors think nothing of paying outlandish prices to own a piece of American business. The cautiousness evident in the early stages of the recovery vanishes, and with it the healthy footing that business and the stock market had been on.

Most important is the change in the fundamentals taking place in the marketplace for money. The booming business conditions fuel a staggering increase in the demand for money that easily outstrips the amount of savings. The outcome, of course: a steep rise in the rate of interest. Some people, perhaps the more rational or the more conservative, or both, are encouraged by the high rate of return on savings to spend less and save more. Some consumers curtail their purchases. A small number of business firms are discouraged by the high cost of borrowing and postpone plans for expansion. A few investors begin to scale back, selling off small portions of their holdings, which depresses prices on the nation's stock exchanges and therefore drains purchasing power. The withdrawal of this modest amount of buying power from the spending stream catches business off-balance. Firms have geared up for a continued expansion in consumer spending, inventories have been increased, capacity expanded, debt loads enlarged, and new and inexperienced workers hired—all on the assumption that the boom of the recent past would continue.

As a bloated business and financial sector is forced to adjust to a lower level of spending, an extremely competitive atmosphere develops. Prices can no longer be raised to offset rising costs. Business people see their profits fall and lose confidence . . . inventories are slashed, capital projects are put on hold, and workers are given pink slips . . . and as the slumping economy frightens still others to cut their spending and save a bit more, even more unsold goods pile up on the shelves . . . a chilling downward spiral in business and the stock market has set in, and not to end until the fall in interest rates is steep enough to encourage a shift from savings to spending . . . and so the cycle goes.

There is another course—call it a detour—that the economy may take when confronted with credit demands that outstrip the supply of savings. The Federal Reserve Bank may step up its creation of money in order to accommodate the ballooning demand for credit. This will usually delay a surge in interest rates and give an aging economic expansion a new lease on life. However, this action only serves to perpetuate the unhealthy conditions already brewing in the economy. Industry is operating near full capacity; most productive workers are already employed; and many raw materials are in short supply; therefore business does not have the wherewithal to expand production nearly enough to satisfy the surging growth in the money stock. The result is a sharp rise in prices—or inflation.

As people catch on to the fact that the purchasing power of their money is falling, they seek refuge in gold and Swiss francs, or diamonds and antiques, which have speculative possibilities vastly preferable to the investment in productive plant and equipment that the nation needs. The result is a diversion of savings from productive investment into the byways and back alleys of investment. The productive power of the economy falls still further, and this widens the discrepancy between the output of goods and money growth even more. To complicate matters, the Fed becomes concerned about the inability of the business sector to attract capital and pumps out money even more vigorously. Soon the financial system is awash in money. Borrowing by individuals and business firms increases enormously. But this money is not used to increase the productive power of the economy. Rather, uncertainty of inflation makes a mockery of long-term investment, and businesspeople begin to act like speculators. They turn their attention to schemes that promise quick payoffs. As a result, bankers end up financing speculative and generally unproductive ventures, and the quality of the debt load deteriorates. Finally, credit demands outstrip the Fed's ability or desire to create money, and interest rates go through the roof, providing an incentive to save rather than spend. As the foundation is now extremely shaky, the resulting fall in spending sends business and investment markets tumbling. A downward spiral sets in and quickly gathers momentum.

This relationship between interest rates and the economy makes a great deal of sense and certainly supports the model. What happens is that during boom times there is a shift of money from savings to spending. After a while the pool of savings is drawn down and can no longer finance the additional expansion in production needed to satisfy the growing demand. It becomes necessary to tempt investors to put more of their money into the financing of new factories and machines. The incentive to induce this shift of money into savings is, of course, high interest rates. However, high interest rates drain purchasing power from the economy, and this catches many business firms that had been betting on continual rises in consumer spending flat-footed. The economy must adjust to a lower level of spending and that means a painful period of unemployment and misery.

However, the slowdown in business activity creates a pool of savings. The inclination to save, initially ignited by the high interest rates, is reinforced by the pain of recession. The good news is that this hoard of funds will finance a new investment boom. And these successive waves of business investment have given us a two-hundred-year period of wealth creation the likes of which the world has never seen before.

If you've kept awake you must have noticed that this process has a "Catch-22" quality about it. When most people view the economic landscape as fraught with danger, the business fundamentals actually become favorable. This perception of risk leads people to become cautious. They save more and spend less, and this will provide business with a cheap and generous amount of capital. The corollary is that when everyone believes the economy has become risk-free, they don't save enough to allow business to get the capital needed to expand. And as sure as night follows day, the economy will be in for a period of rough sledding.

The truth is that *risk is actually lowest when people see it as the greatest, and when most people think of it as absent, it is acutally the highest.* This paradox befuddles most people, and, it appears, a goodly number of economists as well.

The most important determinant of the future course of business activity is the level of interest rates—not the quantity of money, as the monetarists would like you to think, nor shifts in the government's spending and taxing policies, as the Keynesians believe. The cost of money and credit influences the decisions of vast numbers of people to spend or save, to borrow or lend, and this ultimately affects economic activity, just as a rise or fall in the price of hogs, soybeans, or copper affects the production of these commodities. The result is a recurring and self-correcting cycle wherein each contraction carries with it the seeds of its own recovery.

Chapter 16

Designing an Investment Strategy

The most obviously profitable investment strategy is to load up with stocks and other investments when the odds favor an uptrend in the cycle and retreat to a cash portion when a down-phase is indicated. But what if something goes wrong? How much risk do you want to take? And what about investments that often take a long time to sell? While taking advantage of the investment cycle ought to be uppermost in investors' minds, they should also have a larger plan that enables them to take advantage of opportunities while protecting themselves from undue risk.

The first and most important consideration of this master plan is to determine whether we are in an overall environment of secular inflation or deflation. As these two environments each have a different influence on investments, we will outline two plans, one for each environment. Of course, these plans should be considered as general guidelines that investors can modify according to their personal objectives and the risks they feel comfortable in taking.

The Plan for an Inflationary Environment

This environment is generally favorable for investment. Normally, setbacks are not too deep, and lost ground is

191

soon made up. This means if your timing is off, the secular trend will probably bail you out. At this time, investors should be bold and daring. Their focus should be on creating and increasing wealth. To begin with, investors must decide what portion of their assets to hold back in case a situation arises in which cash is required quickly. As economic shocks are not too frequent in this environment, a modest amount will be sufficient, say about 5 percent. This money could be held in very short-term debt instruments—money markets, CDs or T-Bills, probably no longer than six months—that can be easily converted into cash.

The next decision is how large a percentage of funds should be committed to a core holding. As the secular trend is decidedly upward, with each rally likely to exceed the previous peak, it makes sense for investors to place a portion of their assets in a core holding that can be maintained throughout the whole inflationary period regardless of the investment climate. There are several advantages to maintaining a core position. Some investments, such as real estate, cannot be bought and sold quickly. It takes a while to find and buy the right kind of apartment buildings, shopping centers and office buildings. As a result, they are not suitable vehicles to capitalize on an inflationary spiral, which normally lasts about eighteen to thirty-six months. Yet frequently these investments experience substantial appreciation throughout the whole period of secularly rising prices. Secondly, investors will at least have some percentage of their capital working for them if the market should continue up after a sell signal is rendered. Although our model has an almost unblemished record during the past sixty-nine years, it would be unreasonable to expect it to continue to be flawless. Finally, a downswing in the investment cycle doesn't always take the wind out of the better investments. For instance, during the down-phase of the cycle that ran from early 1960 to June 1962, the Dow slid 20 percent. Yet IBM, the leading company in the fast-growing computer field, actually appreciated by approximately 20 percent.

A core position of about 25 percent of one's investment capital would seem about right. Fifteen percent of the total funds might be put to work in various inflation hedges, because these investments in particular reflect the long-term secular uptrend in prices that occur during this environment. An investor could concentrate on those hedges, which, because of the nonliquidity, are unsuitable for short bursts of inflation but are likely to do very well over a longer period of time. The other 10 percent of funds could be deployed in stocks that appear to have very favorable long-term fundamentals. Of course, one may vary this core position depending upon other considerations.

This leaves investors with approximately 70 percent of their investment funds to take advantage of the up-phases in the investment cycle, shifting from cash to stocks to inflation hedges. However, investors might consider varying this plan a bit. They might note that when long-term interest rates decline into a fifteen-month low, the odds favor a prolonged and powerful upswing in the investment cycle. If stocks are already in a buy zone at this time, it makes sense to become more aggressive. Investors could increase their stake by going on margin. If the fifteen-month low in long-term interest rates occurs before the stock market reaches a buy zone (that is, the bull market has not actually begun), it wouldn't hurt to put an additional 15 percent into stocks since it is likely that the market will at least experience a discounting phase. When added to core stock holdings, this would bring security portfolios up to 25 percent and provide additional protection just in case the Dow failed to sink into a two-year low.

Also, as soon as investors spot a shift in the environment to one of secularly rising prices, it is a good idea to do as much long-term borrowing as possible. Long-term rates usually experience a very steep rise during these periods, and those who act quickly will be locking in their financing costs at a cheap rate. A typical plan for an inflationary environment is shown in Table 43. One thing to remember: long-term bonds are generally a poor investment during this time, as there

Table 43 Typical Plan for an Inflationary Environment

	Cash	Stocks	Inflation Hedges	Long-Term Bonds
I. Downphase in Investment Cycle				
A. Before long-term interest rates make a 15-month low	75%	10%	15%	0
B. After long-term interest rates make a 15-month low	60%	25%	15%	0
II. Up-phase in Investment Cycle				
A. Buy signal in stocks	5%	80%	15%	0
B. Buy signal in stocks and long-term interest rates have made a 15-month low	5%	80-135%[a]	15%	0
C. Inflationary spiral begins	5%	10%	85%	0

[a] Aggressive investors may go on margin at this time.

is a decided and unequivocal trend to higher interest rates. The only time to own them would be for brief periods after upward pressure on interest rates had eased.

A *general hint*: after long-term interest rates reach a forty-year high, most inflationary environments are not likely to last very long unless propelled up by repeated bouts of inflation. Therefore, if AAA Corporate Bonds rates make a forty-year high, it might be wise to shift one's entire core holding into inflation hedges. Preferably, this should be done on the next sell signal in stocks. For example, a smart investor would have dumped core stock holdings in December 1968. Not a bad time to unload, and the next fourteen years proved to be a turbulent period for stock market investors.

The Plan for Deflationary Times

Typically, this is a treacherous period for investors. Most investments are buffeted by successive waves of selling and suffer nasty breaks from which they do not fully recover. Some, in fact, may disappear into a black hole. This is the time to be cautious and adopt a defensive posture, concentrating on preserving capital. In general, buying opportunities will not occur until stocks and real assets have become dirt cheap.

During this environment, economic surprises are often unpleasant, and recessions may be unexpectedly severe. The chances of losing a job, a business going sour, of a family member being in trouble and needing assistance increase. Therefore, it would be prudent to hold back a larger portion of one's wealth from investments. To be on the safe side, cash reserves should probably be on the order of 20 percent. This should be held in the safest investments—T-Bills or CDs of the strongest banks.

As investment markets are likely to suffer big breaks during this environment, it is not wise to keep core holdings in stocks or inflation hedges. However, investors should maintain a core holding in long-term bonds—ten to twenty years—of very high quality backed either by the government or extremely strong companies, to profit by the pronounced trend to lower interest rates that generally occurs throughout this period. This trend, of course, means higher bond prices. About 30 percent of funds in this core holding seems sufficient. That leaves 50 percent of funds available to take advantage of the upswings in the investment cycle.

Again, investors can vary the plan somewhat. For instance, investors can begin to nibble at stocks shortly after a level of extreme pessimism is reached—the Dow falls into a five-year low—even if the investment climate is still unfavorable, provided, of course, that a deflationary spiral has not set in. A commitment of 10 percent of one's funds does not seem to be reckless. On the other hand, it is probably unwise to buy inflation hedges just because they appear to have become cheap; because they reflect the general deflationary environment, they may sink much, much lower. Also, when there is a deflationary tilt to the environment, an inflationary spiral does not usually pick up a real head of steam. Therefore, it would be sensible to deploy a smaller percentage, say about 35 percent, of funds into inflation hedges, such as gold, silver, commodities and currencies, which can be sold quickly.

A typical plan for a deflationary environment may look something like the one presented in Table 44. In general, it is not wise to take on leverage during this kind of environment (except for real estate). After interest rates on AAA Corporate Bonds have fallen the equivalent of 50 percent from the high rate, investors might think about shifting a portion of their core holdings from long-term bonds into stocks and real assets. By that time, bond prices will have already experienced a substantial rise and will no longer be the good investment they were. On the other hand, stocks and tangibles are likely to have been beaten down to bargain-basement levels. Preferably, this switch should be made on the next buy signal in stocks. Smart investors would have put in core positions in stocks and real

Table 44   Typical Plan for an Deflationary Environment

	Cash	Stocks	Inflation Hedges	Long-Term Bonds
I. Downphase in Investment Cycle				
A. Before Dow falls into a 5-year low	70%	0	0	30%
B. After Dow falls into a 5-year low	60%	10%	0	30%
II. Up-phase in Investment Cycle				
A. Buy signal in stocks	20%	50%	0	30%
B. Inflationary spiral begins	35%	0	35%	30%

assets in April 1942. This was a very good time to make long-term commitments, as most assets were selling at fire-sale prices.

We have outlined plans, one for each overall environment. During an inflationary environment, the plan should favor a more aggressive stance toward stocks and real assets. It might include the use of credit or margin. The idea is to be more daring and take on greater risks. On the other hand, the program for a deflationary environment ought to emphasize a more defensive posture. At that time, risk is much greater, and as a result, investors should be more cautious, and reserves should play a larger role.

Investors should, of course, vary these plans according to their own objectives and their attitudes toward risk. They should define their objectives as clearly as possible. They should not attempt to take on more risks than they are comfortable with. But above all, their plans should be in tune with the prevailing overall environment and whether it demands an aggressive or defensive posture.

Chapter 17

A Different View of the World

Most people are at the mercy of the twists and turns of a capitalist economy. Investors, bankers, businesspeople and economists are wrong just when it counts most—at major turning points. Etched into the folklore of Wall Street is the notion that important bottoms occur only when most people see the future as bleak. When there is a widespread conviction that good times are here to stay,the stage is being set for a chilling decline in the stock market. It is also well documented that most of our economic seers have failed to predict accurately the timing of and intensity of all eight postwar recessions. Since the beginning of the industrial revolution two hundred years ago, during each expansion and recession, during each bull and bear market, during each real estate boom and bust, people keep repeating the same mistakes.

This record is so depressing because it is at odds with the very way we view the world. We have been taught to consider ourselves creatures of reason. The discoveries of our great thinkers in the physical sciences enabled us to unlock the secrets of thermodynamics, put rockets into orbit, and begin an age of material abundance. Surely, we thought, once the best minds tackle the subject of the economy, the riddle of the business cycle will be solved and all of us would become winners in the game of economics and finance.

The best and brightest have taken up the challenge. They have put the economy under a microscope and studied it. Countless books have been written on the subject. And still . . . we are unable to prevent the pendulum swings from prosperity to recession. Nor have we produced a savvy group of financial experts to manage the public's money in a way that would make us all winners in the game of investments.

Why, after two hundred years of observing a capitalistic economy in action, hasn't our economics sector yielded to the use of reason, as our physical world has? I submit that it is because of the way we approach the subject. Economists take their cue from the great strides made in the physical sciences, which are subject to clear-cut cause-and-effect rules. Economists ask what factor or combination of factors are responsible for a business contraction . . . or an expansion. In their view, the economy is a mechanism, and once they find the broken part, they will be able to fix it, like a plumber fixes a leaky faucet. But the economy does not function like that. Instead, it operates like an organism, endowed with the power to grow, along with the vulnerability to contract. There are two parts to this system: human psychology and the economic fundamentals. Yet neither is the casual variable; *both affect and in turn are affected by the other.*

Let us take a look at how this system operates. The essential element needed to begin a period of rapid industrial growth is a healthy business and investment climate. That only comes about when most participants in the economy have adopted a cautious attitude that emphasizes risk avoidance. When this occurs, people rebuild their savings, and businesspeople throughout the economy tighten their belts. They pare inventories, retire debt, hand out pink slips, and shut down unprofitable and outmoded facilities. This reduces the demand for money, labor and raw materials, and naturally, the price of these items plummet. Yet, a substantial fall in interest rates stimulates a modest uptick in spending and promotes an increase in the value of financial assets—which in turn boosts the buying power of consumers. The market for the products of business firms expands at the very time that the cost of doing business has been sharply reduced, and this creates a very profitable business climate. Massive gains in production and employment throughout the economy will follow. Yet because of this widely held cautious psychology, the fall in interest rates will not totally dispense with the inclination to save, and business will continue to keep inventories lean and hold down costs. Consequently, the return to a high-spending economy will be gradual.

A period of vigorous economic growth does not result because the money managers at the Fed have put their foot on the monetary accelerator, or because an administration in Washington pumps dollars into the economy, or because the government cuts taxes. Although these factors may aid a recovery, they are not sufficient in and of themselves to ignite the fire. A surge in business growth depends upon a healthy atmosphere that results only when the cautious side of human nature reigns supreme.

But there is another side to human nature. This is the acquisitive side, the desire for gain. When the appetite for gain is aroused, we are willing to take chances for a share of the spoils. We will make economic commitments based on continuing business growth. Business people increase inventories, take on debt, hire additional workers, and attempt to expand market share. Consumers dip into savings and up their standard of living. This results in further increases in spending and investment, which in turn refresh and reinforce a business recovery. This transformation in psychology from general cautiousness to one of acquisitiveness is, in fact, the driving force that feeds and keeps an expanding economy on an upward trajectory.

However, when this acquisitive side of human nature is clearly in the driver's seat, it produces a climate that will undermine the profitability and performance of the American economy. Men and women throughout all areas of the economy spend and borrow up a storm, and the reservoir of savings becomes depleted. Businesspeople become bolder, laying in inventories and expanding capacity in order to accommodate further growth in spending. The demand for capital, labor and raw materials balloons, and this drives up their cost. Interest rates reach towering levels, putting a damper on spending. The market for the products of business firms shrinks, and as this is occurring at the same time that the cost of doing business is undergoing a whopping increase, there comes an end to the climate in which business profits were easy to come by. Business can no longer generate the earnings needed to keep the economy afloat and the nation's output of goods and services contracts.

The behavior of the participants has an enormous effect on the economy itself. The fertile breeding ground of an economic expansion is an atmosphere of caution. The transformation in psychology from caution to acquisitiveness is what propels the expansion along an uphill track. However once acquisitiveness is clearly in the driver's seat, the economy is deprived of the healthy atmosphere needed to nourish it and topples. As the psychology is rapidly transformed from one of acquisitiveness to one of caution, the contraction in output snowballs.

But what causes the emphasis on one side and then another side of human nature? It is the other part of the equation, economic reality. That is, the performance of the economy also has a pervasive effect on mass psychology. The cautious side of people's nature only comes to dominate after large numbers of people undergo a traumatic experience, such as a recession, which is invariably accompanied by the pain of unemployment, vanishing profits, corporate bankruptcies, and a chilling decline in the value of assets. Very understandably, people see the business and stock market world as more risky. This change in the way we all perceive risk subtly affects the way we think and act. When risk looms larger, fear takes over, and people instinctively formulate survival strategies. In order to avoid further pain, they cut commitments to economic growth and build up reserves—that is, savings. They become less willing to accept economic risks. They become cautious.

Yet we do not feel comfortable with our actions unless we have some rationale to justify them. This perception of increased risk, which makes us cautious, also sways us to accept a rationale that posits a gloomy view of the future. This is because when the world appears threatening and people feel vulnerable, lines of thinking that emphasize a pessimistic assessment of the future win out in the marketplace for ideas. Most of us come to believe that business conditions will remain bad indefinitely because it rationalizes the way we see risk in our economic world. The widespread adoption of cautious behavior is a result of being mugged by an economic recession.

On the flip side of the coin, the acquisitive side of nature springs to life on the heels of an important success experience. A sustained period of prosperity, which brings with it increases in profits, job opportunities and living standards, along with mouth-watering returns on investments, is a very pleasant experience for most of us. And it leads us to view our economic world in a different light. It appears much less risky. This change in the way we perceive our immediate economic world again colors the way we think and act. When risk appears diminished we feel invincible and unconsciously formulate a strategy to march out and bite the apple of prosperity. We become willing to spend, borrow and invest so as to increase our wealth and living standards.

But to muster up the confidence to march out and make commitments based on economic growth, we must first put on rose-colored glasses and take an optimistic view of the future. We are easily convinced that the future will be rosy and the good times will last indefinitely because this line of thinking legitimizes the way most of us see risk in our economic world and gives us confidence to build commitments. Forecasters who warn of the bad times ahead are out of line with the way the average person sees his economic world, and like the Trojan princess Cassandra, are fated not to be believed—no matter how logical or sophisticated their arguments are. The acquisitive side of man's nature is aroused by a long period of prosperity and its promise of riches.

There is a subtle interaction between man's state of mind and economic reality. People see things in a different light depending on what has happened in the economy. But people's mindset *also affects what happens to the economy.* When most people see the economy and financial markets as fraught with danger and are afraid to make commitments based on business growth, an economic reality different from what had been expected is created—a return to prosperity. The pleasure that flows from the revival in business activity provides the incentive to get the animal spirits flowing again. As people shift their views and consequently their behavior to bring them back into line with the new economic reality, the expansion is fueled along its course. This in turn justifies and furthers the emerging perception of the economy as relatively risk-free. Economic trends change behavior to conform to their direction. Because of this, trends tend to persist for a considerable length of time once set in motion.

Once the majority has caught on to prosperity and sees the economy as risk-free, people begin spending and investing recklessly. But businesspeople gear up and increase supplies even more, and the outcome will be just the opposite of what is expected. The economy begins to contract, and as this has an untoward effect on jobs, wages and asset values, people unexpectedly see their goals frustrated. The lesson of pain imposes a discipline that businesspeople, bankers and workers were unwilling to accept before. They shift their views once more and cut economic commitments, and this puts further downward pressure on the economy. Finally, the cautiousness is overdone, and the wheel is ready to turn once more. By this process, our economy continually regenerates itself.

To be sure, in the real economic world things do not work so smoothly. People obviously prefer the up-phases to the down-phases, and the powers that be attempt to extend the expansion phase of the cycle. In modern times, the government or the Fed attempts to feed money into the economy when a boom seems to be flagging, so as to ensure that purchasing power does not sag. The result: the swings from expansion to recession and back to expansion are not symmetrical. Expansions are noticeably longer than contractions. However, when the government attempts to extend prosperity, it has an unintended consequence on the other side of the equation. As the period of prosperity lengthens, more and more people receive reinforcing success experiences, and the acquisitive side of human nature is stretched to its limit. Making money in business or the stock market looks so easy that nearly everyone wants to have a go at it. Confidence turns into mass feelings of omnipotence. Rational business people begin to take leave of their senses and behave with an irrational optimism. They accumulate inventories that are far too large, overexpand productive capacity, take on too much debt, and in general behave like adolescents out on a binge. When this happens, business commitments to the economy become overextended, and the economy acquires an immunity to further expansion.

Most worrisome is the threat this poses to the long-term growth of the economy. The available resources—manpower, capital, and materials—will either become locked into the older industries or channeled into short-term money-making schemes, thus blocking the way for promising new industries of the future. Lest we forget, it has been the continuing creation of new industries that provides the dynamic thrust to industrial capitalism, If we hope to keep making economic strides like those of the past two hundred years, resources must be made available to the new up-and-comers. How do we get the obsolete, the less productive and redundant business to give up their claim on resources? An appeal to reason? No chance! In an atmosphere in which consumers, businesspeople and bankers feel omnipotent and think they can do no wrong, they are not likely to voluntarily put old and dying industries out to pasture. Besides, most bankers and prospective entrepreneurs recognize that of the multitude of new untired business ventures, only a few really succeed. Quite understandably, they prefer to stick with the old, which because of their financial muscle and string of past successes, appear to be less risky. The only way to change behavior and create an atmosphere wherein new industry can gain access to scarce labor, capital and materials is to undergo an honest-to-goodness recession.

But not to worry. This will occur, because expectations will have become too high in relation to what the economy can realistically deliver. Businesspeople will have geared up on the assumption that the market for their products is insatiable. Consumers will have piled on debt in the belief that the growth in their earning power is unlimited. Investors, drooling at the thought of mushrooming corporate profits, will have bid up prices on the nation's stock exchanges to levels far beyond what are considered rational standards of value. Perhaps the economy is able to maintain its forward momentum, but it will certainly not be able to duplicate the rapid growth rate of the recent past. The result will be disappointment for those businesspeople, consumers and investors who have bet heavily on growth, and some will be forced to liquidate. This provides the ripple that starts the economy on a downhill course. As business conditions turn sour, the psychology changes to reflect the new reality. People throughout the economy become cautious and abandon economic commitments, and the economic setback turns into a full-fledged recession.

The government can intervene and extend an expansion, but in so doing it invariably leads to overconfidence and expectations that become unrealistic and cannot possibly be satisfied. The disappointment of unfulfilled expectations triggers a wave of inventory liquidation, and this tips the economy into recession. The

Greeks, a long time ago, had a saying: "whom the gods choose to destroy, they first make overconfident."

The economy seems to operate in accordance with the immutable laws of growth and decay similar to those found in biology, rather than the cause-and-effect type logic associated with the physical sciences. It is a hopelessly cyclical economy. This is because the mind plays tricks on people. Most people see risk as the highest after the economy has already contracted, and therefore it is actually the least. When the economy has been running at full throttle and is actually in a high-risk area wherein the odds are heavily against investors, very few people recognize that there is a great deal of risk. Unfortunately, there is not much that can be done about this. If most people caught on during an economic contraction and saw that there was actually very little risk, they would not adopt a cautious mode of behavior, and there would in fact still be a great deal of risk—presto, "Catch 22." The idea that everyone can win is a cruel hoax. We cannot fix the economy without also attempting to influence people's behavior.[1]

The wellsprings of human behavior are psychological in origin. In the clutch, most of us operate more by gut instinct than by cool reason. The way we think and the way we act are colored by those recent experiences that are sufficiently painful or pleasurable. *That is a law of human nature.* Because of it, we expect what we have just seen and experienced to keep happening on and on into the future. In short, people are much less rational than they perceive themselves to be.

The problem in the game of investment is obvious. We are all caught off-balance by the twists and turns of markets because we put on blinkers that blind us. These faulty perceptions of risk are likely to cloud

---

[1] That, of course, requires controlling behavior so completely that greed is held in check during good times and fear and panic are not allowed to prevail during bad times. A couple of governments seem to be fairly successful at accomplishing this task. Of course, they have needed a system of surveillance and torture, such as a secret police, a rifle in the back and a gulag to succeed.

the judgment of each and every one of us. To win at this game of investing, you must keep the blinkers off so that you will be able to see what others don't. How do you accomplish this? Although there is no surefire answer, several things might help. One is to develop a good historical perspective. Those with a sense of history recognize that our current experience is never quite as unique as we think. A second tack is to remain flexible. Don't overcommit yourself to any course of action. In this game, there is no certainty. Things are always changing. Investors loaded down with excessive baggage will be slow to respond to new and changing circumstances. A third tactic is to recognize that the opponent in this game is not nature but people. We are trying to outguess others, and this will be a lot easier if we understand what moves people. About two hundred years ago, the English philosopher, Jeremy Bentham, said, "Nature has placed man under the governance of two sovereign masters, pain and pleasure. It is for them alone to point out what we should do." Unless this author's vision of the world is significantly out of focus, the one thing you can depend upon is that people will respond to pain and pleasure. They will change their behavior and play out their allotted roles. And this is what makes markets predictable.

Finally, and probably most important, is the ability to recognize that we are not the objective creatures we like to think. We are just as likely as anyone else to be blinded by our most recent experiences, particularly those that are unexpectedly traumatic or pleasant. We must try to overcome the pull of what most people are saying and doing. That is, when euphoria is running rampant and forecasts of the future are glowing, we should tone down the enthusiasm and consider the possibility that out there on the horizon, storm clouds may be gathering. And when all others have lost hope, there is no reason to despair. Rather, at this time, we should keep an eye out for the silver lining.

If you succeed in removing those blinkers . . . you might be able to see what others don't.

Appendices

Appendix A   Yields of High Grade Railroad Bonds

Year	Jan.	Feb.	Mar.	Apr.	May	Jun.	Jul.	Aug.	Sep.	Oct.	Nov.	Dec.
1910	3.73	3.74	3.76	3.80	3.82	3.84	3.87	3.86	3.82	3.80	3.83	3.83
1911	3.82	3.83	3.84	3.84	3.83	3.84	3.84	3.86	3.87	3.87	3.85	3.85
1912	3.85	3.84	3.85	3.86	3.87	3.88	3.89	3.91	3.92	3.92	3.92	3.93
1913	3.92	3.93	3.99	4.04	4.08	4.13	4.12	4.08	4.05	4.08	4.13	4.14
1914	4.06	4.00	4.02	4.01	4.01	4.00	4.04	a	a	a	a	4.23
1915	4.17	4.16	4.19	4.15	4.15	4.18	4.24	4.27	4.29	4.19	4.06	4.05
1916	4.03	4.02	4.03	4.05	4.06	4.06	4.07	4.09	4.07	4.02	3.98	3.99
1917	3.92	3.99	4.03	4.12	4.24	428	4.32	4.35	4.44	4.49	4.62	4.70
1918	4.66	4.61	4.68	4.73	4.66	4.72	4.77	4.77	4.82	4.71	4.42	4.44
1919	4.53	4.57	4.63	4.67	4.62	4.62	4.68	4.84	4.87	4.75	4.87	4.93
1920	4.91	5.07	5.07	5.27	5.49	5.44	5.41	5.25	5.06	4.91	4.99	5.15

a Markets closed, World War I began.

Source: Frederick R. Macaulay, *The Movements of Interest Rates, Bond Yields and Stock Prices in The United States Since 1856.* New York: National Bureau of Economic Research, 1938, pp. A155-157.

APPENDIX B

AAA Corporate Bond Rates—1919–1989

	1919		1920		1921		1922		1923
Jan	5.35%	Jan	5.75%	Jan	6.14%	Jan	5.34%	Jan	5.04%
Feb	5.35	Feb	5.86	Feb	6.08	Feb	5.29	Feb	5.07
Mar	5.39	Mar	5.92	Mar	6.08	Mar	5.23	Mar	5.18
Apr	5.44	Apr	6.04	Apr	6.06	Apr	5.15	Apr	5.22
May	5.39	May	6.25	May	6.11	May	5.13	May	5.16
Jun	5.40	Jun	6.38	Jun	6.18	Jun	5.08	Jun	5.15
Jul	5.44	Jul	6.34	Jul	6.12	Jul	5.00	Jul	5.14
Aug	5.56	Aug	6.30	Aug	5.99	Aug	4.96	Aug	5.08
Sep	5.60	Sep	6.22	Sep	5.93	Sep	4.93	Sep	5.12
Oct	5.54	Oct	6.05	Oct	5.84	Oct	4.97	Oct	5.11
Nov	5.66	Nov	6.08	Nov	5.60	Nov	5.09	Nov	5.09
Dec	5.73	Dec	6.26	Dec	5.50	Dec	5.08	Dec	5.09

	1924		1925		1926		1927		1928
Jan	5.09%	Jan	4.95%	Jan	4.82%	Jan	4.66%	Jan	4.46%
Feb	5.09	Feb	4.95	Feb	4.77	Feb	4.67	Feb	4.46
Mar	5.10	Mar	4.91	Mar	4.79	Mar	4.62	Mar	4.46
Apr	5.08	Apr	4.87	Apr	4.74	Apr	4.58	Apr	4.46
May	5.04	May	4.83	May	4.71	May	4.57	May	4.49
Jun	4.99	Jun	4.83	Jun	4.72	Jun	4.58	Jun	4.57
Jul	4.95	Jul	4.87	Jul	4.71	Jul	4.60	Jul	4.61
Aug	4.95	Aug	4.90	Aug	4.72	Aug	4.56	Aug	4.64
Sep	4.95	Sep	4.87	Sep	4.72	Sep	4.54	Sep	4.61
Oct	4.92	Oct	4.85	Oct	4.71	Oct	4.51	Oct	4.61
Nov	4.94	Nov	4.84	Nov	4.68	Nov	4.49	Nov	4.58
Dec	4.95	Dec	4.85	Dec	4.68	Dec	4.46	Dec	4.61

	1929		1930		1931		1932		1933
Jan	4.62%	Jan	4.66%	Jan	4.42%	Jan	5.20%	Jan	4.44%
Feb	4.66	Feb	4.69	Feb	4.43	Feb	5.23	Feb	4.48
Mar	4.70	Mar	4.62	Mar	4.39	Mar	4.98	Mar	4.68
Apr	4.69	Apr	4.60	Apr	4.40	Apr	5.17	Apr	4.78
May	4.70	May	4.60	May	4.37	May	5.36	May	4.63
Jun	4.77	Jun	4.57	Jun	4.36	Jun	5.41	Jun	4.46
Jul	4.77	Jul	4.52	Jul	4.36	Jul	5.26	Jul	4.36
Aug	4.79*	Aug	4.47	Aug	4.40	Aug	4.91	Aug	4.30
Sep	4.80	Sep	4.42	Sep	4.55	Sep	4.70	Sep	4.36
Oct	4.77	Oct	4.42	Oct	4.99*	Oct	4.64	Oct	4.34
Nov	4.76	Nov	4.47	Nov	4.94	Nov	4.63	Nov	4.54
Dec	4.67	Dec	4.52	Dec	5.32	Dec	4.59	·Dec	4.50

1934

Week Ended		Week Ended		Week Ended	
Jan 06	4.43%	May 05	4.04%	Sep 01	3.93%
13	4.41	12	4.03	08	3.93
20	4.34	19	4.02	15	3.95
27	4.30	26	3.99	22	3.98
				29	3.96
Feb 03	4.26	Jun 02	3.97	Oct 06	3.95
10	4.22	09	3.94	13	3.93
17	4.20	16	3.93	20	3.90
24	4.17	23	3.92	27	3.87
		30	3.91		
Mar 03	4.17	Jul 07	3.91	Nov 03	3.87
10	4.15	14	3.88	10	3.87
17	4.12	21	3.87	17	3.86
24	4.13	28	3.89	24	3.86
31	4.13				
Apr 07	4.12	Aug 04	3.90	Dec 01	3.85
14	4.09	11	3.91	08	3.84
21	4.06	18	3.95	15	3.81
28	4.04	25	3.93	22	3.81
				29	3.80

AAA Corporate Bond Rates (continued)

1935	1936	1937	1938	1939
Week Ended	Week Ended	Week Ended	Week Ended	Week Ended
Jan 05 3.80%	Jan 04 3.42%	Jan 02 3.10%	Jan 01 3.19%	Jan 07 3.04%
12 3.78	11 3.39	09 3.08	08 3.16	14 3.01
19 3.78	18 3.37	16 3.08	15 3.15	21 3.00
26 3.76	25 3.35	23 3.08	22 3.16	28 3.02
		30 3.13	29 3.21	
Feb 02 3.74	Feb 01 3.35	Feb 06 3.17	Feb 05 3.23	Feb 04 3.01
09 3.73	08 3.34	13 3.20	12 3.21	11 3.00
16 3.70	15 3.32	20 3.26	19 3.19	18 3.00
23 3.68	22 3.31	27 3.23	26 3.19	25 3.00
	29 3.32			
Mar 02 3.66	Mar 07 3.30	Mar 06 3.24	Mar 05 3.18	Mar 04 2.99
09 3.65	14 3.30	13 3.29	12 3.19	11 2.97
16 3.68	21 3.30	20 3.34	19 3.22	18 2.97
23 3.67	28 3.29	27 3.37	26 3.24	25 3.00
30 3.67				
Apr 06 3.68	Apr 04 3.28	Apr 03 3.38	Apr 02 3.30	Apr 01 3.00
13 3.66	11 3.27	10 3.44*	09 3.32	08 3.02
20 3.65	18 3.29	17 3.43	16 3.33	15 3.04
27 3.65	25 3.30	24 3.39	23 3.30	22 3.03
			30 3.26	29 3.02
May 04 3.65	May 02 3.31	May 01 3.40	May 07 3.25	May 06 3.00
11 3.64	09 3.29	08 3.36	14 3.23	13 2.98
18 3.66	16 3.29	15 3.34	21 3.21	20 2.96
25 3.65	23 3.26	22 3.33	28 3.22	27 2.96
	30 3.25	29 3.30		
Jun 01 3.64	Jun 06 3.24	Jun 05 3.30	Jun 04 3.23	Jun 03 2.95
08 3.64	13 3.24	12 3.27	11 3.22	10 2.93
15 3.62	20 3.25	19 3.27	18 3.26	17 2.93
22 3.60	27 3.24	26 3.27	25 3.29	24 2.92
29 3.59				
Jul 06 3.57	Jul 04 3.24	Jul 03 3.29	Jul 02 3.27	Jul 01 2.91
13 3.55	11 3.22	10 3.27	09 3.24	08 2.90
20 3.56	18 3.22	17 3.25	16 3.23	15 2.89
27 3.56	25 3.23	24 3.25	23 3.22	22 2.89
		31 3.23	30 3.20	29 2.90
Aug 03 3.56	Aug 01 3.23	Aug 07 3.22	Aug 06 3.18	Aug 05 2.90
10 3.57	08 3.22	14 3.21	13 3.18	12 2.91
17 3.59	15 3.22	21 3.24	20 3.18	19 2.92
24 3.62	22 3.21	28 3.26	27 3.18	26 2.95
31 3.64	29 3.21			
Sep 07 3.63	Sep 05 3.19	Sep 04 3.26	Sep 03 3.18	Sep 02 3.00
14 3.60	12 3.18	11 3.28	10 3.19	09 3.20
21 3.59	19 3.17	18 3.29	17 3.20	16 3.24
28 3.58	26 3.17	25 3.28	24 3.21	23 3.28
				30 3.31*
Oct 05 3.56	Oct 03 3.19	Oct 02 3.29	Oct 01 3.25	Oct 07 3.24
12 3.54	10 3.19	09 3.28	08 3.17	14 3.20
19 3.53	17 3.19	16 3.28	15 3.14	21 3.14
26 3.51	24 3.18	23 3.29	22 3.14	28 3.09
	31 3.18	30 3.27	29 3.14	
Nov 02 3.49	Nov 07 3.17	Nov 06 3.23	Nov 05 3.12	Nov 04 3.07
09 3.48	14 3.15	13 3.24	12 3.10	11 3.01
16 3.47	21 3.14	20 3.24	19 3.09	18 2.99
23 3.47	28 3.13	27 3.25	26 3.10	25 2.98
30 3.47				
Dec 07 3.46	Dec 05 3.11	Dec 04 3.24	Dec 03 3.10	Dec 02 2.97
14 3.44	12 3.10	11 3.22	10 3.09	09 2.96
21 3.45	19 3.09	18 3.22	17 3.09	16 2.95
28 3.43	26 3.11	25 3.20	24 3.09	23 2.93
			31 3.07	30 2.92

AAA Corporate Bond Rates (continued)

1940 Week Ended		1941 Week Ended		1942 Week Ended		1943 Week Ended		1944 Week Ended	
Jan 06	2.89%	Jan 04	2.72%	Jan 03	2.86%	Jan 02	2.81%	Jan 01	2.74%
13	2.87	11	2.75	10	2.83	09	2.81	08	2.73
20	2.88	18	2.74	17	2.83	16	2.80	15	2.71
27	2.87	25	2.76	24	2.83	23	2.79	22	2.72
				31	2.84	30	2.78	29	2.73
Feb 03	2.87	Feb 01	2.76	Feb 07	2.84	Feb 06	2.77	Feb 05	2.74
10	2.87	08	2.76	14	2.84	13	2.77	12	2.73
17	2.85	15	2.76	21	2.85	20	2.77	19	2.74
24	2.85	22	2.79	28	2.86	27	2.77	26	2.74
Mar 02	2.86	Mar 01	2.79	Mar 07	2.87	Mar 06	2.77	Mar 04	2.74
09	2.85	08	2.78	14	2.87	13	2.77	11	2.74
16	2.85	15	2.78	21	2.87	20	2.76	18	2.74
23	2.84	22	2.78	28	2.85	27	2.76	25	2.73
30	2.83	29	2.83						
Apr 06	2.82	Apr 05	2.82	Apr 04	2.84	Apr 03	2.76	Apr 01	2.74
13	2.82	12	2.82	11	2.83	10	2.76	08	2.74
20	2.83	19	2.83	18	2.83	17	2.76	15	2.74
27	2.83	26	2.82	25	2.83	24	2.76	22	2.74
								29	2.73
May 04	2.82	May 03	2.81	May 02	2.84	May 01	2.75	May 06	2.73
11	2.82	10	2.81	09	2.84	08	2.75	13	2.73
18	2.92	17	2.82	16	2.85	15	2.75	20	2.73
25	3.02	24	2.82	23	2.85	22	2.74	27	2.72
		31	2.82	30	2.85	29	2.74		
Jun 01	3.04	Jun 07	2.81	Jun 06	2.85	Jun 05	2.73	Jun 03	2.72
08	3.03	14	2.78	13	2.86	12	2.73	10	2.73
15	2.98	21	2.77	20	2.84	19	2.72	17	2.73
22	2.92	28	2.75	27	2.84	26	2.72	24	2.73
29	2.91								
Jul 06	2.88	Jul 05	2.75	Jul 04	2.83	Jul 03	2.71	Jul 01	2.72
13	2.88	12	2.74	11	2.83	10	2.70	08	2.72
20	2.87	19	2.74	18	2.83	17	2.69	15	2.72
27	2.87	26	2.74	25	2.83	24	2.69	22	2.72
						31	2.69	29	2.72
Aug 03	2.87	Aug 02	2.74	Aug 01	2.82	Aug 07	2.69	Aug 05	2.71
10	2.85	09	2.74	08	2.82	14	2.69	12	2.72
17	2.86	16	2.75	15	2.81	21	2.69	19	2.72
24	2.85	23	2.75	22	2.81	28	2.69	26	2.72
31	2.84	30	2.74	29	2.80				
Sep 07	2.84	Sep 06	2.74	Sep 05	2.81	Sep 04	2.69	Sep 02	2.71
14	2.83	13	2.74	12	2.81	11	2.69	09	2.71
21	2.82	20	2.75	19	2.80	18	2.69	16	2.71
28	2.81	27	2.75	26	2.80	25	2.70	23	2.72
								30	2.72
Oct 05	2.79	Oct 04	2.74	Oct 03	2.80	Oct 02	2.71	Oct 07	2.72
12	2.79	11	2.73	10	2.80	09	2.70	14	2.72
19	2.78	18	2.73	17	2.80	16	2.70	21	2.72
26	2.78	25	2.73	24	2.80	23	2.70	28	2.73
				31	2.80	30	2.70		
Nov 02	2.79	Nov 01	2.73	Nov 07	2.80	Nov 06	2.69	Nov 04	2.73
09	2.78	08	2.72	14	2.79	13	2.71	11	2.73
16	2.76	15	2.72	21	2.80	20	2.71	18	2.73
23	2.74	22	2.72	28	2.80	27	2.72	25	2.72
30	2.73	29	2.72						
Dec 07	2.71	Dec 06	2.72	Dec 05	2.81	Dec 04	2.74	Dec 02	2.71
14	2.71	13	2.79	12	2.81	11	2.74	09	2.71
21	2.71	20	2.81	19	2.82	18	2.74	16	2.70
28	2.72	27	2.84	26	2.81	25	2.74	23	2.70
								30	2.70

AAA Corporate Bond Rates (continued)

1945		1946		1947		1948		1949	
Week Ended		Week Ended		Week Ended		Week Ended		Week Ended	
Jan 06	2.70%	Jan 05	2.58%	Jan 04	2.59%	Jan 03	2.90%*	Jan 01	2.76
13	2.70	12	2.57	11	2.58	10	2.85	08	2.74
20	2.69	19	2.54	18	2.57	17	2.85	15	2.71
27	2.69	26	2.52	25	2.56	24	2.85	22	2.70
						31	2.86	29	2.70
Feb 03	2.68	Feb 02	2.50	Feb 01	2.56	Feb 07	2.87	Feb 05	2.71
10	2.66	09	2.49	08	2.56	14	2.86	12	2.71
17	2.65	16	2.48	15	2.55	21	2.85	19	2.71
24	2.65	23	2.48	22	2.55	28	2.83	26	2.71
Mar 03	2.63	Mar 02	2.48	Mar 01	2.55	Mar 06	2.83	Mar 05	2.71
10	2.62	09	2.48	08	2.55	13	2.83	12	2.71
17	2.62	16	2.47	15	2.55	20	2.84	19	2.71
24	2.61	23	2.47	22	2.55	27	2.83	26	2.70
31	2.60	30	2.46	29	2.54				
Apr 07	2.61	Apr 06	2.46	Apr 05	2.53	Apr 03	2.81	Apr 02	2.70
14	2.61	13	2.46	12	2.53	10	2.79	09	2.70
21	2.61	20	2.46	19	2.53	17	2.78	16	2.70
28	2.61	27	2.48	26	2.53	24	2.78	23	2.70
								30	2.70
May 05	2.61	May 04	2.50	May 03	2.53	May 01	2.78	May 07	2.70
12	2.61	11	2.51	10	2.53	08	2.77	14	2.70
19	2.62	18	2.51	17	2.53	15	2.77	21	2.71
26	2.62	25	2.51	24	2.53	22	2.76	28	2.71
				31	2.53	29	2.75		
Jun 02	2.62	Jun 01	2.51	Jun 07	2.53	Jun 05	2.75	Jun 04	2.72
09	2.62	08	2.50	14	2.55	12	2.74	11	2.71
16	2.61	15	2.49	21	2.55	19	2.75	18	2.71
23	2.61	22	2.48	28	2.56	26	2.77	25	2.71
30	2.61	29	2.49						
Jul 07	2.60	Jul 06	2.49	Jul 05	2.56	Jul 03	2.79	Jul 02	2.70
14	2.60	13	2.48	12	2.55	10	2.80	09	2.69
21	2.60	20	2.49	19	2.55	17	2.80	16	2.67
28	2.60	27	2.49	26	2.55	24	2.82	23	2.65
						31	2.82	30	2.64
Aug 04	2.61	Aug 03	2.50	Aug 02	2.55	Aug 07	2.83	Aug 06	2.64
11	2.60	10	2.50	09	2.55	14	2.85	13	2.62
18	2.61	17	2.51	16	2.55	21	2.85	20	2.61
25	2.62	24	2.51	23	2.56	28	2.84	27	2.61
		31	2.51	30	2.56				
Sep 01	2.62	Sep 07	2.53	Sep 06	2.57	Sep 04	2.84	Sep 03	2.61
08	2.62	14	2.57	13	2.58	11	2.84	10	2.60
15	2.62	21	2.59	20	2.62	18	2.84	17	2.61
22	2.63	28	2.60	27	2.64	25	2.84	24	2.60
29	2.62								
Oct 06	2.61	Oct 05	2.59	Oct 04	2.68	Oct 02	2.83	Oct 01	2.61
13	2.61	12	2.60	11	2.69	09	2.84	08	2.61
20	2.62	19	2.60	18	2.71	16	2.83	15	2.61
27	2.62	26	2.60	25	2.71	23	2.84	22	2.61
						30	2.86	29	2.61
Nov 03	2.61	Nov 02	2.60	Nov 01	2.71	Nov 06	2.87	Nov 05	2.61
10	2.62	09	2.59	08	2.73	13	2.86	12	2.61
17	2.62	16	2.59	15	2.75	20	2.83	19	2.60
24	2.61	23	2.59	22	2.78	27	2.81	26	2.59
		30	2.60	29	2.83				
Dec 01	2.61	Dec 07	2.61	Dec 06	2.83	Dec 04	2.81	Dec 03	2.60
08	2.62	14	2.62	13	2.86	11	2.80	10	2.59
15	2.62	21	2.61	20	2.84	18	2.80	17	2.59
22	2.61	28	2.60	27	2.86	25	2.78	24	2.58
29	2.60							31	2.57

AAA Corporate Bond Rates (continued)

1950		*1951*		*1952*		*1953*		*1954*	
Week Ended		Week Ended		Week Ended		Week Ended		Week Ended	
Jan 07	2.57%	Jan 06	2.66%	Jan 05	3.03%	Jan 03	2.99%	Jan 02	3.12%
14	2.57	13	2.66	12	3.01	10	2.99	09	3.09
21	2.57	20	2.66	19	2.99	17	3.01	16	3.08
28	2.58	27	2.65	26	2.97	24	3.04	23	3.06
						31	3.05	30	3.03
Feb 04	2.58	Feb 03	2.66	Feb 02	2.95	Feb 07	3.05	Feb 06	2.99
11	2.58	10	2.66	09	2.93	14	3.06	13	2.94
18	2.58	17	2.65	16	2.91	21	3.08	20	2.93
25	2.58	24	2.66	23	2.93	28	3.09	27	2.92
Mar 04	2.58	Mar 03	2.69	Mar 01	2.95	Mar 07	3.11	Mar 06	2.89
11	2.58	10	2.73	08	2.96	14	3.10	13	2.86
18	2.59	17	2.78	15	2.97	21	3.12	20	2.85
25	2.59	24	2.80	22	2.97	28	3.14	27	2.85
		31	2.83	29	2.96				
Apr 01	2.59	Apr 07	2.87	Apr 05	2.95	Apr 04	3.18	Apr 03	2.85
08	2.59	14	2.87	12	2.94	11	3.19	10	2.85
15	2.59	21	2.87	19	2.93	18	3.22	17	2.85
22	2.60	28	2.89	26	2.93	25	3.25	24	2.85
29	2.60								
May 06	2.60	May 05	2.88	May 03	2.92	May 02	3.28	May 01	2.87
13	2.61	12	2.88	10	2.93	09	3.33	08	2.87
20	2.61	19	2.89	17	2.92	16	3.35	15	2.87
27	2.62	26	2.89	24	2.93	23	3.35	22	2.87
				31	2.93	30	3.35	29	2.89
Jun 03	2.62	Jun 02	2.89	Jun 07	2.93	Jun 06	3.39	Jun 05	2.91
10	2.62	09	2.90	14	2.93	13	3.41	12	2.91
17	2.62	16	2.92*	21	2.94	20	3.42	19	2.90
24	2.61	23	2.96	28	2.93	27	3.41	26	2.90
		30	2.99						
Jul 01	2.63	Jul 07	2.97	Jul 05	2.94	Jul 04	3.36	Jul 03	2.90
08	2.65	14	2.95	12	2.95	11	3.31	10	2.90
15	2.66	21	2.93	19	2.95	18	3.28	17	2.89
22	2.66	28	2.92	26	2.95	25	3.26	24	2.88
29	2.65							31	2.88
Aug 05	2.62	Aug 04	2.91	Aug 02	2.94	Aug 01	3.24	Aug 07	2.87
12	2.61	11	2.89	09	2.95	08	3.22	14	2.87
19	2.61	18	2.87	16	2.94	15	3.22	21	2.86
26	2.61	25	2.86	23	2.95	22	3.24	28	2.87
				30	2.95	29	3.26		
Sep 02	2.61	Sep 01	2.85	Sep 06	2.94	Sep 05	3.29	Sep 04	2.88
09	2.62	08	2.84	13	2.94	12	3.30	11	2.89
16	2.64	15	2.84	20	2.95	19	3.31	18	2.89
23	2.67	22	2.83	27	2.97	26	3.30	25	2.89
30	2.66	29	2.83						
Oct 07	2.66	Oct 06	2.86	Oct 04	2.99	Oct 03	3.24	Oct 02	2.89
14	2.66	13	2.87	11	3.01	10	3.19	09	2.88
21	2.67	20	2.88	18	3.02	17	3.16	16	2.88
28	2.68	27	2.92	25	3.02	24	3.14	23	2.87
						31	3.12	30	2.87
Nov 04	2.68	Nov 03	2.95	Nov 01	3.01	Nov 07	3.09	Nov 06	2.88
11	2.67	10	2.96	08	3.00	14	3.10	13	2.89
18	2.66	17	2.96	15	2.98	21	3.13	20	2.89
25	2.66	24	2.97	22	2.98	28	3.13	27	2.88
				29	2.97				
Dec 02	2.67	Dec 01	2.97	Dec 06	2.97	Dec 05	3.14	Dec 04	2.89
09	2.68	08	2.99	13	2.96	12	3.13	11	2.89
16	2.67	15	3.00	20	2.98	19	3.12	18	2.90
23	2.67	22	3.01	27	2.98	26	3.12	25	2.91
30	2.66	29	3.03						

AAA Corporate Bond Rates (continued)

1955		*1956*		*1957*		*1958*		*1959*	
Week Ended		Week Ended		Week Ended		Week Ended		Week Ended	
Jan 01	2.92%	Jan 07	3.14%	Jan 05	3.82%	Jan 04	3.68%	Jan 03	4.10%
08	2.91	14	3.13	12	3.81	11	3.65	10	4.09
15	2.92	21	3.11	19	3.78	18	3.61	17	4.11
22	2.93	28	3.09	26	3.73	25	3.57	24	4.12
29	2.94							31	4.16*
Feb 05	2.97	Feb 04	3.09	Feb 02	3.72	Feb 01	3.56	Feb 07	4.15
12	2.97	11	3.08	09	3.69	08	3.59	14	4.14
19	2.99	18	3.07	16	3.67	15	3.59	21	4.14
26	3.02	25	3.07	23	3.66	22	3.58	28	4.13
Mar 05	3.03	Mar 03	3.07	Mar 02	3.66	Mar 01	3.60	Mar 07	4.11
12	3.04	10	3.08	09	3.66	08	3.62	14	4.13
19	3.03	17	3.10	16	3.66	15	3.62	21	4.13
26	3.01	24	3.12	23	3.67	22	3.63	28	4.14
		31	3.14	30	3.66	29	3.64		
Apr 02	3.01	Apr 07	3.16	Apr 06	3.66	Apr 05	3.64	Apr 04	4.17
09	3.01	14	3.21	13	3.66	12	3.62	11	4.20
16	3.01	21	3.27	20	3.67	19	3.61	18	4.22
23	3.01	28	3.30	27	3.69	26	3.57	25	4.26
30	3.01								
May 07	3.02	May 05	3.30	May 04	3.71	May 03	3.55	May 02	4.30
14	3.04	12	3.27	11	3.72	10	3.57	09	4.33
21	3.04	19	3.27	18	3.73	17	3.57	16	4.36
28	3.05	26	3.27	25	3.75	24	3.57	23	4.39
						31	3.57	30	4.42
Jun 04	3.05	Jun 02	3.27	Jun 01	3.79	Jun 07	3.56	Jun 06	4.44
11	3.04	09	3.27	08	3.82	14	3.56	13	4.47
18	3.05	16	3.26	15	3.88	21	3.57	20	4.46
25	3.05	23	3.26	22	3.94	28	3.61	27	4.47
		30	3.27	29	3.97				
Jul 02	3.05	Jul 07	3.26	Jul 06	4.00	Jul 05	3.62	Jul 04	4.48
09	3.05	14	3.27	13	3.97	12	3.63	11	4.48
16	3.05	21	3.28	20	3.98	19	3.67	18	4.47
23	3.05	28	3.30	27	4.01	26	3.70	25	4.46
30	3.07								
Aug 06	3.09	Aug 04	3.35	Aug 03	4.05	Aug 02	3.71	Aug 01	4.45
13	3.10	11	3.38	10	4.07	09	3.77	08	4.43
20	3.12	18	3.42	17	4.09	16	3.83	15	4.42
27	3.12	25	3.47*	24	4.11	23	3.89	22	4.42
				31	4.12	30	3.94	29	4.44
Sep 03	3.13	Sep 01	3.49	Sep 07	4.12	Sep 06	4.03	Sep 05	4.47
10	3.14	08	3.53	14	4.11	13	4.07	12	4.49
17	3.13	15	3.55	21	4.12	20	4.10	19	4.52
24	3.13	22	3.56	28	4.14	27	4.11	26	4.54
		29	3.58						
Oct 01	3.12	Oct 06	3.58	Oct 05	4.12	Oct 04	4.13	Oct 03	4.57
08	3.12	13	3.57	12	4.09	11	4.13	10	4.57
15	3.11	20	3.57	19	4.07	18	4.09	17	4.56
22	3.10	27	3.61	26	4.11	25	4.10	24	4.56
29	3.10							31	4.56
Nov 05	3.10	Nov 03	3.65	Nov 02	4.12	Nov 01	4.12	Nov 07	4.57
12	3.08	10	3.66	09	4.12	08	4.11	14	4.57
19	3.08	17	3.67	16	4.12	15	4.10	21	4.57
26	3.11	24	3.71	23	4.06	22	4.08	28	4.55
				30	4.02	29	4.07		
Dec 03	3.12	Dec 01	3.73	Dec 07	3.97	Dec 06	4.06	Dec 05	4.55
10	3.13	08	3.72	14	3.84	13	4.06	12	4.56
17	3.17	15	3.72	21	3.77	20	4.07	19	4.59
24	3.17	22	3.76	28	3.73	27	4.09	26	4.59
31	3.16	29	3.79						

AAA Corporate Bond Rates (continued)

1960 Week Ended		1961 Week Ended		1962 Week Ended		1963 Week Ended		1964 Week Ended	
Jan 02	4.61%	Jan 07	4.34%	Jan 06	4.43%	Jan 05	4.22%	Jan 04	4.37%
09	4.61	14	4.33	13	4.42	12	4.21	11	4.37
16	4.61	21	4.32	20	4.42	19	4.20	18	4.38
23	4.61	28	4.31	27	4.41	26	4.21	25	4.38
30	4.61								
Feb 06	4.60	Feb 04	4.30	Feb 03	4.42	Feb 02	4.21	Feb 01	4.37
13	4.57	11	4.38	10	4.42	09	4.19	08	4.36
20	4.54	18	4.27	17	4.43	16	4.19	15	4.36
27	4.54	25	4.25	24	4.42	23	4.19	22	4.36
								29	4.35
Mar 05	4.54	Mar 04	4.23	Mar 03	4.42	Mar 02	4.19	Mar 07	4.36
12	4.51	11	4.22	10	4.40	09	4.19	14	4.37
19	4.48	18	4.21	17	4.39	16	4.19	21	4.38
26	4.46	25	4.22	24	4.39	23	4.19	28	4.39
				31	4.38	30	4.19		
Apr 02	4.45	Apr 01	4.22	Apr 07	4.37	Apr 06	4.20	Apr 04	4.40
09	4.44	08	4.23	14	4.34	13	4.20	11	4.40
16	4.45	15	4.24	21	4.33	20	4.21	18	4.40
23	4.45	22	4.26	28	4.31	27	4.22	25	4.41
30	4.46	29	4.28						
May 07	4.46	May 06	4.29	May 05	4.30	May 04	4.22	May 02	4.41
14	4.45	13	4.27	12	4.29	11	4.22	09	4.41
21	4.46	20	4.25	19	4.28	18	4.21	16	4.41
28	4.47	27	4.27	26	4.27	25	4.22	23	4.41
								30	4.41
Jun 04	4.48	Jun 03	4.29	Jun 02	4.28	Jun 01	4.23	Jun 06	4.41
11	4.44	10	4.31	09	4.28	08	4.23	13	4.41
18	4.45	17	4.33	16	4.28	15	4.23	20	4.41
25	4.45	24	4.34	23	4.29	22	4.22	27	4.41
				30	4.29	29	4.22		
Jul 02	4.44	Jul 01	4.36	Jul 07	4.32	Jul 06	4.23	Jul 04	4.40
09	4.44	08	4.39	14	4.34	13	4.24	11	4.40
16	4.43	15	4.41	21	4.33	20	4.27	18	4.41
23	4.40	22	4.41	28	4.35	27	4.29	25	4.40
30	4.38	29	4.42						
Aug 06	4.34	Aug 05	4.45	Aug 04	4.37	Aug 03	4.29	Aug 01	4.40
13	4.30	12	4.45	11	4.36	10	4.29	08	4.41
20	4.26	19	4.45	18	4.36	17	4.29	15	4.42
27	4.23	26	4.44	25	4.34	24	4.29	22	4.41
						31	4.29	29	4.41
Sep 03	4.23	Sep 02	4.44	Sep 01	4.33	Sep 07	4.30	Sep 05	4.42
10	4.23	09	4.46	08	4.33	14	4.31	12	4.42
17	4.26	16	4.46	15	4.32	21	4.32	19	4.42
24	4.26	23	4.45	22	4.31	28	4.32	26	4.42
		30	4.45	29	4.31				
Oct 01	4.27	Oct 07	4.43	Oct 06	4.29	Oct 05	4.32	Oct 03	4.42
08	4.28	14	4.42	13	4.28	12	4.31	10	4.43
15	4.29	21	4.42	20	4.27	19	4.31	17	4.42
22	4.31	28	4.42	27	4.27	26	4.32	24	4.42
29	4.30							31	4.43
Nov 05	4.30	Nov 04	4.40	Nov 03	4.26	Nov 02	4.32	Nov 07	4.43
12	4.29	11	4.39	10	4.25	09	4.33	14	4.43
19	4.30	18	4.39	17	4.25	16	4.33	21	4.42
26	4.32	25	4.39	24	4.24	23	4.33	28	4.44
						30	4.33		
Dec 03	4.33	Dec 02	4.38	Dec 01	4.25	Dec 07	4.33	Dec 05	4.45
10	4.35	09	4.39	08	4.26	14	4.34	12	4.45
17	4.34	16	4.42	15	4.25	21	4.36	19	4.43
24	4.34	23	4.44	22	4.24	28	4.37	26	4.43
31	4.35	30	4.44	29	4.23				

AAA Corporate Bond Rates (continued)

1965		1966		1967		1968		1969	
Week Ended		Week Ended		Week Ended		Week Ended		Week Ended	
Jan 02	4.43%	Jan 01	4.73%	Jan 07	5.38%	Jan 06	6.24	Jan 04	6.55
09	4.44	08	4.73	14	5.32	13	6.20	11	6.58
16	4.43	15	4.74	21	5.15	20	6.14	18	6.59
23	4.43	22	4.74	28	5.04	27	6.12	25	6.59
30	4.42	29	4.74						
Feb 06	4.41	Feb 05	4.75	Feb 04	5.02	Feb 03	6.12	Feb 01	6.59
13	4.41	12	4.76	11	5.00	10	6.11	08	6.63
20	4.41	19	4.79	18	5.01	17	6.10	15	6.66
27	4.41	26	4.82	25	5.05	24	6.09	22	6.66
Mar 06	4.41	Mar 05	4.85	Mar 04	5.11	Mar 02	6.09	Mar 01	6.68
13	4.41	12	4.88	11	5.12	09	6.07	08	6.72
20	4.42	19	4.93	18	5.13	16	6.08	15	6.75
27	4.43	26	4.97	25	5.13	23	6.13	22	6.94
						30	6.17	29	6.99
Apr 03	4.42	Apr 02	4.99	Apr 01	5.12	Apr 06	6.20	Apr 05	6.99
10	4.42	09	4.98	08	5.11	13	6.19	12	6.97
17	4.43	16	4.95	15	5.12	20	6.20	19	6.88
24	4.43	23	4.95	22	5.11	27	6.22	26	6.81
		30	4.95	29	5.11				
May 01	4.43	May 07	4.94	May 06	5.16	May 04	6.25	May 03	6.80
08	4.43	14	4.95	13	5.19	11	6.25	10	6.79
15	4.45	21	5.01	20	5.26	18	6.27	17	6.75
22	4.43	28	5.02	27	5.31	25	6.28	24	6.78
29	4.44							31	6.83
Jun 05	4.45	Jun 04	5.04	Jun 03	5.36	Jun 01	6.29	Jun 07	6.90
12	4.46	11	5.06	10	5.38	08	6.29	14	6.96
19	4.47	18	5.06	17	5.39	15	6.28	21	7.03
26	4.47	25	5.07	24	5.45	22	6.29	28	7.03
						29	6.27		
Jul 03	4.46	Jul 02	5.10	Jul 01	5.56*	Jul 06	6.27	Jul 05	7.03
10	4.47	09	5.12	08	5.59	13	6.27	12	7.08
17	4.48	16	5.14	15	5.59	20	6.26	19	7.10
24	4.48	23	5.17	22	5.56	27	6.22	26	7.10
31	4.48	30	5.22	29	5.57		.		
Aug 07	4.47	Aug 06	5.24	Aug 05	5.59	Aug 03	6.14	Aug 02	7.05
14	4.48	13	5.25	12	5.58	10	6.07	09	7.00
21	4.50	20	5.31	19	5.62	17	6.00	16	6.96
28	4.51	27	5.37	26	5.65	24	5.98	23	6.95
						31	5.97	30	6.98
Sep 04	4.51	Sep 03	5.44	Sep 02	5.68	Sep 07	5.95	Sep 06	7.05
11	4.52	10	5.52	09	5.66	14	5.95	13	7.12
18	4.52	17	5.51	16	5.65	21	5.98	20	7.16
25	4.52	24	5.49	23	5.64	28	6.00	27	7.19
				30	5.66				
Oct 02	4.53	Oct 01	5.47	Oct 07	5.72	Oct 05	6.02	Oct 04	7.28
09	4.57	08	5.44	14	5.76	12	6.06	11	7.37
16	4.57	15	5.43	21	5.83	19	6.10	18	7.39
23	4.57	22	5.40	28	5.90	26	6.13	25	7.31
30	4.57	29	5.37						
Nov 06	4.58	Nov 05	5.35	Nov 04	5.95	Nov 02	6.15	Nov 01	7.25
13	4.60	12	5.35	11	6.02	09	6.16	08	7.26
20	4.61	19	5.36	18	6.10	16	6.15	15	7.29
27	4.61	26	5.36	25	6.08	23	6.17	22	7.38
						30	6.28	29	7.50
Dec 04	4.60	Dec 03	5.37	Dec 02	6.13	Dec 07	6.33	Dec 06	7.60
11	4.64*	10	5.38	09	6.14	14	6.45	13	7.64
18	4.69	17	5.38	16	6.16	21	6.48	20	7.73
25	4.71	24	5.39	23	6.22	28	6.53	27	7.84
		31	5.40	30	6.24				

220   Appendix B

AAA Corporate Bond Rates (continued)

	1970		1971		1972		1973		1974
Week Ended		**Week Ended**		**Week Ended**		**Week Ended**		**Week Ended**	
Jan 03	7.90%	Jan 02	7.48%	Jan 01	7.22%	Jan 06	7.11%	Jan 05	7.73%
10	7.91	09	7.45	08	7.19	13	7.12	12	7.77
17	7.92	16	7.42	15	7.17	20	7.15	19	7.85
24	7.90	23	7.36	22	7.16	27	7.18	26	7.88
31	7.91	30	7.19	29	7.22				
Feb 07	7.97	Feb 06	7.10	Feb 05	7.25	Feb 03	7.20	Feb 02	7.87
14	7.97	13	7.06	12	7.29	10	7.22	09	7.82
21	7.93	20	7.07	19	7.28	17	7.23	16	7.85
28	7.83	27	7.10	26	7.26	24	7.22	23	7.87
Mar 07	7.79	Mar 06	7.13	Mar 04	7.25	Mar 03	7.25	Mar 02	7.87
14	7.80	13	7.20	11	7.24	10	7.27	09	7.92
21	7.88	20	7.26	18	7.22	17	7.29	16	7.99
28	7.92	27	7.25	25	7.24	24	7.31	23	8.05
						31	7.31	30	8.11
Apr 04	7.85	Apr 03	7.22	Apr 01	7.24	Apr 07	7.27	Apr 06	8.17
11	7.80	10	7.23	08	7.25	14	7.25	13	8.25
18	7.82	17	7.24	15	7.28	21	7.25	20	8.26
25	7.83	24	7.24	22	7.33	28	7.27	27	8.28
				29	7.36				
May 02	7.92	May 01	7.30	May 06	7.34	May 05	7.26	May 04	8.34
09	7.99	08	7.43	13	7.33	12	7.26	11	8.38
16	8.09	15	7.48	20	7.30	19	7.29	18	8.36
23	8.16	22	7.57	27	7.27	26	7.32	25	8.38
30	8.21	29	7.66						
Jun 06	8.30	Jun 05	7.69	Jun 03	7.23	Jun 02	7.35	Jun 01	8.39
13	8.42	12	7.66	10	7.24	09	7.36	08	8.40
20	8.55	19	7.63	17	7.25	16	7.36	15	8.40
27	8.60	26	7.62	24	7.23	23	7.38	22	8.49
						30	7.40	29	8.57
Jul 04	8.60	Jul 03	7.63	Jul 01	7.21	Jul 07	7.41	Jul 06	8.62 *
11	8.55	10	7.65	08	7.20	14	7.44	13	8.66
18	8.49	17	7.64	15	7.20	21	7.45	20	8.71
25	8.40	24	7.63	22	7.20	28	7.48	27	8.77
		31	7.66	29	7.22				
Aug 01	8.26	Aug 07	7.69	Aug 05	7.22	Aug 04	7.53	Aug 03	8.86
08	8.17	14	7.71	12	7.20	11	7.61	10	8.93
15	8.10	21	7.49	19	7.19	18	7.71	17	8.98
22	8.12	28	7.50	26	7.17	25	7.77	24	9.03
29	8.13							31	9.07
Sep 05	8.13	Sep 04	7.45	Sep 02	7.19	Sep 01	7.73	Sep 07	9.13
12	8.13	11	7.42	09	7.19	08	7.64	14	9.20
19	8.09	18	7.44	16	7.23	15	7.63	21	9.29
26	8.06	25	7.44	23	7.23	22	7.65	28	9.32
				30	7.24	29	7.60		
Oct 03	8.05	Oct 02	7.46	Oct 07	7.23	Oct 06	7.59	Oct 05	9.37
10	8.02	09	7.44	14	7.22	13	7.56	12	9.38
17	8.01	16	7.42	21	7.21	20	7.58	19	9.29
24	8.03	23	7.37	28	7.19	27	7.64	26	9.19
31	8.07	30	7.31						
Nov 07	8.09	Nov 06	7.25	Nov 04	7.18	Nov 03	7.65	Nov 02	9.09
14	8.07	13	7.24	11	7.16	10	7.67	09	8.99
21	8.05	20	7.27	18	7.12	17	7.69	16	8.89
28	8.02	27	7.28	25	7.09	24	7.68	23	8.84
								30	8.84
Dec 04	7.85	Dec 04	7.28	Dec 02	7.07	Dec 01	7.64	Dec 07	8.90
11	7.78	11	7.27	09	7.05	08	7.65	14	8.87
18	7.59	18	7.24	16	7.08	15	7.67	21	8.85
25	7.51	25	7.23	23	7.10	22	7.68	28	8.90
				30	7.11	29	7.73		

AAA *Corporate Bond Rates (continued)*

1975		*1976*		*1977*		*1978*		*1979*	
Week Ended		Week Ended		Week Ended		Week Ended		Week Ended	
Jan 04	8.93%	Jan 03	8.66%	Jan 08	7.88%	Jan 07	8.30%	Jan 06	9.26%
11	8.91	10	8.63	15	7.94	14	8.40	13	9.26
18	8.84	17	8.60	22	7.99	21	8.44	20	9.28
25	8.78	24	8.58	29	8.01	28	8.47	27	9.24
		31	8.57						
Feb 01	8.74	Feb 07	8.56	Feb 05	8.03	Feb 04	8.46	Feb 03	9.19
08	8.68	14	8.57	12	8.01	11	8.46	10	9.23
15	8.63	21	8.56	19	8.04	18	8.47	17	9.25
22	8.58	28	8.51	26	8.04	25	8.49	24	9.28
Mar 01	8.57	Mar 06	8.55	Mar 05	8.10	Mar 04	8.49	Mar 03	9.36
08	8.59	13	8.55	12	8.12	11	8.48	10	9.35
15	8.61	20	8.54	19	8.09	18	8.45	17	9.38
22	8.69	27	8.50	26	8.09	25	8.45	24	9.38
29	8.78							31	9.38
Apr 05	8.87	Apr 03	8.46	Apr 02	8.10	Apr 01	8.48	Apr 07	9.31
12	8.94	10	8.42	09	8.10	08	8.53	14	9.37
19	8.95	17	8.36	16	8.05	15	8.56	21	9.39*
26	8.97	24	8.36	23	7.99	22	8.57	28	9.44
				30	8.01	29	8.59		
May 03	9.01	May 01	8.41	May 07	8.04	May 06	8.62	May 05	9.51
10	8.96	08	8.48	14	8.07	13	8.65	12	9.52
17	8.88	15	8.56	21	8.06	20	8.69	19	9.51
24	8.85	22	8.62	28	8.04	27	8.76	26	9.49
31	8.89	29	8.65						
Jun 07	8.85	Jun 05	8.63	Jun 04	8.00	Jun 03	8.79	Jun 02	9.48
14	8.76	12	8.63	11	7.98	10	8.74	09	9.41
21	8.73	19	8.61	18	7.94	17	8.72	16	9.25
28	8.75	26	8.60	25	7.94	24	8.76	23	9.23
								30	9.23
Jul 05	8.82	Jul 03	8.63	Jul 02	7.91	Jul 01	8.82	Jul 07	9.16
12	8.84	10	8.57	09	7.93	08	8.85	14	9.17
19	8.82	17	8.53	16	7.94	15	8.90	21	9.19
26	8.85	24	8.55	23	7.94	22	8.89	28	9.23
		31	8.55	30	7.96	29	8.88		
Aug 02	8.86	Aug 07	8.51	Aug 06	8.00	Aug 05	8.76	Aug 04	9.24
09	8.93	14	8.48	13	8.00	12	8.66	11	9.20
16	8.95	21	8.42	20	7.99	19	8.70	18	9.20
23	8.96	28	8.43	27	7.96	26	8.69	25	9.23
30	8.96								
Sep 06	8.93	Sep 04	8.41	Sep 03	7.92	Sep 02	8.67	Sep 01	9.30
13	8.94	11	8.38	10	7.90	09	8.67	08	9.34
20	8.98	18	8.39	17	7.89	16	8.63	15	9.42
27	8.94	25	8.36	24	7.92	23	8.70	22	9.49
						30	8.77	29	9.50
Oct 04	8.96	Oct 02	8.37	Oct 01	7.96	Oct 07	8.81	Oct 06	9.66
11	8.93	09	8.33	08	7.99	14	8.85	13	9.91
18	8.86	16	8.30	15	8.04	21	8.88	20	10.09
25	8.81	23	8.31	22	8.05	28	8.94	27	10.50
		30	8.33	29	8.06				
Nov 01	8.77	Nov 06	8.30	Nov 05	8.08	Nov 04	9.04	Nov 03	10.73
08	8.76	13	8.31	12	8.10	11	9.06	10	10.83
15	8.75	20	8.27	19	8.08	18	9.02	17	10.75
22	8.81	27	8.17	26	8.07	25	9.00	24	10.83
29	8.81								
Dec 06	8.83	Dec 04	8.09	Dec 03	8.08	Dec 02	9.04	Dec 01	10.63
13	8.86	11	8.01	10	8.13	09	9.06	08	10.58
20	8.81	18	8.00	17	8.18	16	9.12	15	10.70
27	8.72	24	7.96	24	8.23	23	9.24	22	10.79
		31	7.91	31	8.28	30	9.27	29	10.87

AAA Corporate Bond Rates (continued)

1980		*1981*		*1982*		*1983*	
Week Ended		Week Ended		Week Ended		Week Ended	
Jan 05	10.88%	Jan 02	12.83%	Jan 01	14.50%	Jan 07	11.77%
12	10.91	09	12.59	08	14.81	14	11.70
19	10.99	16	12.76	15	15.29	21	11.70
26	11.22	23	12.91	22	15.36	28	11.94
		30	12.98	29	15.27		
Feb 02	11.49	Feb 06	13.07	Feb 05	15.34	Feb 04	12.06
09	11.95	13	13.41	12	15.49	11	12.11
16	12.19	20	13.51	19	15.34	18	12.08
23	12.74	27	13.45	26	14.92	25	11.82
Mar 01	12.88	Mar 06	13.61	Mar 05	14.61	Mar 04	11.63
08	13.00	13	13.31	12	14.55	11	11.72
15	13.00	20	13.06	19	14.55	18	11.79
22	12.83	27	13.32	26	14.53	25	11.76
29	13.00						
Apr 05	12.95	Apr 03	13.41	Apr 02	14.66	Apr 01	11.75
12	12.57	10	13.72	09	14.68	08	11.66
19	11.87	17	13.89	16	14.53	15	11.51
26	11.51	24	14.02	23	14.31	22	11.46
				30	14.31	29	11.43
May 03	11.38	May 01	14.26	May 07	14.36	May 06	11.29
10	10.93	08	14.50	14	14.22	13	11.29
17	10.96	15	14.53	21	14.23	20	11.54
24	11.02	22	14.18	28	14.21	27	11.67
31	10.90	29	14.00				
Jun 07*	10.88	Jun 05	13.84	Jun 04	14.50	Jun 03	11.76
13	10.53	12	13.76	11	14.62	10	11.77
20	10.34	19	13.61	18	14.79	17	11.66
27	10.53	26	13.77	24	15.10	24	11.71
Jul 04	10.84	Jul 03	14.04	Jul 02	15.07	Jul 01	11.85
11	10.94	10	14.19	09	14.96	08	12.02
18	11.09	17	14.25	16	14.65	15	12.13
25	11.11	24	14.55	23	14.32	22	12.17
		31	14.61	30	14.39	29	12.31
Aug 01	11.33	Aug 07	14.82	Aug 06	14.22	Aug 05	12.62
08	11.44	14	14.62	13	14.14	12	12.71
15	11.57	21	14.78	20	13.48	19	12.40
22	11.70	28	15.21	27	13.15	26	12.32
29	11.88						
Sep 05	11.88	Sep 04	15.50	Sep 03	13.20	Sep 02	12.54
12	11.90	11	15.61	10	13.03	09	12.47
19	12.00	18	15.30	17	13.08	16	12.40
26	12.15	25	15.35	24	12.83	23	12.31
						30	12.22
Oct 03	12.30	Oct 02	15.85	Oct 01	12.66	Oct 07	12.20
10	12.18	09	15.40	08	12.49	14	12.22
17	12.11	16	15.18	15	11.94	21	12.21
24	12.27	23	15.36	22	11.95	28	12.34
31	12.72	30	15.51	29	12.00		
Nov 07	12.96	Nov 06	14.88	Nov 05	11.68	Nov 04	12.42
14	12.93	13	14.18	12	11.62	11	12.47
21	12.96	20	13.91	19	11.70	18	12.42
28	13.03*	27	13.92	26	11.67	25	12.36
Dec 05	13.15	Dec 04	13.99	Dec 03	11.83	Dec 02	12.39
12	13.47	11	14.16	10	11.79	09	12.51
19	13.49	18	14.11	17	11.82	16	12.66
26	12.89	25	14.36	24	11.91	23	12.61
				31	11.82	30	12.56

*Beginning here, week ending is on Friday.

AAA Corporate Bond Rates (continued)

1984		1985		1986	
Week Ended		Week Ended		Week Ended	
Jan 06	12.53%	Jan 04	12.21%	Jan 03	9.92%
13	12.43	11	12.16	10	9.95
20	12.01	18	12.20	17	10.18
27	11.98	25	11.97	24	10.13
				31	10.00
Feb 03	11.94	Feb 01	11.85	Feb 07	9.90
10	11.96	08	11.95	11	9.84
17	12.06	15	12.01	21	9.64
24	12.22	22	12.21	28	9.29
Mar 02	12.30	Mar 01	12.47	Mar 07	9.08
09	12.46	08	12.55	14	8.98
16	12.58	15	12.58	21	9.03
23	12.65	22	12.64	28	8.94
30	12.71	29	12.50		
Apr 06	12.74	Apr 05	12.44	Apr 04	8.74
13	12.71	12	12.46	11	8.75
20	12.79	19	12.09	18	8.66
27	12.95	26	12.09	25	8.90
May 04	13.00	May 03	12.15	May 02	8.97
11	13.15	10	12.03	09	8.98
18	13.33	17	11.77	16	9.12
25	13.42	24	11.50	23	9.17
		31	11.27	30	9.14
Jun 01	13.56	Jun 07	10.93	Jun 06	9.29
08	13.46	14	10.88	13	9.19
15	13.48	21	10.86	20	9.08
22	13.55	28	11.09	27	9.01
29	13.71				

AAA Corporate Bond Rates (continued)

	1984		*1985*		*1986*
Week Ended		Week Ended		Week Ended	
Jul 06	13.69	Jul 05	10.91	Jul 04	8.93
13	13.53	12	10.85	11	8.89
20	13.36	19	10.87	18	8.84
27	13.32	26	11.07	25	8.86
Aug 03	13.05	Aug 02	11.21	Aug 01	8.88
10	12.84	09	11.20	08	8.85
17	12.86	16	11.08	15	8.74
24	12.85	23	10.95	22	8.66
31	12.88	30	10.90	29	8.62
Sep 07	12.87	Sep 06	10.94	Sep 05	8.74
14	12.72	13	11.13	12	8.85
21	12.52	20	11.11	19	8.95
28	12.56	27	11.05	26	8.97
Oct 05	12.62	Oct 04	11.07	Oct 03	8.90
12	12.52	11	11.12	10	8.86
19	12.51	18	11.03	17	8.88
26	12.54	25	10.94	24	8.89
				31	8.80
Nov 02	12.50	Nov 01	10.87	Nov 07	8.73
09	12.43	08	10.67	14	8.77
16	12.42	15	10.56	21	8.65
23	12.20	22	10.47	28	8.55
30	12.05	29	10.43		
Dec 07	12.20	Dec 06	10.43	Dec 05	8.52
14	12.21	13	10.26	12	8.48
21	12.04	20	10.04	19	8.51
28	12.05	27	9.97	26	8.47

AAA Corporate Bond Rates (continued)

1987 Week Ended		*1988* Week Ended		*1989* Week Ended	
Jan 02	8.49%	Jan 01	10.06%	Jan 06	9.66%
09	8.40	08	10.00	13	9.69
16	8.33	15	10.00	20	9.61
23	8.31	22	9.88	27	9.56
30	8.37	29	9.64		
Feb 06	8.38	Feb 05	9.46	Feb 03	9.56
13	8.40	12	9.42	10	9.56
20	8.40	19	9.41	17	9.65
27	8.36	26	9.33	24	9.70
Mar 06	8.34	Mar 04	9.27	Mar 03	9.75
13	8.36	11	9.34	10	9.73
20	8.36	18	9.36	17	9.79
27	8.36	25	9.44	24	9.85
				31	9.88
Apr 03	8.50	Apr 01	9.53	Apr 07	9.81
10	8.56	08	9.61	14	9.80
17	8.82	15	9.61	21	9.80
24	9.07	22	9.73	28	9.75
		29	9.73		
May 01	9.21	May 06	9.78	May 05	9.73
08	9.21	13	9.85	12	9.69
15	9.25	20	9.94	19	9.54
22	9.49	27	10.01	26	9.41
29	9.40				
Jun 05	9.38	Jun 03	10.00	Jun 02	9.37
12	9.36	10	9.93	09	9.16
19	9.29	17	9.80	16	9.02
26	9.25	24	9.79	23	9.09
				30	9.02

AAA Corporate Bond Rates (continued)

	1987			*1988*			*1989*	
Week Ended			Week Ended			Week Ended		
Jul 03	9.33		Jul 01	9.82		Jul 07	8.97	
10	9.31		08	9.84		14	8.94	
17	9.36		15	9.95		21	8.93	
24	9.46		22	10.03		28	8.91	
31	9.56		29	10.03				
Aug 07	9.65		Aug 05	10.00		Aug 04	8.81	
14	9.63		12	10.10		11	8.92	
21	9.68		19	10.15		18	8.99	
28	9.70		26	10.16		25	9.02	
Sep 04	9.87		Sep 02	10.14		Sep 01	9.05	
11	10.15		09	9.95		08	9.02	
18	10.28		16	9.84		15	8.98	
25	10.25		23	9.73		22	8.98	
			30	9.67		29	9.03	
Oct 02	10.34		Oct 07	9.58		Oct 06	9.02	
09	10.48		14	9.54		13	8.95	
16	10.73		21	9.49		20	8.88	
23	10.68		28	9.44		27	8.85	
30	10.25							
Nov 06	10.08		Nov 04	9.39		Nov 03	8.91	
13	9.97		11	9.38		10	8.90	
20	9.97		18	9.45		17	8.86	
27	10.01		25	9.52		24	8.89	
Dec 04	10.06		Dec 02	9.55		Dec 01	8.88	
11	10.14		09	9.52				
18	10.19		16	9.57				
25	10.08		23	9.59				
			30	9.60				

APPENDIX C

Prime Banker's Acceptances—90-Day—1919–1946

1919		1920		1921		1922		1923	
Week Ended		Week Ended		Week Ended		Week Ended		Week Ended	
Jan 04	4.22%	Jan 03	5.31%	Jan 01	6.25%	Jan 07	4.13	Jan 06	4.00%
11	4.22	10	5.31	08	6.19	14	3.94	13	4.00
18	4.28	17	5.19	15	6.00	21	3.75	20	4.00
25	4.28	24	5.25	22	5.81	28	4.00	27	4.00
		31	5.31	29	5.81				
Feb 01	4.28	Feb 07	5.63	Feb 05	6.06	Feb 04	4.00	Feb 03	3.94
08	4.28	14	5.63	12	6.06	11	4.00	10	3.94
15	4.28	21	5.63	19	6.06	18	4.00	17	4.00
22	4.28	28	5.63	26	5.94	25	4.00	24	4.00
Mar 01	4.28	Mar 06	6.00	Mar 05	5.94	Mar 04	4.00	Mar 03	4.00
08	4.28	13	6.00	12	6.06	11	4.00	10	4.00
15	4.28	20	6.06	19	6.06	18	3.88	17	4.00
22	4.28	27	6.00	26	6.06	25	3.50	24	4.00
29	4.28							31	4.00
Apr 05	4.28	Apr 03	6.19	Apr 02	6.00	Apr 01	3.50	Apr 07	4.00
12	4.28	10	6.00	09	5.75	08	3.38	14	4.00
19	4.28	17	6.00	16	5.81	15	3.38	21	4.25*
26	4.28	24	6.00	23	5.81	22	3.31	28	4.19
				30	5.69	29	3.25		
May 03	4.28	May 01	6.00	May 07	5.81	May 06	3.25	May 05	4.13
10	4.28	08	6.00	14	5.69	13	3.13	12	4.13
17	4.28	15	6.13	21	5.75	20	3.13	19	4.13
24	4.28	22	6.19	28	5.75	27	3.13	26	4.13
31	4.28	29	6.38						
Jun 07	4.28	Jun 05	6.50	Jun 04	5.81	Jun 03	3.13	Jun 02	4.13
14	4.28	12	6.38	11	5.88	10	3.13	09	4.13
21	4.28	19	6.25	18	5.69	17	3.06	16	4.13
28	4.28	26	6.25	25	5.50	24	3.00	23	4.13
								30	4.13
Jul 05	4.28	Jul 03	6.25	Jul 02	5.38	Jul 01	3.00	Jul 07	4.13
12	4.28	10	6.25	09	5.31	08	3.00	14	4.13
19	4.28	17	6.25	16	5.25	15	3.00	21	4.13
26	4.34	24	6.25	23	5.25	22	3.00	28	4.13
		31	6.19	30	5.13	29	3.00		
Aug 02	4.34	Aug 07	6.13	Aug 06	5.00	Aug 05	3.00	Aug 04	4.13
09	4.34	14	6.13	13	5.00	12	3.00	11	4.13
16	4.28	21	6.13	20	5.00	19	3.00	18	4.13
23	4.34	28	6.13	27	5.00	26	3.00	25	4.13
30	4.34								
Sep 06	4.34	Sep 04	6.13	Sep 03	5.00	Sep 02	3.00	Sep 01	4.13
13	4.31	11	6.13	10	5.00	09	3.00	08	4.13
20	4.28	18	6.13	17	5.00	16	3.06	15	4.13
27	4.22	25	6.13	24	4.81	23	3.19	22	4.13
						30	3.31	29	4.13
Oct 04	4.34	Oct 02	6.25	Oct 01	4.75	Oct 07	3.50	Oct 06	4.13
11	4.34	09	6.25	08	4.75	14	3.50	13	4.13
18	4.28	16	6.25	15	4.50	21	3.63	20	4.13
25	4.28	23	6.25	22	4.50	28	3.94	27	4.13
		30	6.25	29	4.50				
Nov 01	4.28	Nov 06	6.25	Nov 05	4.44	Nov 04	4.00	Nov 03	4.13
08	4.28	13	6.25	12	4.38	11	4.00	10	4.13
15	4.53	20	6.25	19	4.31	18	4.00	17	4.13
22	4.56	27	6.19	26	4.25	25	4.00	24	4.13
29	4.88								
Dec 06	5.13	Dec 04	6.13	Dec 03	4.13	Dec 02	4.00	Dec 01	4.13
13	5.13	11	6.25	10	4.13	09	4.00	08	4.13
20	5.13	18	6.25	17	4.13	16	4.00	15	4.13
27	5.13	25	6.25	24	4.19	23	4.00	22	4.13
				31	4.13	30	4.00	29	4.13

Prime Banker's Acceptances—90-Day (continued)

1924		1925		1926		1927		1928	
Week Ended		Week Ended		Week Ended		Week Ended		Week Ended	
Jan 05	4.13%	Jan 03	3.00%	Jan 02	3.50%	Jan 01	3.75%	Jan 07	3.25%
12	4.13	10	3.00	09	3.50	08	3.75	14	3.38
19	4.06	17	3.00	16	3.75	15	3.63	21	3.38
26	4.06	24	3.00	23	3.69	22	3.69	28	3.38
		31	3.00	30	3.69	29	3.69		
Feb 02	4.00	Feb 07	3.00	Feb 06	3.63	Feb 05	3.69	Feb 04	3.50
09	4.00	14	3.06	13	3.63	12	3.63	11	3.50
16	4.13	21	3.13	20	3.63	19	3.75	18	3.50
23	4.13	28	3.19	27	3.63	26	3.75	25	3.50
Mar 01	4.13	Mar 07	3.25	Mar 06	3.63	Mar 05	3.69	Mar 03	3.50
08	4.13	14	3.25	13	3.63	12	3.63	10	3.50
15	4.13	21	3.25	20	3.63	19	3.63	17	3.50
22	4.00	28	3.25	27	3.63	26	3.63	24	3.50
29	3.94							31	3.50
Apr 05	4.00	Apr 04	3.19	Apr 03	3.63	Apr 02	3.63	Apr 07	3.69
12	4.00	11	3.19	10	3.56	09	3.63	14	3.75
19	4.00	18	3.06	17	3.50	16	3.63	21	3.88
26	3.94	25	3.13	24	3.31	23	3.63	28	3.88
						30	3.63		
May 03	3.63	May 02	3.13	May 01	3.13	May 07	3.63	May 05	3.88
10	3.50	09	3.13	08	3.13	14	3.63	12	3.88
17	3.44	16	3.13	15	3.13	21	3.63	19	3.88
24	3.00	23	3.19	22	3.25	28	3.63	26	4.06
31	3.00	30	3.25	29	3.31				
Jun 07	2.94	Jun 06	3.25	Jun 05	3.25	Jun 04	3.63	Jun 02	4.06
14	2.56	13	3.25	12	3.25	11	3.63	09	4.00
21	2.38	20	3.25	19	3.25	18	3.63	16	4.00
28	2.19	27	3.25	26	3.31	25	3.69	23	4.06
								30	4.13
Jul 05	2.00	Jul 04	3.25	Jul 03	3.38	Jul 02	3.69	Jul 07	4.13
12	2.00	11	3.25	10	3.38	09	3.63	14	4.25
19	2.00	18	3.25	17	3.38	16	3.63	21	4.38
26	2.00	25	3.25	24	3.38	23	3.56	28	4.50
				31	3.38	30	3.38		
Aug 02	2.00	Aug 01	3.25	Aug 07	3.38	Aug 06	3.13	Aug 04	4.63
09	2.00	08	3.25	14	3.44	13	3.13	11	4.63
16	2.00	15	3.25	21	3.63	20	3.13	18	4.63
23	2.13	22	3.25	28	3.75	27	3.13	25	4.63
30	2.25	29	3.25						
Sep 06	2.25	Sep 05	3.50*	Sep 04	3.88	Sep 03	3.13	Sep 01	4.63
13	2.25	12	3.50	11	3.88	10	3.13	08	4.50
20	2.19	19	3.50	18	3.88	17	3.13	15	4.50
27	2.13	26	3.50	25	3.88	24	3.13	22	4.50
								29	4.50
Oct 04	2.13	Oct 03	3.50	Oct 02	3.88	Oct 01	3.13	Oct 06	4.50
11	2.25	10	3.50	09	3.88	08	3.19	13	4.50
18	2.25	17	3.50	16	3.88	15	3.25	20	4.50
25	2.25	24	3.50	23	3.88	22	3.25	27	4.50
		31	3.50	30	3.88	29	3.25		
Nov 01	2.25	Nov 07	3.50	Nov 06	3.88	Nov 05	3.25	Nov 03	4.50
08	2.25	14	3.50	13	3.81	12	3.25	10	4.50
15	2.25	21	3.50	20	3.75	19	3.25	17	4.50
22	2.50	28	3.50	27	3.75	26	3.25	24	4.50
29	2.56								
Dec 06	2.69	Dec 05	3.50	Dec 04	3.75	Dec 03	3.25	Dec 01	4.50
13	2.94	12	3.50	11	3.88	10	3.25	08	4.50
20	2.94	19	3.50	18	3.88	17	3.25	15	4.50
27	3.00	26	3.50	25	3.88	24	3.25	22	4.50
						31	3.25	29	4.50

Prime Banker's Acceptances—90-Day (continued)

1929		1930		1931		1932		1933	
Week Ended		Week Ended		Week Ended		Week Ended		Week Ended	
Jan 05	4.50%	Jan 04	3.94%	Jan 03	1.88%	Jan 02	3.00%	Jan 07	.38%
12	4.75	11	3.88	10	1.75	09	3.00	14	.38
19	4.75	18	4.00	17	1.63	16	2.94	21	.38
26	5.00	25	4.00	24	1.50	23	2.75	28	.25
				31	1.44	30	2.75		
Feb 02	5.00	Feb 01	4.00	Feb 07	1.38	Feb 06	2.75	Feb 04	.25
09	5.00	08	3.81	14	1.25	13	2.31	11	.25
16	5.13	15	3.75	21	1.44	20	2.31	18	.44
23	5.25	22	3.75	28	1.50	27	2.75	25	.63
Mar 02	5.25	Mar 01	3.75	Mar 07	1.50	Mar 05	2.63	Mar 04	2.25
09	5.25	08	3.56	14	1.50	12	2.63	11	*
16	5.25	15	3.25	21	1.50	19	2.50	18	3.25*
23	5.38	22	2.81	28	1.50	26	2.38	25	2.00
30	5.56	29	2.63						
Apr 06	5.50	Apr 05	2.88	Apr 04	1.50	Apr 02	2.38	Apr 01	2.00
13	5.50	12	2.88	11	1.50	09	2.13	08	1.50
20	5.50	19	2.94	18	1.50	16	1.50	15	.88
27	5.38	26	3.00	25	1.44	23	1.00	22	.56
						30	.88	29	.50
May 04	5.38	May 03	2.81	May 02	1.25	May 07	1.00	May 06	.50
11	5.50	10	2.56	09	1.19	14	1.00	13	.50
18	5.50	17	2.50	16	1.06	21	.88	20	.50
25	5.50	24	2.38	23	.88	28	.88	27	.50
		31	2.38	30	.88				
Jun 01	5.50	Jun 07	2.25	Jun 06	.88	Jun 04	.88	Jun 03	.44
08	5.50	14	2.13	13	.88	11	.88	10	.38
15	5.50	21	2.13	20	.88	18	.88	17	.38
22	5.50	28	1.94	27	.88	25	.88	24	.38
29	5.50								
Jul 06	5.31	Jul 05	1.88	Jul 04	.88	Jul 02	.81	Jul 01	.38
13	5.13	12	1.88	11	.88	09	.75	08	.38
20	5.13	19	1.88	18	.88	16	.75	15	.50
27	5.13	26	1.88	25	.88	23	.75	22	.50
						30	.75	29	.50
Aug 03	5.13	Aug 02	1.88	Aug 01	.88	Aug 06	.75	Aug 05	.50
10	5.13	09	1.88	08	.88	13	.75	12	.50
17	5.13	16	1.88	15	.88	20	.75	19	.50
24	5.13	23	1.88	22	.88	27	.75	26	.44
31	5.13	30	1.88	29	.88				
Sep 07	5.13	Sep 06	1.88	Sep 05	.88	Sep 03	.75	Sep 02	.31
14	5.13	13	1.88	12	.88	10	.75	09	.25
21	5.13	20	1.88	19	.88	17	.75	16	.25
28	5.13	27	1.88	26	1.06	24	.75	23	.25
								30	.25
Oct 05	5.13	Oct 04	1.88	Oct 03	1.25	Oct 01	.75	Oct 07	.25
12	5.13	11	1.88	10	1.25	08	.75	14	.25
19	5.13	18	1.88	17	2.75*	15	.63	21	.25
26	4.94	25	1.88	24	3.25	22	.50	28	.25
				31	3.25	29	.50		
Nov 02	4.63	Nov 01	1.88	Nov 07	3.25	Nov 05	.50	Nov 04	.25
09	4.63	08	1.88	14	3.00	12	.50	11	.31
16	4.38	15	1.88	21	2.88	19	.50	18	.38
23	3.81	22	1.88	28	2.94	26	.50	25	.50
30	3.81	29	1.88						
Dec 07	3.81	Dec 06	1.88	Dec 05	3.00	Dec 03	.50	Dec 02	.50
14	3.88	13	1.88	12	3.00	10	.38	09	.63
21	3.88	20	1.88	19	3.00	17	.38	16	.63
28	4.00	27	1.88	26	3.00	24	.38	23	.63
						31	.38	30	.63

*Bank holiday, markets closed.

Prime Banker's Acceptances—90-Day (continued)

1934		1935		1936		1937		1938	
Week Ended		Week Ended		Week Ended		Week Ended		Week Ended	
Jan 06	.50%	Jan 05	.13%	Jan 04	.13%	Jan 02	.19%	Jan 01	.44%
13	.50	12	.13	11	.13	09	.19	08	.44
20	.50	19	.13	18	.13	16	.22	15	.44
27	.50	26	.13	25	.13	23	.25	22	.44
						30	.25	29	.44
Feb 03	.50	Feb 02	.13	Feb 01	.13	Feb 06	.31	Feb 05	.44
10	.50	09	.13	08	.13	13	.31	12	.44
17	.50	16	.13	15	.13	20	.31	19	.44
24	.50	23	.13	22	.13	27	.31	26	.44
				29	.13				
Mar 03	.50	Mar 02	.13	Mar 07	.13	Mar 06	.31	Mar 05	.44
10	.38	09	.13	14	.13	13	.31	12	.44
17	.25	16	.13	21	.13	20	.33	19	.44
24	.25	23	.13	28	.13	27	.56	26	.44
31	.25	30	.13						
Apr 07	.25	Apr 06	.13	Apr 04	.13	Apr 03	.56	Apr 02	.44
14	.19	13	.13	11	.13	10	.56	09	.44
21	.19	20	.13	18	.13	17	.56	16	.44
28	.19	27	.13	25	.13	24	.56	23	.44
								30	.44
May 05	.19	May 04	.13	May 02	.13	May 01	.56	May 07	.44
12	.19	11	.13	09	.13	08	.56	14	.44
19	.19	18	.13	16	.13	15	.50	21	.44
26	.19	25	.13	23	.13	22	.50	28	.44
				30	.13	29	.50		
Jun 02	.19	Jun 01	.13	Jun 06	.13	Jun 05	.50	Jun 04	.44
09	.19	08	.13	13	.13	12	.50	11	.44
16	.19	15	.13	20	.13	19	.50	18	.44
23	.19	22	.13	27	.13	26	.44	25	.44
30	.19	29	.13						
Jul 07	.19	Jul 06	.13	Jul 04	.13	Jul 03	.44	Jul 02	.44
14	.19	13	.13	11	.13	10	.44	09	.44
21	.19	20	.13	18	.13	17	.44	16	.44
28	.19	27	.13	25	.19*	24	.44	23	.44
						31	.44	30	.44
Aug 04	.19	Aug 03	.13	Aug 01	.19	Aug 07	.44	Aug 06	.44
11	.19	10	.13	08	.19	14	.44	13	.44
18	.19	17	.13	15	.19	21	.44	20	.44
25	.19	24	.13	22	.19	28	.44	27	.44
		31	.13	29	.19				
Sep 01	.19	Sep 07	.13	Sep 05	.19	Sep 04	.44	Sep 03	.44
08	.19	14	.13	12	.19	11	.44	10	.44
15	.19	21	.13	19	.19	18	.44	17	.44
22	.19	28	.13	26	.19	25	.44	24	.44
29	.19								
Oct 06	.19	Oct 05	.13	Oct 03	.19	Oct 02	.44	Oct 01	.44
13	.19	12	.13	10	.19	09	.44	08	.44
20	.19	19	.13	17	.19	16	.44	15	.44
27	.16	26	.13	24	.19	23	.44	22	.44
				31	.19	30	.44	29	.44
Nov 03	.13	Nov 02	.13	Nov 07	.19	Nov 06	.44	Nov 05	.44
10	.13	09	.13	14	.19	13	.44	12	.44
17	.13	16	.13	21	.19	20	.44	19	.44
24	.13	23	.13	28	.19	27	.44	26	.44
		30	.13						
Dec 01	.13	Dec 07	.13	Dec 05	.19	Dec 04	.44	Dec 03	.44
08	.13	14	.13	12	.19	11	.44	10	.44
15	.13	21	.13	19	.19	18	.44	17	.44
22	.13	28	.13	26	.19	25	.44	24	.44
29	.13							31	.44

Prime Banker's Acceptances—90-Day (continued)

1939		1940		1941		1942		1943	
Week Ended		Week Ended		Week Ended		Week Ended		Week Ended	
Jan 07	.44%	Jan 06	.44%	Jan 04	.44%	Jan 03	.44%	Jan 02	.44%
14	.44	13	.44	11	.44	10	.44	09	.44
21	.44	20	.44	18	.44	17	.44	16	.44
28	.44	27	.44	25	.44	24	.44	23	.44
						31	.44	30	.44
Feb 04	.44	Feb 03	.44	Feb 01	.44	Feb 07	.44	Feb 06	.44
11	.44	10	.44	08	.44	14	.44	13	.44
18	.44	17	.44	15	.44	21	.44	20	.44
25	.44	24	.44	22	.44	28	.44	27	.44
Mar 04	.44	Mar 02	.44	Mar 01	.44	Mar 07	.44	Mar 06	.44
11	.44	09	.44	08	.44	14	.44	13	.44
18	.44	16	.44	15	.44	21	.44	20	.44
25	.44	23	.44	22	.44	28	.44	27	.44
		30	.44	29	.44				
Apr 01	.44	Apr 06	.44	Apr 05	.44	Apr 04	.44	Apr 03	.44
08	.44	13	.44	12	.44	11	.44	10	.44
15	.44	20	.44	19	.44	18	.44	17	.44
22	.44	27	.44	26	.44	25	.44	24	.44
29	.44								
May 06	.44	May 04	.44	May 03	.44	May 02	.44	May 01	.44
13	.44	11	.44	10	.44	09	.44	08	.44
20	.44	18	.44	17	.44	16	.44	15	.44
27	.44	25	.44	24	.44	23	.44	22	.44
				31	.44	30	.44	29	.44
Jun 03	.44	Jun 01	.44	Jun 07	.44	Jun 06	.44	Jun 05	.44
10	.44	08	.44	14	.44	13	.44	12	.44
17	.44	15	.44	21	.44	20	.44	19	.44
24	.44	22	.44	28	.44	27	.44	26	.44
		29	.44						
Jul 01	.44	Jul 06	.44	Jul 05	.44	Jul 04	.44	Jul 03	.44
08	.44	13	.44	12	.44	11	.44	10	.44
15	.44	20	.44	19	.44	18	.44	17	.44
22	.44	27	.44	26	.44	25	.44	24	.44
29	.44							31	.44
Aug 05	.44	Aug 03	.44	Aug 02	.44	Aug 01	.44	Aug 07	.44
12	.44	10	.44	09	.44	08	.44	14	.44
19	.44	17	.44	16	.44	15	.44	21	.44
26	.44	24	.44	23	.44	22	.44	28	.44
		31	.44	30	.44	29	.44		
Sep 02	.44	Sep 07	.44	Sep 06	.44	Sep 05	.44	Sep 04	.44
09	.44	14	.44	13	.44	12	.44	11	.44
16	.44	21	.44	20	.44	19	.44	18	.44
23	.44	28	.44	27	.44	26	.44	25	.44
30	.44								
Oct 07	.44	Oct 05	.44	Oct 04	.44	Oct 03	.44	Oct 02	.44
14	.44	12	.44	11	.44	10	.44	09	.44
21	.44	19	.44	18	.44	17	.44	16	.44
28	.44	26	.44	25	.44	24	.44	23	.44
						31	.44	30	.44
Nov 04	.44	Nov 02	.44	Nov 01	.44	Nov 07	.44	Nov 06	.44
11	.44	09	.44	08	.44	14	.44	13	.44
18	.44	16	.44	15	.44	21	.44	20	.44
25	.44	23	.44	22	.44	28	.44	27	.44
		30	.44	29	.44				
Dec 02	.44	Dec 07	.44	Dec 06	.44	Dec 05	.44	Dec 04	.44
09	.44	14	.44	13	.44	12	.44	11	.44
16	.44	21	.44	20	.44	19	.44	18	.44
23	.44	28	.44	27	.44	26	.44	25	.44
30	.44								

Prime Banker's Acceptances—90-Day (continued)

1944		1945		1946	
Week Ended		Week Ended		Week Ended	
Jan 01	.44%	Jan 06	.44%	Jan 05	.44%
08	.44	13	.44	12	.44
15	.44	20	.44	19	.44
22	.44	27	.44	26	.44
29	.44				
Feb 05	.44	Feb 03	.44	Feb 02	.44
12	.44	10	.44	09	.44
19	.44	17	.44	16	.44
26	.44	24	.44	23	.44
Mar 04	.44	Mar 03	.44	Mar 02	.44
11	.44	10	.44	09	.44
18	.44	17	.44	16	.44
25	.44	24	.44	23	.44
		31	.44	30	.44
Apr 01	.44	Apr 07	.44	Apr 06	.44
08	.44	14	.44	13	.44
15	.44	21	.44	20	.44
22	.44	28	.44	27	.44
29	.44				
May 06	.44	May 05	.44	May 04	.44
13	.44	12	.44	11	.46*
20	.44	19	.44	18	.50
27	.44	26	.44	25	.50
Jun 03	.44	Jun 02	.44	Jun 01	.50
10	.44	09	.44	08	.50
17	.44	16	.44	15	.50
24	.44	23	.44	22	.50
		30	.44	29	.50
Jul 01	.44	Jul 07	.44	Jul 06	.50
08	.44	14	.44	13	.50
15	.44	21	.44	20	.69
22	.44	28	.44	27	.69
29	.44				
Aug 05	.44	Aug 04	.44	Aug 03	.69
12	.44	11	.44	10	.69
19	.44	18	.44	17	.69
26	.44	25	.44	24	.74
				31	.81
Sep 02	.44	Sep 01	.44	Sep 07	.81
09	.44	08	.44	14	.81
16	.44	15	.44	21	.81
23	.44	22	.44	28	.81
30	.44	29	.44		
Oct 07	.44	Oct 06	.44	Oct 05	.81
14	.44	13	.44	12	.81
21	.44	20	.44	19	.81
28	.44	27	.44	26	.81
Nov 04	.44	Nov 03	.44	Nov 02	.81
11	.44	10	.44	09	.81
18	.44	17	.44	16	.81
25	.44	24	.44	23	.81
				30	.81
Dec 02	.44	Dec 01	.44	Dec 07	.81
09	.44	08	.44	14	.81
16	.44	15	.44	21	.81
23	.44	22	.44	28	.81
30	.44	29	.44		

APPENDIX D

90-Day T-Bills at Weekly Auction—1945–1989

1945		1946		1947		1948		1949	
Jan 02	.373%	Jan 07	.375%	Jan 06	.375%	Jan 05	.950%	Jan 03	1.155%
08	.375	14	.375	13	.376	12	.976	10	1.160
15	.375	21	.375	20	.376	19	.981	17	1.160
22	.375	28	.375	27	.376	26	.990	24	1.160
29	.375							31	1.161
Feb 05	.375	Feb 04	.375	Feb 03	.376	Feb 02	.990	Feb 07	1.163
12	.375	11	.375	10	.376	09	.994	14	1.163
19	.376	18	.375	17	.376	16	.996	21	1.164
26	.375	25	.375	24	.376	24	.997	28	1.163
Mar 05	.375	Mar 04	.375	Mar 03	.376	Mar 01	.997	Mar 07	1.162
12	.375	11	.375	10	.376	08	.997	14	1.162
19	.375	18	.375	17	.376	15	.996	21	1.162
26	.375	25	.375	24	.376	22	.996	28	1.162
				31	.376	29	.996		
Apr 02	.376	Apr 01	.375	Apr 07	.376	Apr 05	.997	Apr 04	1.160
09	.375	08	.375	14	.376	12	.998	11	1.153
16	.375	15	.375	21	.376	19	.997	18	1.157
23	.375	22	.375	28	.376	26	.997	25	1.156
30	.375	29	.375						
May 07	.375	May 06	.375	May 05	.376	May 03	.998	May 02	1.147
14	.375	13	.375	12	.376	10	.998	09	1.148
21	.375	20	.375	19	.376	17	.997	16	1.157
28	.375	27	.376	26	.376	24	.997	23	1.159
						31	.997	31	1.159
Jun 04	.375	Jun 03	.375	Jun 02	.376	Jun 07	.998	Jun 06	1.158
11	.375	10	.375	09	.376	14	.998	13	1.158
18	.375	17	.375	16	.376	21	.998	20	1.158
25	.375	24	.375	23	.376	28	.997	27	1.158
				30	.376				
Jul 02	.375	Jul 01	.376	Jul 07	.594	Jul 06	.997	Jul 05	1.052
09	.375	08	.375	14	.737	12	.997	11	.923
16	.375	15	.375	21	.740	19	.997	18	.928
23	.375	22	.375	28	.740	26	.997	25	1.017
30	.375	29	.376						
Aug 06	.375	Aug 05	.376	Aug 04	.740	Aug 02	.997	Aug 01	1.032
13	.375	12	.376	11	.741	09	.997	08	1.007
20	.375	19	.375	18	.741	16	1.066	15	1.017
27	.375	26	.375	25	.752	23	1.072	22	1.031
						30	1.075	29	1.054
Sep 04	.375	Sep 03	.375	Sep 02	.766	Sep 07	1.076	Sep 06	1.055
10	.375	09	.375	08	.789	13	1.083	12	1.058
17	.375	16	.375	15	.802	20	1.092	19	1.062
24	.375	23	.375	22	.808	27	1.109	26	1.076
		30	.375	29	.817				
Oct 01	.375	Oct 07	.375	Oct 06	.827	Oct 04	1.114	Oct 03	1.059
08	.375	14	.375	14	.835	11	1.118	10	1.050
15	.375	21	.375	20	.855	18	1.118	17	1.027
22	.375	28	.376	27	.873	25	1.120	24	1.036
29	.375							31	1.063
Nov 05	.375	Nov 04	.376	Nov 03	.895	Nov 01	1.129	Nov 07	1.074
13	.375	12	.376	10	.912	08	1.138	14	1.056
19	.376	18	.376	17	.931	15	1.141	21	1.052
26	.375	25	.376	24	.940	22	1.147	28	1.108
						29	1.150		
Dec 03	.375	Dec 02	.376	Dec 01	.944	Dec 06	1.152	Dec 05	1.115
10	.375	09	.375	08	.948	13	1.153	12	1.115
17	.375	16	.375	15	.949	20	1.154	19	1.087
26	.375	23	.375	22	.951	27	1.157	27	1.087
31	.373	30	.374	29	.952				

90-Day T-Bills at Weekly Auction (continued)

1950		1951		1952		1953		1954	
Jan 03	1.081%	Jan 02	1.381%	Jan 07	1.686%	Jan 05	1.986%	Jan 04	1.314%
09	1.076	08	1.387	14	1.684	12	2.124	11	1.336
16	1.101	15	1.391	21	1.599	19	2.097	18	1.208
23	1.103	22	1.389	28	1.589	26	1.961	25	.998
30	1.118	29	1.391						
Feb 06	1.119	Feb 05	1.391	Feb 04	1.584	Feb 02	2.031	Feb 01	1.031
14	1.131	13	1.391	11	1.643	09	1.993	08	.893
20	1.132	19	1.390	18	1.507	16	1.976	15	1.024
27	1.137	26	1.390	25	1.563	24	2.070	23	.986
Mar 06	1.139	Mar 05	1.406	Mar 03	1.656	Mar 02	2.164	Mar 01	1.059
13	1.131	12	1.402	10	1.784	09	2.098	08	1.066
20	1.138	19	1.405	17	1.601	16	2.029	15	1.056
27	1.145	26	1.507	24	1.592	23	2.036	22	1.030
				31	1.598	30	2.029	29	1.063
Apr 03	1.148	Apr 02	1.517	Apr 07	1.629	Apr 06	2.073	Apr 05	1.013
10	1.160	09	1.528	14	1.650	13	2.219	12	1.066
17	1.160	16	1.529	21	1.616	20	2.320	19	1.027
24	1.166*	23	1.506	28	1.691	27	2.243	26	.886
		30	1.508						
May 01	1.166	May 07	1.566	May 05	1.710	May 04	2.352	May 03	.773
08	1.166	14	1.626	12	1.725	11	2.271	10	.825
15	1.165	21	1.591	19	1.694	18	2.092	17	.813
22	1.167	28	1.600	26	1.728	25	2.084	24	.718
29	1.169								
Jun 05	1.179	Jun 04	1.555	Jun 02	1.737	Jun 01	2.416	Jun 01	.714
12	1.177	11	1.467	09	1.753	08	2.324	07	.616
19	1.174	18	1.445	16	1.626	15	2.229	14	.633
26	1.172	25	1.527	23	1.682	22	1.954	21	.635
				30	1.788	29	2.107	28	.646
Jul 03	1.174	Jul 02	1.604	Jul 07	1.793	Jul 06	2.007	Jul 06	.671
10	1.168	09	1.615	14	1.810	13	2.106	12	.701
17	1.173	16	1.562	21	1.850	20	2.126	19	.731
24	1.174	23	1.591	28	1.877	27	2.157	26	.800
31	1.174	30	1.611						
Aug 07	1.174	Aug 06	1.652	Aug 04	1.860	Aug 03	2.136	Aug 02	.797
14	1.173	13	1.660	11	1.903	10	2.116	09	.892
21	1.247	20	1.651	18	1.841	17	2.101	16	.898
28	1.285	27	1.645	25	1.899	24	2.001	23	.983
						31	1.961	30	1.023
Sep 05	1.308	Sep 04	1.646	Sep 02	1.884	Sep 08	1.953	Sep 07	1.016
11	1.311	10	1.646	08	1.850	14	1.957	13	1.024
18	1.317	17	1.644	15	1.774	21	1.634	20	.986
25	1.324	24	1.647	22	1.635	28	1.583	27	.984
				29	1.760				
Oct 02	1.324	Oct 01	1.646	Oct 06	1.829	Oct 05	1.397	Oct 04	.966
09	1.337	08	1.576	13	1.836	12	1.438	11	.966
16	1.337	15	1.615	20	1.735	19	1.372	18	1.009
23	1.316	22	1.593	29	1.757	26	1.220	25	1.007
30	1.341	29	1.617						
Nov 06	1.350	Nov 05	1.610	Nov 03	1.796	Nov 02	1.306	Nov 01	1.023
13	1.366	13	1.619	10	1.843	09	1.482	08	.940
20	1.380	19	1.585	17	1.877	16	1.433	15	.931
27	1.383	26	1.609	21	1.931	23	1.488	22	.897
						30	1.589	29	1.029
Dec 04	1.366	Dec 03	1.632	Dec 01	2.049	Dec 07	1.603	Dec 06	1.087
11	1.351	10	1.700	08	2.091	14	1.682	13	1.247
18	1.368	17	1.725	15	2.138	21	1.704	20	1.333
26	1.382	24	1.865	22	2.228	28	1.574	27	1.175
		31	1.883	29	2.191				

90-Day T-Bills at Weekly Auction (continued)

1955		1956		1957		1958		1959	
Jan 03	1.049%	Jan 03	2.489%	Jan 07	3.197%	Jan 06	2.858%	Jan 05	2.678%
10	1.222	09	2.596	14	3.223	13	2.591	12	2.808
17	1.407	16	2.493	21	3.085	20	2.587	19	3.035
24	1.349	23	2.245	28	3.283	27	2.202	26	2.975
31	1.134	30	2.402						
Feb 07	1.088	Feb 06	2.271	Feb 04	3.132	Feb 03	1.583	Feb 02	2.721
14	1.130	13	2.388	11	3.057	10	1.730	09	2.810
21	1.355	20	2.429	18	3.182	17	1.731	16	2.726
28	1.417	27	2.409	25	3.288	24	1.202	24	2.589
Mar 07	1.231	Mar 05	2.173	Mar 04	3.246	Mar 03	1.351	Mar 02	2.816
14	1.286	12	2.374	11	3.238	10	1.532	09	3.062
21	1.366	19	2.422	18	3.041	17	1.343	16	2.763
28	1.374	26	2.173	25	3.034	24	1.189	23	2.766
						31	1.148	30	2.841
Apr 04	1.466	Apr 02	2.397	Apr 01	3.050	Apr 07	1.074	Apr 06	2.948
11	1.652	09	2.497	08	3.154	14	1.225	13	3.075
18	1.664	16	2.769	15	3.194	21	1.055	20	3.105
25	1.697	23	2.788	22	3.054	28	1.367	27	2.831
		30	2.741	29	3.039				
May 02	1.627	May 07	2.524	May 06	2.909	May 05	1.187	May 04	2.935
09	1.440	14	2.708	13	2.894	12	1.112	11	2.722
16	1.427	21	2.702	20	3.122	19	.931	18	2.869
23	1.471	28	2.573	27	3.245	26	.635	25	2.878
31	1.434								
Jun 06	1.390	Jun 04	2.562	Jun 03	3.374	Jun 02	.723	Jun 01	3.149
13	1.514	11	2.581	10	3.256	09	.841	08	3.283
20	1.420	18	2.430	17	3.404	16	.953	15	3.276
27	1.401	25	2.535	24	3.231	23	1.006	22	3.281
						30	.768	29	3.164
Jul 05	1.541	Jul 02	2.409	Jul 01	3.238	Jul 07	.934	Jul 06	3.266
11	1.606	09	2.387	08	3.171	14	1.137	13	3.401
18	1.620	16	2.237	15	3.092	21	.988	20	3.337
25	1.720	23	2.303	22	3.158	28	.984	27	3.047
		30	2.378	29	3.363				
Aug 01	1.850	Aug 06	2.399	Aug 05	3.308	Aug 04	1.165	Aug 03	3.043
08	1.889	13	2.603	12	3.498	11	1.524	10	3.150
15	1.888	20	2.818	19	3.354	18	1.895	17	3.417
22	1.875	27	2.832	26	3.497	25	2.162	24	3.824*
29	2.088							31	3.889
Sep 06	2.134	Sep 04	2.736	Sep 03	3.571	Sep 02	2.462	Sep 08	3.979
12	2.104	10	2.770	09	3.575	08	2.359	14	4.166
19	1.981	17	2.908	16	3.633	15	2.605	21	3.958
26	2.122	24	2.985	23	3.534	22	2.511	28	4.194
				30	3.528	29	2.920		
Oct 03	2.214	Oct 01	2.899	Oct 07	3.525	Oct 06	2.668	Oct 05	4.007
10	2.257	08	3.013	14	3.660	13	2.927	12	4.262
17	2.333	15	3.024	21	3.619	20	2.804	19	4.099
24	2.231	22	2.907	28	3.622	27	2.647	26	4.022
31	2.179	29	2.889						
Nov 07	2.034	Nov 05	2.914	Nov 04	3.571	Nov 03	2.649	Nov 02	4.137
14	2.248	12	2.979	11	3.473	10	2.774	09	4.089
21	2.440*	19	3.043	18	3.145	17	2.876	16	4.332
28	2.450	26	3.174	25	3.158	24	2.723	23	4.279
								30	4.501
Dec 05	2.471	Dec 03	3.102	Dec 02	3.105	Dec 01	2.806	Dec 07	4.638
12	2.591	10	3.268	09	2.991	08	2.805	14	4.535
19	2.618	17	3.331	16	3.140	15	2.904	21	4.670
27	2.688	26	3.217	23	3.174	22	2.739	28	4.516
		31	3.262	30	2.752	29	2.690		

90-Day T-Bills at Weekly Auction (continued)

1960		1961		1962		1963		1964	
Jan 04	4.602%	Jan 03	2.234%	Jan 02	2.703%	Jan 07	2.920%	Jan 06	3.534%
11	4.590	09	2.385	08	2.823	14	2.884	13	3.549
18	4.436	16	2.358	15	2.770	21	2.923	20	3.538
25	4.116	23	2.230	22	2.688	28	2.917	27	3.501
		30	2.299	29	2.705				
Feb 01	4.039	Feb 06	2.374	Feb 05	2.695	Feb 04	2.946	Feb 03	3.505
08	3.563	13	2.462	12	2.759	11	2.944	10	3.540
15	4.045	20	2.496	19	2.849	18	2.905	17	3.534
23	4.168	27	2.594	26	2.664	25	2.870	24	3.547
29	4.278								
Mar 07	3.641	Mar 06	2.485	Mar 05	2.721	Mar 04	2.897	Mar 02	3.589
14	3.451	13	2.352	12	2.804	11	2.870	09	3.534
21	3.033	20	2.278	19	2.689	18	2.902	16	3.538
28	2.792	27	2.392	26	2.719	25	2.919	23	3.550
								30	3.525
Apr 04	2.731	Apr 03	2.470	Apr 02	2.757	Apr 01	2.922	Apr 06	3.503
11	3.622	10	2.360	09	2.720	08	2.913	13	3.484
17	3.306	17	2.292	16	2.723	15	2.917	20	3.463
25	3.317	24	2.186	23	2.740	22	2.884	27	3.446
				30	2.748	29	2.898		
May 02	3.003	May 01	2.300	May 07	2.720	May 06	2.905	May 04	3.482
09	3.274	08	2.232	14	2.646	13	2.903	11	3.491
16	3.793	15	2.264	21	2.700	20	2.922	18	3.482
23	3.497	22	2.354	28	2.656	27	2.974	25	3.475
31	3.184	31	2.438						
Jun 06	2.716	Jun 05	2.516	Jun 04	2.691	Jun 03	3.028	Jun 01	3.478
13	2.292	12	2.295	11	2.671	10	2.975	08	3.462
20	2.613	19	2.325	18	2.721	17	2.997	15	3.496
27	2.399	26	2.219	25	2.792	24	2.979	22	3.478
								29	3.479
Jul 05	2.307	Jul 03	2.305	Jul 02	2.930	Jul 01	3.011	Jul 06	3.492
11	2.567	10	2.322	09	2.974	08	3.164	13	3.448
18	2.307	17	2.200	16	2.983	15	3.192	20	3.503
25	2.404	24	2.244	23	2.892	22	3.206	27	3.475
		31	2.300	30	2.874	29	3.263		
Aug 01	2.131	Aug 07	2.366	Aug 06	2.802	Aug 05	3.253	Aug 03	3.488
08	2.215	14	2.519	13	2.867	12	3.335	10	3.510
15	2.278	21	2.503	20	2.837	19	3.355	17	3.511
22	2.518	28	2.321	27	2.806	26	3.396	24	3.513
29	2.550							31	3.512
Sep 06	2.520	Sep 05	2.392	Sep 04	2.834	Sep 03	3.384	Sep 08	3.514
12	2.654	11	2.328	10	2.789	09	3.343	14	3.541
19	2.434	18	2.262	17	2.796	16	3.409	21	3.542
26	2.286	25	2.233	24	2.749	23	3.379	28	3.555
						30	3.408		
Oct 03	2.473	Oct 02	2.302	Oct 01	2.752	Oct 07	3.459	Oct 05	3.582
10	2.698	09	2.389	08	2.760	14	3.458	12	3.580
17	2.406	16	2.382	15	2.749	21	3.488	19	3.592
24	2.129	23	2.325	22	2.742	28	3.452	26	3.567
31	2.127	30	2.280	29	2.686				
Nov 07	2.390	Nov 06	2.349	Nov 05	2.841	Nov 04	3.517	Nov 02	3.562
14	2.624	13	2.516	12	2.801	11	3.565	09	3.574
21	2.396	20	2.537	19	2.833	18	3.524	16	3.600
28	2.326	27	2.606	26	2.853	26	3.480	23	3.758
								30	3.868
Dec 05	2.328	Dec 04	2.625	Dec 03	2.861	Dec 02	3.531	Dec 07	3.815
12	2.334	11	2.579	10	2.807	09	3.500	14	3.864
19	2.222	18	2.670	17	2.861	16	3.538	21	3.868
27	2.148	26	2.594	24	2.894	23	3.522	28	3.867
				31	2.926	30	3.524		

90-Day T-Bills at Weekly Auction (continued)

1965		1966		1967		1968		1969	
Jan 04	3.829%	Jan 03	4.532%	Jan 03	4.822%	Jan 02	5.103%	Jan 06	6.227%
11	3.814	10	4.585	09	4.818	08	5.080	13	6.215
18	3.821	17	4.673*	16	4.716	15	5.072	20	6.076
25	3.848	24	4.596	23	4.680	22	5.068	27	6.167
		31	4.638	30	4.486	29	4.846		
Feb 01	3.888	Feb 07	4.650	Feb 06	4.530	Feb 05	4.957	Feb 03	6.251
08	3.903	14	4.695	13	4.577	12	5.040	11	6.199
15	3.936	21	4.696	20	4.621	19	4.940	17	6.092
23	3.989	28	4.661	27	4.538	26	5.063	24	6.080
Mar 01	3.982	Mar 07	4.620	Mar 06	4.344	Mar 04	5.000	Mar 03	6.215
08	3.948	14	4.718	13	4.308	11	5.107	10	6.049
15	3.917	21	4.576	20	4.102	18	5.285	17	6.108
22	3.922	28	4.555	27	4.150	25	5.186	24	5.946
29	3.921								
Apr 05	3.942	Apr 04	4.531	Apr 03	3.976	Apr 01	5.146	Apr 01	6.065
12	3.937	11	4.618	10	3.810	08	5.309	07	6.167
19	3.946	18	4.664	17	3.905	15	5.463	14	6.195
26	3.916	25	4.630	24	3.715	22	5.542	21	6.175
						29	5.499	28	6.053
May 03	3.901	May 02	4.674	May 01	3.770	May 06	5.507	May 05	5.978
10	3.893	09	4.630	08	3.671	13	5.558	12	6.084
17	3.897	16	4.626	15	3.628	20	5.847*	19	6.148
24	3.889	23	4.638	22	3.493	27	5.696	26	6.124
		31	4.641	29	3.477				
Jun 01	3.870	Jun 06	4.573	Jun 05	3.386	Jun 03	5.649	Jun 02	6.191
07	3.781	13	4.575	12	3.505	10	5.713	09	6.591
14	3.799	20	4.470	19	3.572	17	5.578	16	6.666
21	3.789	27	4.435	26	3.462	24	5.238	23	6.524
28	3.784							30	6.456
Jul 06	3.853	Jul 05	4.731	Jul 03	4.280	Jul 01	5.400	Jul 07	7.069
12	3.883	11	4.876	10	4.285	08	5.368	14	7.105
19	3.833	18	4.996	17	4.245	15	5.467	22	7.220
26	3.803	25	4.818	24	4.423	22	5.293	28	7.172
				31	4.182	29	5.190		
Aug 02	3.832	Aug 01	4.834	Aug 07	4.174	Aug 05	4.905	Aug 04	6.994
09	3.846	08	4.826	14	4.193	12	5.084	11	7.081
16	3.813	15	5.048	21	4.336	19	5.123	18	6.856
23	3.855	22	5.020	28	4.490	26	5.173	25	7.098
30	3.886	29	5.087						
Sep 07	3.898	Sep 06	5.155	Sep 05	4.324	Sep 03	5.194	Sep 02	7.014
13	3.887	12	5.447	11	4.360	09	5.246	08	7.184
20	3.905	19	5.586	18	4.490	16	5.218	15	7.156
27	3.983	26	5.503	25	4.629	23	5.151	22	7.161
						30	5.182	29	7.106
Oct 04	4.050	Oct 03	5.408	Oct 02	4.514	Oct 07	5.277	Oct 06	7.046
11	4.006	10	5.471	09	4.564	14	5.345	13	7.042
18	4.034	17	5.424	16	4.676	21	5.396	20	6.975
25	4.040	24	5.246	23	4.597	28	5.471	27	7.030
		31	5.234	30	4.542				
Nov 01	4.082	Nov 07	5.432	Nov 06	4.672	Nov 04	5.554	Nov 03	6.998
08	4.045	14	5.459	13	4.648	12	5.483	10	7.157
15	4.097	21	5.252	20	4.989	18	5.483	17	7.141
22	4.104	28	5.202	27	4.957	25	5.448	24	7.476
29	4.115								
Dec 06	4.344	Dec 05	5.198	Dec 04	4.989	Dec 02	5.633	Dec 01	7.453
13	4.391	12	5.048	11	4.941	09	5.788	08	7.702
20	4.505	19	4.842	18	5.127	16	5.966	15	7.920
27	4.457	27	4.747	26	4.989	23	6.278	22	7.804
						30	6.199	29	8.096

90-Day T-Bills at Weekly Auction (continued)

1970		1971		1972		1973		1974	
Jan 05	7.960%	Jan 04	4.921%	Jan 03	3.735%	Jan 02	5.163%	Jan 07	7.615%
12	7.837	11	4.640	10	3.109	08	5.155	14	7.983
19	7.789	18	4.213	17	3.276	15	5.277	21	7.995
26	7.888	25	4.201	24	3.493	22	5.633	28	7.778
				31	3.367	29	5.689		
Feb 02	7.754	Feb 01	4.110	Feb 07	3.141	Feb 05	5.665	Feb 04	6.951
09	7.312	08	3.845	14	3.066	12	5.424	11	7.081
16	6.777	16	3.640	22	3.145	20	5.455	19	7.018
24	6.812	22	3.497	28	3.446	26	5.811	25	7.188
Mar 02	6.868	Mar 01	3.347	Mar 06	3.553	Mar 05	5.879	Mar 04	7.675
07	6.876	08	3.307	13	3.845	12	5.997	11	7.920
16	6.836	15	3.307	20	3.920	19	6.334	18	8.047
23	6.262	22	3.331	27	3.845	26	6.251	25	8.300
30	6.330	29	3.521						
Apr 06	6.409	Apr 05	3.703	Apr 03	3.798	Apr 02	6.531	Apr 01	8.358
13	6.310	12	4.039	10	3.731	09	6.187	08	8.648
20	6.476	19	3.770	17	3.849	16	6.187	15	8.051
27	6.876	26	3.865	24	3.513	23	6.251	22	7.857
						30	6.278	29	8.909
May 04	7.184	May 03	3.865	May 01	3.604	May 07	6.136	May 06	9.036
11	6.994	10	3.861	08	3.462	14	6.179	13	8.023
18	6.828	17	4.352	15	3.699	21	6.452	20	8.197
25	7.133	24	4.478	22	3.825	29	6.694	28	7.983
				30	3.762				
Jun 01	6.824	Jun 01	4.344	Jun 05	3.861	Jun 04	7.133	Jun 03	8.300
08	6.785	07	4.510	12	3.798	11	7.129	10	8.260
15	6.733	14	4.989	19	3.924	18	7.263	17	8.177
22	6.626	21	4.953	26	4.023	25	7.228	24	7.841
29	6.421	28	5.080						
Jul 06	6.642	Jul 06	5.467	Jul 03	4.138	Jul 02	7.987	Jul 01	7.808
13	6.547	12	5.376	10	4.102	09	7.991	08	7.892
20	6.385	19	5.546	17	3.948	16	7.967	15	7.702
27	6.345	26	5.554	24	4.047	23	8.114*	22	7.604
				31	3.794	30	8.320	29	7.698
Aug 03	6.413	Aug 02	5.273	Aug 07	3.928	Aug 06	8.486	Aug 05	8.505
10	6.512	09	5.372	14	3.956	13	8.976	12	8.763
17	6.527	16	4.921	21	4.058	20	8.910	19	8.846
24	6.198	23	4.747	28	4.332	27	8.668	26	9.908
31	6.342	30	4.549						
Sep 08	6.365	Sep 07	4.538	Sep 05	4.569	Sep 04	8.778	Sep 03	9.167
14	6.314	13	4.834	11	4.759	10	9.016	09	9.099
21	5.954	20	4.743	18	4.633	17	8.786	16	8.185
28	5.807	27	4.676	25	4.644	24	7.331	23	7.002
								30	6.385
Oct 05	6.025	Oct 04	4.534	Oct 02	4.601	Oct 01	7.149	Oct 07	6.698
12	6.029	11	4.486	09	4.743	08	7.323	14	7.722
19	5.942	18	4.494	16	4.818	15	7.188	21	7.524
26	5.831	25	4.443	23	4.712	22	6.959	28	7.892
				30	4.767	29	7.196		
Nov 02	5.653	Nov 01	4.233	Nov 06	4.668	Nov 05	8.098	Nov 04	7.880
09	5.459	08	4.174	13	4.775	12	8.636	11	7.604
16	5.281	15	4.122	20	4.776	19	7.074	18	7.528
23	4.760	22	4.236	27	4.886	26	7.695	25	7.328
30	5.084	29	4.324						
Dec 07	4.882	Dec 06	4.091	Dec 04	4.945	Dec 03	7.358	Dec 02	7.524
14	4.775	13	3.944	11	5.099	10	7.386	09	7.172
21	4.727	20	4.023	18	5.087	17	7.366	16	7.058
28	4.830	27	3.731	26	5.111	24	7.346	23	6.963
						31	7.406	30	7.113

90-Day T-Bills at Weekly Auction (continued)

1975		1976		1977		1978		1979	
Jan 06	6.698%	Jan 05	5.226%	Jan 03	4.407%	Jan 03	6.144%	Jan 02	9.388%
13	6.678	12	4.826	10	4.613	09	6.682	08	9.316
20	6.369	19	4.783	17	4.668	16	6.535	15	9.411
27	5.606	26	4.763	24	4.700	23	6.429	22	9.289
				31	4.720	30	6.440	29	9.324
Feb 03	5.669	Feb 02	4.811	Feb 07	4.625	Feb 06	6.476	Feb 05	9.186
10	5.800	09	4.872	14	4.633	13	6.452	12	9.257
18	5.408	17	4.854	21	4.668	21	6.460	20	9.293
24	5.455	23	4.870	28	4.708	27	6.429	26	9.451
Mar 03	5.637	Mar 01	5.258	Mar 07	4.652	Mar 06	6.349	Mar 05	9.364
10	5.622	08	5.060	14	4.545	13	6.302	12	9.475
17	5.376	15	4.981	21	4.553	20	6.207	19	9.498
24	5.542	22	4.890	28	4.609	27	6.310	26	9.498
31	5.562	29	4.929						
Apr 07	6.021	Apr 05	4.957	Apr 04	4.585	Apr 03	6.417	Apr 02	9.593
14	5.538	12	4.830	11	4.561	10	6.373	09	9.649
21	5.653	19	4.763	18	4.494	17	6.140	16	9.613
28	5.716	26	4.909	25	4.518	24	6.294	23	9.115
								30	9.498
May 05	5.356	May 03	4.921	May 02	4.807	May 01	6.460	May 07	9.621
12	5.182	10	5.072	09	4.822	08	6.464	14	9.506
19	5.115	17	5.250	16	4.996	15	6.318	21	9.744
27	5.206	24	5.495	23	5.143	22	6.476	29	9.526
				31	4.993	30	6.658		
Jun 02	5.528	Jun 01	5.578	Jun 06	5.048	Jun 05	6.626	Jun 05	9.554
09	5.080	07	5.459	13	5.000	12	6.618	11	8.956
16	4.767	14	5.380	20	5.012	19	6.666	18	8.869
23	5.665	21	5.356	27	4.965	26	6.967	25	8.802
30	6.009	28	5.368						
Jul 07	6.203	Jul 06	5.412	Jul 05	5.044	Jul 03	7.058	Jul 02	8.968
14	6.045	12	5.163	11	5.163	10	7.188	09	9.265
21	6.247	19	5.226	18	5.214	17	7.113	16	9.336
28	6.318	26	5.194	25	5.163	24	6.935	23	9.479
						31	6.895	30	9.154
Aug 04	6.456	Aug 02	5.151	Aug 01	5.424	Aug 07	6.808	Aug 06	9.320
11	6.349	09	5.181	08	5.353	14	6.887	13	9.495
18	6.452	16	5.143	15	5.669	21	7.267	20	9.599
25	6.593	23	5.138	22	5.553	28	7.323	27	9.680
		30	5.091	29	5.574				
Sep 02	6.381	Sept 07	5.087	Sep 06	5.554	Sep 05	7.659	Sep 04	9.855
08	6.389	13	5.099	12	5.887	11	7.695	10	10.531*
15	6.444	20	5.028	19	5.851	18	7.884	17	10.353
22	6.315	27	5.072	26	5.982	25	8.106	24	9.989
29	6.457								
Oct 06	6.239	Oct 04	5.087	Oct 03	6.108	Oct 02	8.161	Oct 01	10.313
13	6.045	11	4.905	10	6.156	09	8.256	08	10.808
20	5.887	18	4.797	17	6.282	16	8.209	15	11.836
27	5.685	25	4.929	24	6.207	23	7.900	22	12.932
				31	6.278	30	8.454	29	12.256
Nov 03	5.602	Nov 01	4.862	Nov 07	6.187	Nov 06	9.028	Nov 05	12.098
10	5.279	08	4.892	14	6.092	13	8.593	12	12.026
17	5.471	15	4.890	21	6.084	20	8.696	19	11.944
24	5.520	22	4.596	28	6.057	27	9.166	26	11.018
		29	4.466						
Dec 01	5.550	Dec 06	4.383	Dec 05	6.049	Dec 04	8.984	Dec 03	11.927
08	5.633	13	4.360	12	6.073	11	8.929	10	12.054
15	5.491	20	4.269	19	5.985	18	9.237	17	12.228
22	5.340	27	4.296	27	6.152	26	9.336	24	12.074
29	5.208							31	12.105

90-Day T-Bills at Weekly Auction (continued)

1980		1981		1982		1983	
Jan 07	11.943%	Jan 05	13.601%	Jan 04	11.658%	Jan 03	7.896%
14	11.904	12	15.318	11	12.121	10	7.671
21	12.189	19	15.595	18	12.505	17	7.619
28	12.038	26	15.199	25	13.364	24	8.055
						31	8.122
Feb 04	12.086	Feb 02	14.657	Feb 01	13.850	Feb 07	8.252
11	12.307	09	15.397	08	14.099	14	8.256
19	13.162	16	15.464	15	14.740	21	7.888
25	13.700	23	14.103	22	12.430	28	7.944
Mar 08	15.136	Mar 02	14.463	Mar 01	12.450	Mar 07	8.205
10	15.381	09	13.996	08	12.058	14	8.256
17	15.053	16	12.758	15	12.909	21	8.434
24	16.532	23	12.695	22	12.553	28	8.680
31	15.073	30	12.501	29	13.399		
Apr 07	14.424	Apr 06	14.147	Apr 05	12.893	Apr 04	8.664
14	13.818	13	13.783	12	12.849	11	8.165
21	12.731	20	13.553	19	12.497	18	8.030
28	10.788	27	14.190	26	12.469	25	8.150
May 05	9.728	May 04	15.963	May 03	12.675	May 02	8.040
12	8.604	11	16.433	10	12.248	09	8.140
19	8.953	18	16.034	17	12.189	16	8.100
27	7.675	25	16.750	24	11.480	23	8.460
				31	11.520	30	8.650
Jun 02	8.035	Jun 01	14.456	Jun 07	12.074	Jun 06	8.640
09	6.500	08	14.982	14	12.248	13	8.730
16	6.369	15	13.451	21	12.588	20	8.980
23	7.077	22	14.337	28	13.269	27	9.090
30	8.149	29	13.909				
Jul 07	8.209	Jul 06	14.400	Jul 05	12.806	Jul 04	9.100
14	8.169	13	14.558	12	11.797	11	9.070
21	7.880	20	14.563	19	11.140	18	9.190
28	8.221	27	15.065	26	10.559	25	9.130
Aug 04	8.877	Aug 03	15.674	Aug 02	9.633	Aug 01	9.360
11	8.723	10	15.235	09	10.025	08	9.570
18	9.411	17	15.705	16	8.616	15	9.430
25	10.025	24	15.832	23	7.748	22	9.180
		31	15.583	30	8.604	29	9.280
Sep 02	10.124	Sep 08	15.611	Sep 07	8.565	Sep 06	9.210
08	10.060	14	14.412	13	8.161	12	9.040
15	10.638	21	14.198	20	7.849	21	8.990
22	10.460	28	14.669	27	7.801	26	8.730
29	11.524						
Oct 06	11.295	Oct 05	14.206	Oct 04	8.102	Oct 03	8.720
13	11.330	12	13.526	12	7.429	10	8.830
20	11.413	19	13.613	18	7.437	17	8.630
27	12.331	26	13.352	25	8.031	24	8.660
						31	8.410
Nov 03	13.344	Nov 02	12.675	Nov 01	7.813	Nov 07	8.830
10	13.517	09	11.128	08	7.964	14	8.780
17	14.309	16	10.693	15	8.446	21	8.810
24	14.384	23	10.560	22	7.944	28	8.900
		30	10.400	29	8.280		
Dec 01	14.649	Dec 07	10.404	Dec 06	7.956	Dec 05	9.000
08	16.335	14	11.101	13	7.995	12	8.930
15	16.667*	21	11.037	20	7.857	19	9.040
22	14.992	28	11.690	27	7.975	26	8.940
29	13.908						

90-Day T-Bills at Weekly Auction (continued)

1984		*1985*		*1986*	
Jan 03	9.04%*	Jan 07	7.78%	Jan 06	7.05%
09	8.92	14	7.74	13	7.23
16	8.82	21	7.68*	21	6.98*
23	8.92	28	7.76	27	6.92
30	8.87				
Feb 06	9.08	Feb 04	8.16	Feb 03	6.99
14	9.04*	11	8.20	10	7.18
21	9.13*	19	8.15*	18	6.97*
27	9.20	25	8.36	24	6.96
Mar 05	9.24	Mar 04	8.73	Mar 03	6.92
12	9.37	11	8.48	10	6.55
19	9.65	18	8.64	17	6.52
26	9.76	25	8.41	24	6.36
				31	6.35
Apr 02	9.67	Apr 01	8.18	Apr 07	6.19
09	9.66	08	8.14	14	5.84
16	9.80	15	8.04	21	5.86
23	9.64	22	7.62	28	6.08
30	9.68	29	7.87		
May 07	9.99	May 06	7.76	May 05	6.07
14	10.07	13	7.69	12	6.07
21	9.95	20	7.28	19	6.22
29	9.83*	28	7.22*	27	6.15*
Jun 04	9.90	Jun 03	7.03	Jun 02	6.33
11	10.07	10	7.21	09	6.31
18	10.01	17	6.73	16	6.11
25	9.77	22	7.06	23	6.09
				30	5.99

90-Day T-Bills at Weekly Auction (continued)

1984			*1985*			*1986*	
Jul 02	10.01		Jul 01	7.00		Jul 07	5.85
09	10.04		08	6.92		14	5.78
16	10.17		15	7.06		21	5.72
23	10.30		22	7.23		28	5.86
30	10.40		29	7.23			
Aug 06	10.55		Aug 05	7.30		Aug 04	5.70
13	10.49		12	7.14		11	5.60
20	10.40		19	7.14		18	5.64
27	10.60		26	7.07		25	5.32
Sep 04	10.63*		Sep 03	7.12*		Sep 02	5.12*
10	10.39		09	7.22		08	5.24
17	10.33		16	7.17		15	5.16
24	10.27		23	6.81		22	5.25
			30	7.07		29	5.20
Oct 01	10.23		Oct 07	7.14		Oct 06	5.08
09	10.11*		15	7.20*		14	5.13*
15	9.98		21	7.18		20	5.30
22	9.54		28	7.24		27	5.18
29	9.38						
Nov 05	8.82		Nov 04	7.21		Nov 03	5.23
13	8.73*		12	7.21*		10	5.41
19	8.59		18	7.24		17	5.39
26	8.43		25	7.15		24	5.35
Dec 03	8.52		Dec 02	7.19		Dec 01	5.40
10	8.38		09	7.05		08	5.51
17	7.97		16	7.00		15	5.55
24	7.75		23	7.02		22	5.49
31	7.86		30	7.04		29	5.68

90-Day T-Bills at Weekly Auction (continued)

1987		*1988*		*1989*	
Jan 05	5.53%	Jan 04	5.90%	Jan 03	8.24%*
12	5.38	11	5.85	09	8.36
20	5.23*	19	5.98*	17	8.30*
26	5.44	25	5.85	23	8.26
				30	8.33
Feb 02	5.58	Feb 01	5.74	Feb 06	8.57
09	5.72	08	5.63	13	8.49
17	5.66*	16	5.73*	20	8.51
23	5.40	22	5.64	27	8.73
		29	5.62		
Mar 02	5.47	Mar 07	5.74	Mar 06	8.65
09	5.63	14	5.65	13	8.69
16	5.58	21	5.76	20	9.00
23	5.55	28	5.69	27	9.10
30	5.72				
Apr 06	5.53	Apr 04	5.98	Apr 03	8.87
13	5.98	11	5.98	10	8.78
20	5.77	18	5.78	17	8.59
27	5.79	25	5.92	24	8.66
May 04	5.81	May 02	6.13	May 01	8.64
11	5.47	09	6.31	08	8.41
18	6.03	16	6.28	15	8.21
26	5.70*	23	6.34	22	8.32
		31	6.53*	30	8.50*
Jun 01	5.80	Jun 06	6.44	Jun 05	8.17
08	5.59	13	6.44	12	8.13
15	5.70	20	6.51	19	8.22
22	5.64	27	6.59	26	8.07
29	5.82				

90-Day T-Bills at Weekly Auction (continued)

1987			*1988*			*1989*	
Jul 06	5.62		Jul 05	6.57*		Jul 03	7.96
13	5.54		11	6.72		10	7.76
20	6.14		18	6.76		17	7.87
27	6.01		25	6.88		24	8.09
						31	7.65
Aug 03	5.96		Aug 01	6.89		Aug 07	7.94
10	5.93		08	6.94		14	8.01
17	5.97		15	7.05		21	7.99
24	6.12		22	7.18		28	7.94
31	6.19		29	7.26			
Sep 08	6.45*		Sep 06	7.26*		Sep 05	7.88
14	6.32		12	7.21		11	7.64
21	6.51		19	7.17		18	7.64
28	6.59		26	7.23		25	7.72
Oct 05	6.49		Oct 03	7.23		Oct 02	7.83
13	6.96*		11	7.32*		10	7.63
19	6.84		17	7.36		16	7.37
26	5.12		24	7.45		23	7.52
			31	7.37		30	7.78
Nov 02	5.80		Nov 07	7.54		Nov 08	7.67*
09	5.74		14	7.82		13	7.68
16	6.01		21	7.97		20	7.61
23	5.70		28	8.05		27	7.63
30	5.49						
Dec 07	5.81		Dec 05	8.04		Dec 04	7.55
14	6.00		12	7.98		11	7.60
21	5.96		19	8.14			
28	5.73		26	8.22			

APPENDIX E

20 Interest-Rate-Sensitive Stocks—1966–1983

	10/3/66–1/8/68	*6/30/70–8/26/71*	*10/1/74–3/8/76*	*5/13/80–3/16/81*	*8/3/82–7/12/83*
Best Products	b	b	3¾–29⅞	19⅞–23⅝	15⅝–34½
Fleetwood	5⅝[a]–21¾	18–53⅞	6⅛–19⅛	7⅜–10½	9–35⅛
General Cinema	14½–36½	21½–60¼	6¾–23⅝	20½–32	23[a]–41¼
Gulf & Western	21[a]–62¼	12⅜–28¾	8⅝[a]–25⅝	15¾–16	12⅛–27¾
Holiday Inn	16⅛[a]–50¼	24⅞–45⅜	7⅜–17¼	15⅜–25½	27¼–53
E. F. Hutton	b	b	4¼[a]–23¼	14⅞[a]–30¾	20½[a]–50½
Kaufman & Broad	7⅜[a]–35⅛	16[a]–37	2⅜–9¼	8⅞–14⅛	7⅛–20¼
Levi Strauss	b	b	16¾–49⅛	36⅛–47⅛	23⅞–51
Levitz	b	34¼–80⅝	2⅜–8⅜	21¼–27⅜	27–83½

Appendix E (Continued)

Lomas & Nettleton Fin.	3–4⅞	8⅝–18¾	4⅛–8⅝	15⅛–22⅝	24⅝–48
Masco	19⅝–32	34⅛–60⅞	9⅞[a]–26¾	24¾–36⅞	16⅛[a]–30¾
Melville	32¼–90¾	30–54¼	6⅞–22¾	29¼–42¾	23⅝–44¼
Merrill Lynch	[b]	[b]	7⅞–32	20¾–35¾	12¼[a]–52⅞
Mohasco	15⅝–24	15½–35½	11⅞–22	7¼–11¾	10¾–22⅜
Outboard Marine	16⅛–29⅝	13–24⅝	13⅞–29½	9⅛–15⅝	23⅜–41
Pulte	[b]	[b]	1¼–3¼	7[a]–17	9⅛[a]–30⅞
Ryder	14¼–32⅝	31⅝–59¼	5–11⅜	18¼–33	31¾–58¾
Time	73½–92⅝	27⅛–52	30¾–64½	39⅞–65¼	29¾–72
U.S. Home	[b]	9⅝[a]–36¾	2⅝–7½	11⅞[a]–31⅜	6⅞[a]–16¼
Walgreen	16⅞[a]–40⅜	16–26⅜	10¼–14¼	30¾–49	16[a]–31⅞

[a] Adjusted for splits and stock distributions.
[b] Not listed.

APPENDIX F

10 Stable Growth Stocks—1961–1984

	7/31/61–12/26/63	*1/8/68–12/20/68*	*8/26/71–11/26/71*	*3/8/76–11/8/76*	*3/16/80–4/20/81*	*7/12/83–2/13/84*
AT & T	101–137⅞	55⅛–54	43⅛–41⅝	55⅝–61	52–55⅛	62⅜–63⅜
Avon	64–133¼	130–133	97½–97½	39⅛–45¼	38⅛–39⅝	31¼–24½
Beatrice Foods	36¼[a]–51½	60⅞–81¼	42⅜–38¾	23–25⅝	20¼–21⅛	27–31
Coca-Cola	76⅛–114	64¼[a]–74	107½–108¼	88–77⅜	37–35⅜	48⅝–50⅛
General Foods	63¾–86¼	72¼–84⅞	35–33⅛	30⅛–30¼	34–34	45–47¼
McDonald's	[b]	43[a]–65⅞	57–62	60⅞–53¼	59⅞–67½	64⅞–63½
Philip Morris	73½–73½	46¾–67½	69⅛–59⅛	52–58⅜	50–52½	58⅜–69⅞
Ralston Purina	31–34	23¾–26⅞	30⅜–31⅜	48⅛–49⅞	13–12¾	22–26¾
Sears	63⅜–97⅜	60⅛–65⅛	95⅝–96	71–68⅛	17⅜–19½	40–35½
Tampax	42½–67½	167½–191	296–301	36¼–34½	33⅞–35⅝	59⅞–53⅞

[a] Adjusted for splits and stock distributions.
[b] Not listed.

APPENDIX G

20 Capital Goods Stocks—1959–1983[c]

	4/22/59–1/4/60	*12/26/63–1/18/66*	*11/26/71–12/15/72*	*11/8/76–3/15/77*
Alcoa	86⅞–106½	67⅜–80½	39⅝–55⅞	51⅝–59¼
Avnet	[b]	13¾–18⅞	10–13	15¼–17¼
Black & Decker	32[a]–38¼	30⅛[a]–59	68¾–108½	16⅞–16¾
Boeing	40⅜–31¼	37⅛–158	14⅜–25¾	42–44⅜
Caterpillar Tractor	31⅝[a]–33½	23⅝[a]–49⅛	39–66¾	54–54¾
Cincinnati Milacron	40⅛–38⅜	43–73¼	33⅞–44	29⅜–36⅜
Cummins Eng.	84–87	36¾–52⅝	50¼–57⅞	40⅛–51⅜
Deere	57¾–46¾	35¼[a]–58¾	21[a]–45¾	30¼–29⅝
Eastman Kodak	87½–107	60⅜[a]–120⅝	87¾–149	83–74¼
Hewlett-Packard	44¾–49¼	19⅝–36¾	41¼–79⅜	82–76⅜
Intel	[b]	[b]	20⅝–54	51–50
IBM	384¾[a]–437	392⅜[a]–483½	298¾–398¼	259½–285¼
Midland Ross	44¾–56¼	31⅜–55¼	14⅞–16½	24¼–30¼
Motorola	84½–170½	52¼[a]–167½	73–131⅞	50–48⅛
Perkin-Elmer	24½[a]–29¾	48¼–85¾	23¾[a]–38⅞	20⅛–18

20 Capital Goods Stocks (continued)

	4/22/59–1/4/60	12/26/63–1/18/66	11/26/71–12/15/72	11/8/76–3/15/77
Stanley Works	$18\frac{1}{4}$–$22\frac{3}{4}$	$19\frac{7}{8}$–$42\frac{3}{4}$	$33\frac{3}{8}$–$42\frac{3}{4}$	$27\frac{1}{2}$–$30\frac{5}{8}$
Tektronix	b	$19\frac{1}{8}$–$34\frac{3}{4}$	$29\frac{7}{8}$–$50\frac{3}{4}$	$59\frac{3}{8}$–60
Texas Instruments	$113\frac{3}{4}$–$165\frac{1}{8}$	$54\frac{1}{2}$ a–$186\frac{1}{8}$	108–$172\frac{1}{2}$	103–$84\frac{3}{4}$
Timken	$55\frac{5}{8}$–$66\frac{7}{8}$	$35\frac{1}{8}$ a–$47\frac{5}{8}$	$38\frac{1}{8}$–$41\frac{7}{8}$	$49\frac{5}{8}$–$54\frac{3}{4}$
Xerox	$28\frac{1}{2}$ a–$30\frac{3}{4}$	84–$216\frac{3}{8}$	$110\frac{1}{2}$–$149\frac{3}{4}$	$58\frac{3}{8}$–50

a Adjusted for splits and stock distributions.
b Not listed.
c Last capital goods phase ended in 1977; as of this writing, there has been no new capital goods phase since.

Index

I

About the Author

Dick Stoken received his M.B.A. from the University of Chicago in 1958. He has been a member of the Chicago Mercantile Exchange since 1959, and a member of the Chicago Board of Trade since 1971. Formerly a partner of Lind-Waldock, a leading investment firm, he is now a partner in Strategic Investments, an investment advisory firm in Chicago. He is the author of *Cycles* (McGraw Hill, 1978), and *The Great Cycle,* Revised Edition (Probus, 1993). *Cycles* and *Strategic Investment Timing in the '90s* were selected by *The Stock Trader's Almanac* as the "Best Investment Book" of their respective years.

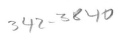